The Army Star (1943 pattern)

Jeanne Poore

Members of St. Luke's United Church of Christ in Independence, Mo., stitched a star pattern patchwork quilt in 1975.

Facing page: **Victory block (1942 pattern) by Edie McGinnis**

One Piece at a Time

A Selection of the Legendary Kansas City Star Quilt Patterns

By the staff of *The Kansas City Star*

Kansas City Star Books
Kansas City, Missouri

ONE PIECE AT A TIME

The Legendary Kansas City Star Quilt Patterns

Consultants and Contributors
Edie McGinnis and Jeanne Poore

Editors
Monroe Dodd
Dru Sefton
Joyce Shirk

Illustrations, design and production
Jean Donaldson Dodd

Photography
Tammy Ljungblad

Cover photo:
Sampler Quilt, pieced by Susan Jarsulic, quilted by Jean Zyck. Blocks made from various *Star* quilt patterns

Back cover photos: Clockwise, from upper left:
■ **Dolly Madison** (1937 pattern), made by Jessie Cuthbertson, owned by Charlotte Crawford
■ **Grape Basket** (1930 pattern), owned by D. Thomas.
■ **Washington Stamp** (1944 pattern), made by Edna Danekas, owned by Jerry Stube.
■ **Hands All Around** (1935 pattern), made by Edna Danekas, owned by Jerry Strube.
■ **Small Triangle** (1945 pattern), made by Ad-dah Menzies, owned by Jeanne Poore.
■ **Flannel Sampler** quilt by D. Thomas.

Published by KANSAS CITY STAR BOOKS
1729 Grand Blvd.
Kansas City, Missouri, USA 64108

First edition

Library of Congress Card Number: 99-068032

ISBN 0-9604884-5-6

Printed in the United States of America
by Walsworth Publishing Co.

To order copies, call StarInfo, (816)-234-4636.
www.kcstar.com

Facing page: **Envelope Quilt Pattern (1943 pattern), quilter unknown, owned by Bonnie Ingram**

TABLE OF CONTENTS

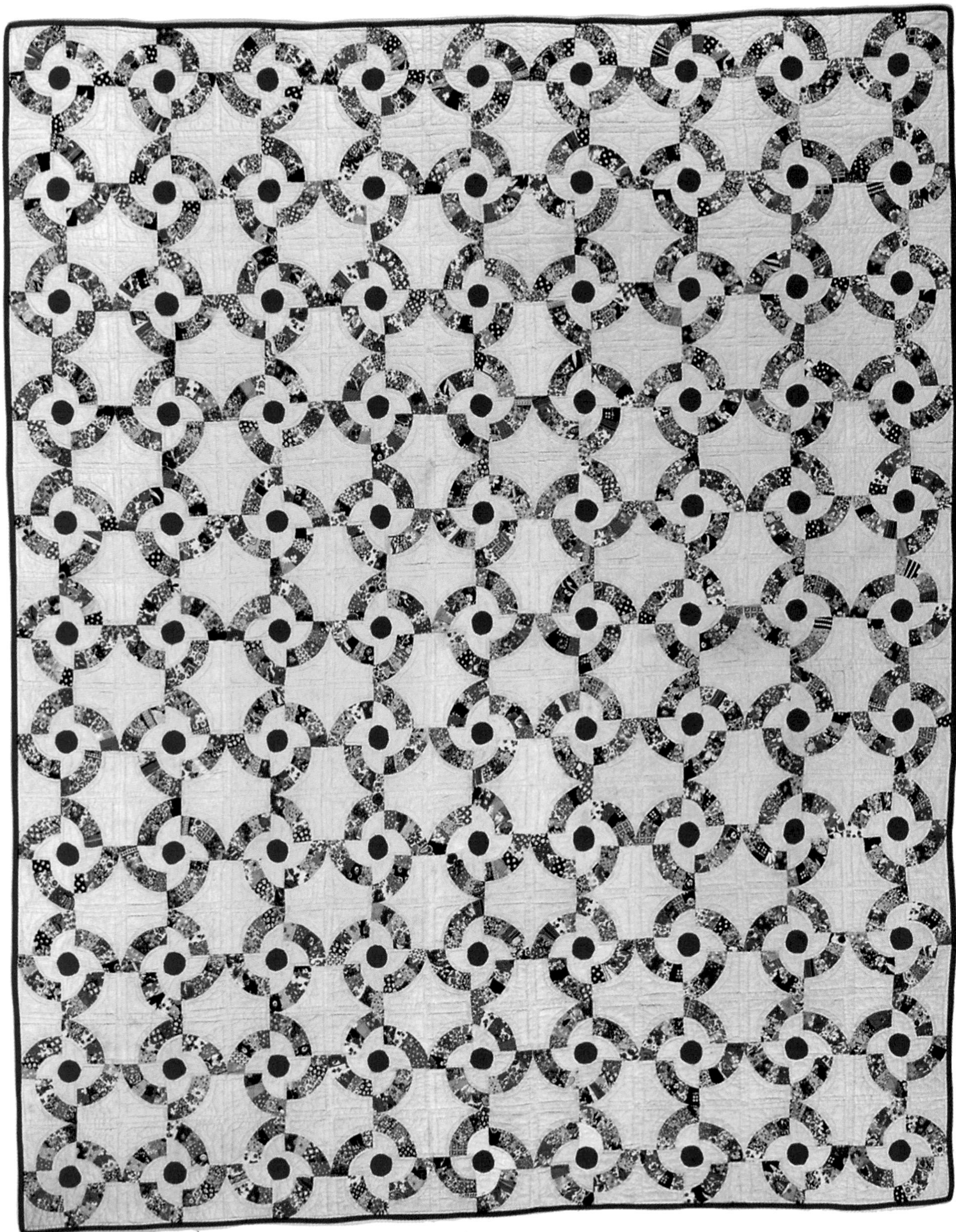

Letha's Electric Fan (1938 pattern) Made by Sarah Suffel Schaefer Courtesy Kansas Quilt Project

Twenty volunteers worked on a fundraising quilt in 1992 at Guardian Angels Church in Kansas City. The pattern is Wild Goose Chase.

Of all the things a woman's hands have made,
The quilt so lightly thrown across her bed —
The quilt that keeps her loved ones warm —
Is woven of her love and dreams and thread.
— Carrie A. Hall, *The Romance of the Patchwork Quilt in America,* 1935

Introduction

If the American Midwest is the heart of quilting country, then Kansas City, Mo., is its soul. There in 1928, *The Kansas City Star* newspaper began running in its pages the traditional quilt patterns that would become world famous and remain favorites for generations to come.

These "Kansas City Stars," as they now are known, have been indexed in several previous books. Never before, however, has the history of the patterns been documented. Until now.

In this book you'll find that and more. Redrafts of dozens of the original patterns, so modern-day quilters can more easily use them. Photographs and reminiscences of women who cherish these quilts. A chapter on quilting basics for beginning quilters, including a simple *Star* pattern. A look at some of the unique — and surprising— ways the patterns are being used today. And there is a chronological list of every pattern, by month and year.

We at *The Kansas City Star* hope you find this book to be a fitting tribute to these historic quilts.

Jeanne Poore's Kansas City Star sampler quilt is made of 12 patterns published from 1928 to 1931. Poore, of Overland Park, Kan., used 1930s reproduction fabric and hand-quilted most of it.

An enduring legacy: The Star

"The pine tree blocks make a very handsome quilt."

That simple sentence marked the beginning of what would become a worldwide phenomenon: *The Kansas City Star* quilt patterns.

The patterns were a weekly feature in *The Star* or sister publications *The Weekly Star* and *The Star Farmer* from 1928 until the mid-1930s, then less regularly until 1961. By the time the last one ran, 1,068 had been published in the papers, which circulated in seven Midwestern states as well as North Carolina, Kentucky and Texas.

The patterns have since become a loving obsession for many quilters.

"I think the *Kansas City Star* patterns influenced more quilts than any other means this century," says Raeann Lenzini, who owns an antiques store in Macon, Mo., and collects original *Star* patterns. "I love to sit and look at the patterns and imagine the farm wife, separated and isolated, waiting each Wednesday for the copy of *The Star Farmer* to arrive."

The influential Central Oklahoma Quilters Guild, 500 members strong, goes even further. A 1990 index that it researched and published states that *Star* patterns "are considered by the quilting world as the premium patterns to collect."

That's saying a lot. In 1998 there were nearly 14 million quilters in America over the age of 18, according to *Quilter's Newsletter Magazine*. It's a multibillion-dollar, international industry, experts say.

The newspaper continues to receive inquiries about *Star* patterns. Readers' representative Miriam Pepper fields some of those calls. "People have so many fond memories of the patterns," she says.

The Star never filed or indexed the patterns. Perhaps that's because, at the time they ran, they were an ordinary feature: Just everyday quilting designs, many submitted by farm wives or church groups. Perhaps it was because of the magnitude of the project — the great number of individual patterns and quilting designs plus numerous repeats.

So now enthusiasts of the "Kansas City Stars," as they are known among quilters, enjoy the thrill of the hunt for the old clippings as much as the nostalgic art of the designs.

Longtime quilter Judy Fleischmann of Higginsville, Mo., has a huge collection of *Star* quilt clippings. Her grandmother's collection started her off years ago. She since has received others from friends, has found some at auctions and sales, or has traded with other quilters "from California to Connecticut, from Wisconsin to Texas." At a family reunion, a cousin passed along 278.

The history is what draws many enthusiasts.

"It is such a thrill to hold a piece of the 1930s in my hand," says Jenny Alcasid from her home in Makati City, the Philippines. "On back of one of the clippings was a news item on (aviator) Charles Lindbergh, that he and some archaeologists discovered 'an ancient city previously unknown to science.' "

Alcasid has quilted two of the designs, Single Wedding Ring and Fence Row.

The names of the patterns reflect their times. Aviation designs were popular in the barnstorming era of the 1920s and '30s;

Edie McGinnis of Kansas City, Mo., a *Kansas City Star* employee, fashioned her award-winning quilt out of antique sacks. The project took her two years.

Air-Ship Propeller, for instance, was published in 1933. During the Depression, one pattern was dubbed Economy. During World War II, patriotic patterns proliferated, such as The Army Star of 1943 and Roads to Berlin of 1944.

As the Oklahoma guild's book says, "If you listen closely, the Kansas City Stars will talk to you, and you can experience a lesson in history."

Quilt historian and author Barbara Brackman of Lawrence, Kan., says hundreds of newspapers ran nationally syndicated patterns in the 1930s and '40s, but "*The Star* was one of the few that actually devoted enough space to put the full pattern in. You didn't have to send off a dime to get the pattern."

Brackman, who has written six books on quilts and quilt history, also collects the Stars. "I collect them casually," she says. "I have 400 or 500 of them."

One reason the Stars were popular then — and have remained so today — is the readers' response. "Many had a quote, such as 'This is my favorite pattern, signed, Mrs. Smith from Nevada, Mo.,' " Brackman says. "So these were done by women who made quilts, rather than just a designer. People knew they were going to work."

Interest in quilting fluctuates. In the 1920s and '30s the hobby underwent a boom, Brackman says, when people "felt like technology was overtaking the world. They wanted a touch of something hand-done." Recent years have brought quilting a new popularity — possibly for the same reason, she adds.

Through it all, the Stars have held a constant fascination for quilters.

Edie McGinnis of Kansas City, Mo., a *Star* employee, exemplifies the dedication of fans of the Stars. She quilted a 1936 pattern, "Whirligig," that won third place at an international quilt show in the early 1990s.

It is hand-stitched of 187 antique sacks. The project took her two years. Her quilt is a colorful conglomeration of feed sacks, flour sacks and sugar sacks. That's exactly the material women in 1936 would have used in the Depression.

To McGinnis, the Stars are more than just historical patterns: "Because there are so many of them, people use them to identify patterns they may not know. They're used as a reference."

Jeanne Poore of Overland Park, Kan., who redrafted the Stars that appear in this book, gives classes and lectures on the patterns through the Prairie Point Quilt Shop in Shawnee, Kan. Her grandmothers and great-grandmother were quilters, and many of her Stars were handed down through them.

Nowadays, she says, there are thousands of quilt patterns, "hundreds of publications and books."

"At the time the Stars were being published," she says, "there was only a handful of really good patterns readily available."

Most came from one Midwestern newspaper, *The Kansas City Star*.

The last pattern, A Fan of Many Colors, was printed May 24, 1961.

The text said the quilt was "long a favorite because of its simplicity of construction and of the possibilities of color combinations." It was contributed anonymously.

About the patterns and redrafts

In the pages to come you'll find 32 *Kansas City Star* quilts and instructions for making them. Each quilt section begins with a reproduction of the original illustration. This illustration is accompanied by its original caption. The type is reset because of the difficulty of reproducing readable print from old newspapers. Next come modern instructions, complete with diagrams of the results you should expect. Finally, templates to help you produce and check your work are shown; you can find them in the appendix.

The artists

■ **Ruby Short McKim** was the original *Star* quilt artist and one of the first illustrators in the country to use the newspaper to syndicate patterns, beginning in the early 1900s.

Ruby Short McKim, circa 1928

An Independence, Mo., businesswoman, she worked as the art needlework editor for *Better Homes & Gardens* magazine before founding McKim Studios in her hometown. McKim Studios grew into a national mail-order business for sewing patterns, kits and materials.

McKim drew *Star* patterns for the first three years.

■ **Eveline Foland** sketched the patterns over the next several years. She was a graphic designer who taught drawing at Manual Training High School, a vocational school in Kansas City, Mo.

Her patterns are known for their art-deco style and her distinctive signature.

One day Foland disappeared. Her last pattern was published unfinished and the following week an apology ran because pieces were missing. Many quilters now think Foland may have married and moved away or perhaps left *The Star* over a disagreement.

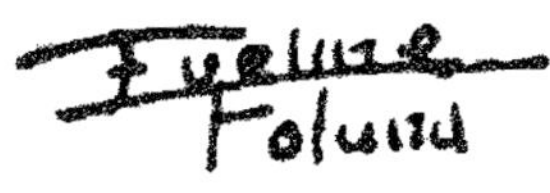

■ **Edna Marie Dunn** probably was Foland's boss and took over the patterns when Foland left.

Dunn was *The Star's* fashion illustrator during her long tenure at the paper, 1914 to 1965. She also owned the Edna Marie Dunn School of Fashion in Kansas City.

Dunn's forte was selecting the most timeless designs from hundreds of quilt patterns readers submitted over the years.

Edna Marie Dunn at her drawing board at *The Kansas City Star* in the 1940s.

A grandmother from Oklahoma proudly displayed her quilt in February 1936 in her new home, Kern County, Calif.

How to make a Kansas City Star Quilt

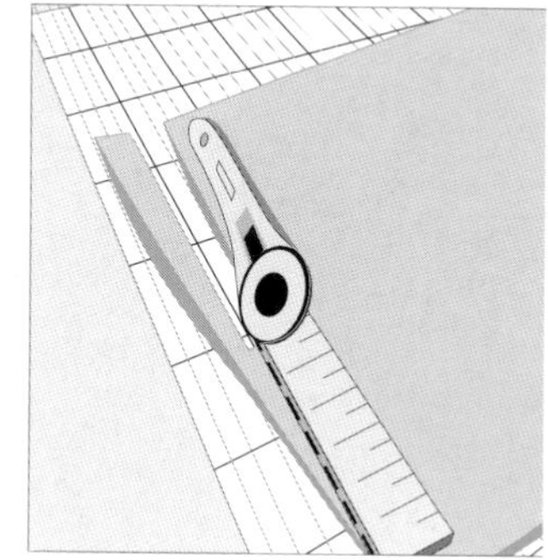

Diagram 1

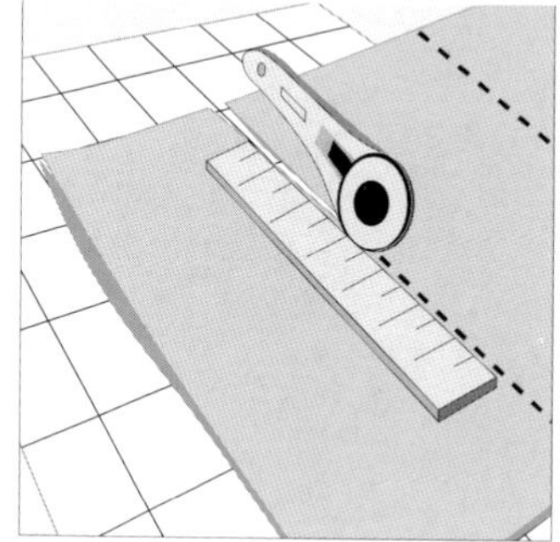

Diagram 2

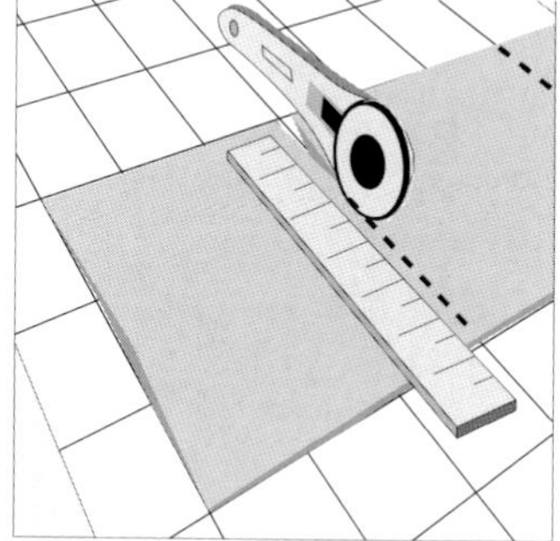

Diagram 3

With more than 1,000 patterns, the Kansas City Stars offer projects for everyone from novices to advanced quilters.

If you're a beginner but would like to try making an entire quilt, here are basic, complete directions for a full-size (72-by-96-inch) Double Square. Quilting books with more detailed instructions are available at quilt shops or your public library.

Terms in boldface are defined in the accompanying glossary.

Materials

These are available at quilt or craft stores. Words in **boldface** are defined in the glossary at the end of this chapter.

- 4½ yards of dark fabric, 100 percent cotton
- 3½ yards of light fabric, 100 percent cotton
- 7½ yards of fabric for **backing**, 100 percent cotton
- Double/queen size **batting** (cotton or polyfill)
- **Template** plastic with grids
- **Rotary cutter**
- **Rotary mat**
- Pins
- **Quilting thread**
- **Quilting needles (betweens)**
- **Quilting thimble**
- Wash-out marking pencils
- 24-by-6-inch clear ruler with grids
- **Quilting hoop**

Cutting

Machine-wash each fabric separately, using the detergent and temperature settings you plan to use to clean it after it becomes a quilt. Check for shrinkage and color fastness. With most modern fabrics, neither of these is a problem, but occasionally fabrics can shrink and colors can run. You don't want to find this out after your quilt is finished. If all is well, press each fabric and trim off **selvages** using your rotary cutter and rotary ruler.

Make sure all fabric edges are straight. Do this by folding the fabric in half lengthwise and aligning the long edges with horizontal lines on a rotary cutting mat. If edges along the width aren't straight, align your rotary-cutting ruler with a vertical line and cut straight across the width as close to the edge as possible to save fabric (Diagram 1).

Now move the ruler 6¾ inches in from the edge and cut across the width of the fabric (Diagram 2). Repeat until you have 16 strips of dark fabric and 16 of light. Set aside remaining dark material for later use. Line up strips and cut into 6¾-inch squares (Diagram 3).

Cut these squares from corner to corner at a 45-degree angle (Diagram 4). You will have 192 dark triangles and 192 light triangles.

Piecing

You can **piece** your quilt by hand or machine. There are advantages to each.

With hand piecing, you don't need a sewing machine. Your project is portable. You can hand-piece just about anywhere, and many quilters enjoy taking their projects along with them.

Machine piecing, however, is a lot faster.

For this quilt, if you're piecing by hand: Place your template plastic over the template pattern for the Double Square. See Page 152 (T 6¾). Trace on dashed lines. Cut out template with scissors.

Place the template on the **wrong side** of the fabric. Trace around the template with marking pencil on each triangular piece of fabric. These are sewing lines.

If you're piecing by machine, marking your sewing lines isn't necessary. Use the ¼-inch **seam guide** on your machine.

With the **right sides** of the fabric facing each other, place together the long sides of 1 light triangle and 1 dark triangle. Match the corners along the long side and pin on the seam line. With a small **running stitch**, sew along the marked seam line. Unfold and you'll have a square that is half dark and half light (Diagram 5).

Repeat on 3 more sets of triangles for a total of 4 squares.

Sew 2 squares together, placing dark triangle against

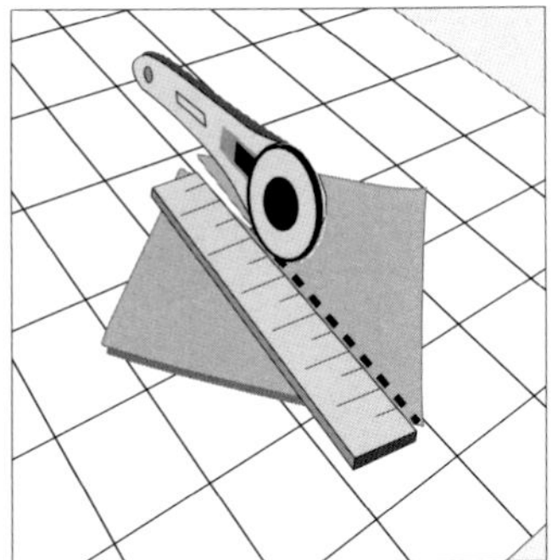

Diagram 4

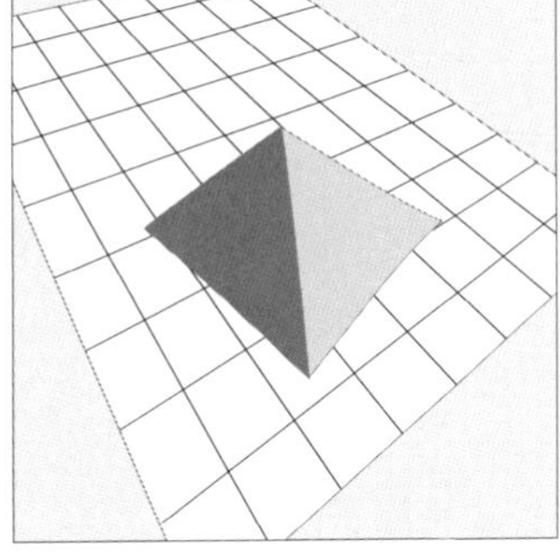

Diagram 5

Diagram 6

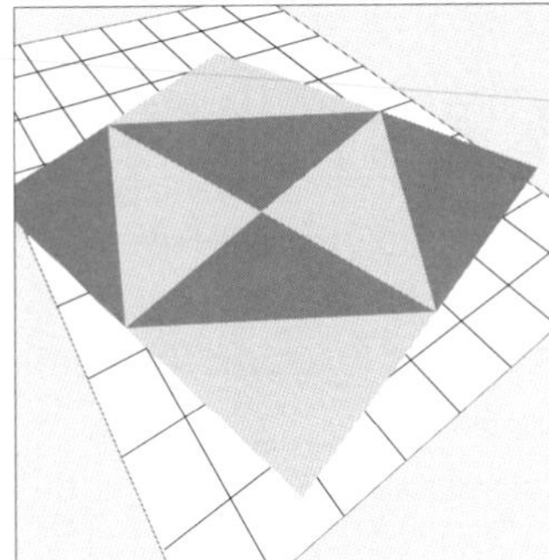

Diagram 7

Diagram 8

Diagram 9

light as shown in Diagram 6. Sew 2 more squares together the same way.

Place those 2 rectangles together and sew as shown in Diagram 7. This makes 1 complete block.

Repeat the process until 48 blocks are complete.

Sew 6 blocks together into strip. Make 8 strips. Sew strips together to complete the **quilt top** (Diagram 8). Before you sew together each block and each strip, pin each part together, taking care to keep all corners and intersecting seams matched.

Backing

Fold the backing fabric in half lengthwise. Cut across the width into two parts, each 3 3/4 yards long. Place the parts together, right sides facing each other. Sew pieces together along the length of fabric. This forms the back of the quilt.

Assembly

Iron the quilt top with all **seams** going toward the dark piece. On the back, press the middle seam open. This makes it easier to quilt through the seam.

Place backing, right side *down*, on a flat surface; smooth out all wrinkles. Place the quilt **batting** atop the backing. Place the top on these, right side *up*. **Baste** all layers together with thread or safety pins 4 to 6 inches apart in a rough grid. If you baste with thread, remove the stitches only after finishing the quilting. If you use safety pins, remove them as you quilt.

Quilting

You are now ready to begin **quilting**.

Place your quilting hoop as near the center as possible. You'll work from the center out toward the edges, moving the hoop as you complete each area.

Thread your quilting needle and put a small knot at one end of the thread. Thread directly from the spool to minimize tangles.

Mark the quilting line on each block ¼ inch in from each seam line with fine-line, wash-out marking pencil or with 1/4-inch quilter's masking tape.

To start the first stitch, slide the needle in anywhere under the first layer and pull the needle up to a marked quilting line. Tug gently until the knot pulls through the starting point and catches between the layers. That way, the knot will be hidden

Continue quilting as shown in Diagram 9. Try to make stitches as small and even as possible.

When you're almost out of thread, tie a knot in the thread closest to the quilt top. Insert your needle through the top layer, through the batting and back out the top, lodging the knot in the batting. Cut the remaining thread, rethread the needle and repeat the process.

Binding

After all quilting is complete, you'll need to **bind** the quilt.

Trim all excess batting and backing from the edges. Using the dark fabric set aside earlier, cut 10 strips horizontally, each 2½ inches wide.

Sew the ends of 2 strips together across their width. The resulting strip will be long enough to go across the top edge of the quilt. Sew 2 more strips together in the same manner to go across the bottom edge of the quilt. Now sew

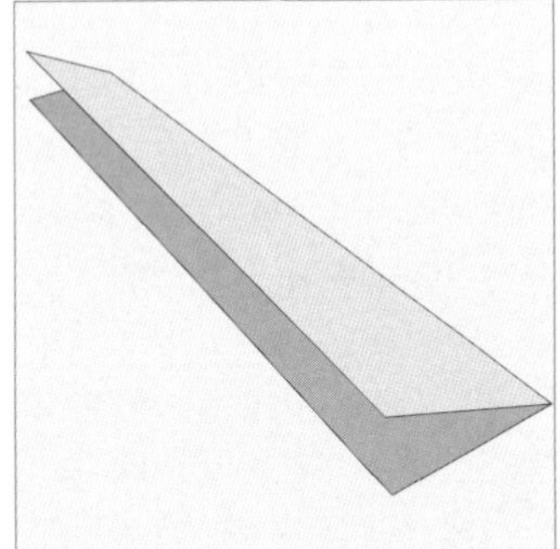

Diagram 10

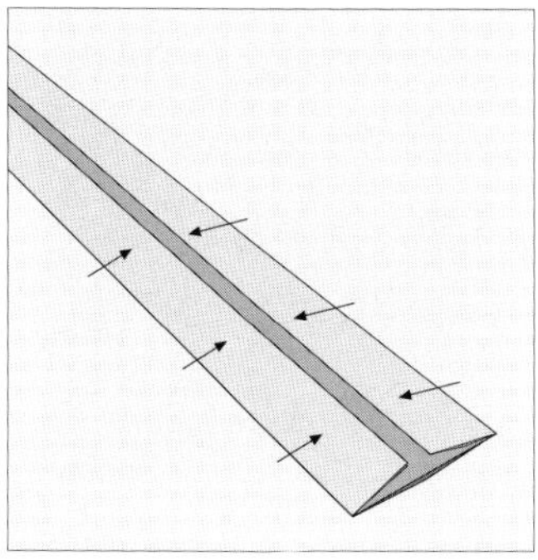

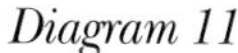

Diagram 11

Diagram 12

3 strips together to go on each side of the quilt. Fold each strip in half lengthwise and press (Diagram 10). Then fold one side of each strip halfway in and press (Diagram 11). Bring the other side over until edges meet and press again (Diagram 12).

Sew the strip to the top of quilt with a running stitch. Turn the remaining binding to the back and stitch. Do the side edges of the quilt first. Then do the top and bottom edges, folding under the raw ends of the binding to make the corners neat.

Your *Kansas City Star* quilt is complete!

Quilt glossary

■ **Background (or secondary)fabric:** A secondary fabric that complements the predominant fabric used in a quilt. (See also *primary fabric.*)

■ **Backing:** The bottom layer of a quilt.

■ **Baste:** Pinning or loosely stitching layers of a quilt together in preparation for quilting. The pins or stitches are later removed and the quilting holds all the layers of the quilt together.

■ **Batting:** The middle layer of the quilt, which provides depth and warmth. Batting, mainly cotton or polyester, is sold in lofts; a high loft is thick, a low loft is thin. The thinner the loft, the easier it is to quilt.

■ **Binding:** A strip of fabric used to enclose the rough edges of all the layers of a finished quilt.

■ **Block:** A square unit consisting of pieces of fabric sewn into a design. Many blocks sewn together make a quilt top.

■ **4-patch:** A square block using four pieces of fabric.

■ **9-patch:** A square block using nine pieces of fabric.

■ **Piecing:** Stitching together quilt pieces.

■ **Press to, press away:** To iron the fabric in a block. "Press to dark" means iron both sides of the seam toward the darker fabric; "press to the edge" means iron both sides of the seam toward the outer edge of the fabric, and so on. "Press away" means the opposite, as in "press away from center."

■ **Primary fabric:** The predominant fabric used in a quilt.

■ **Quilting:** Stitching through the top, middle and bottom layers of a quilt in a design or in straight lines to secure the layers together and add a decorative touch.

■ **Quilting hoop:** A two-part wooden or plastic circle. Placed on either side of the quilt, the hoop holds the fabric taut inside.

■ **Quilting needles:** Smaller than sewing needles, quilting needles are called "betweens." They come in sizes from 7 (longest) to 12 (shortest). Beginning quilters often use a 7 or 8.

■ **Quilting thimble:** A thimble with a ridge around the top to help push the quilting needle.

■ **Quilting thread:** Heavier and stronger than average sewing thread.

■ **Right side:** The front side of the fabric with a pattern or color; the opposite of the "wrong side," or back of a fabric.

■ **Rotary cutter:** A sharp, circular cutting utensil — resembling a pizza cutter — used to cut through layers of fabric.

■ **Rotary mat:** A mat marked with grids and angles, made to be used with a rotary cutter.

■ **Running stitch:** A sewing stitch made by passing the needle in and out repeatedly, using short, even stitches.

■ **Selvages:** The lengthwise, finished edges of a fabric.

■ **Seams:** The line formed by sewing together pieces of fabric.

■ **Seam guide:** A mark or piece on a sewing machine footplate that measures the distance from the needle to the edge of the fabric.

■ **Template:** A pattern, usually plastic, used to trace cutting or sewing lines onto fabric.

■ **Wrong side:** See **Right side.**

**Jacob's Ladder (1928 pattern)
Pattern made and owned by
Martha Schuman**

**Magnolia Bud (1932 pattern)
Made in 1998 by Blue Valley
Quilt Guild
Owned by Jerry Atube**

**Album Quilt (1935 pattern)
Quiltmaker unknown.
Owned by Elizabeth A. Wallis**

**Maple Leaf on Point (1938
pattern). Made by Miriam G
Eads. Owned by Lougene
Eads Geary**

Album quilt No. 364 (1935 pattern)   Quiltmaker unknown   Owned by Elizabeth A. Wallis

1928-1938

Stitching through hard times

Whether as a necessary task or as a creative outlet, women were busy stitching quilts in the Great Depression. They gathered in quilting bees at church groups or social clubs, or created quilts by themselves at home.

The Kansas Quilt Project, a 1986 effort to document the history of quilts and quilters in the state, determined that the quilting frenzy in that state peaked between 1930 and 1936. Magazines and newspapers were quick to take advantage of the trend. Patterns popped up in *Capper's Weekly* in Topeka in 1927, followed by *The Kansas City Star's* series, beginning regularly in 1928.

The greatest number of *Star* patterns to run in one year was in this era: In 1930, 53 patterns were published, many in the daily paper as well as in its weekly editions.

The pattern names, such as Kansas Dust Storm and Depression, reflected the somber tone of the times. Women with little money to buy fabrics turned to quilting any cloth that wasn't too worn; men's shirttails, the inside hems of dresses. Feed-sack manufacturers took to printing fabric bags with attractive patterns, and these became a popular source of fabric for quilters. Women would meet and trade sack fabric to get enough of the patterns they wanted.

This 1937 quilting party in an Alvin, Wis., home is typical of many Midwestern quilting bees of the era. Women gathered to quilt as well as exchange gossip, recipes and advice.

A PATTERN FOR AN ALBUM QUILT

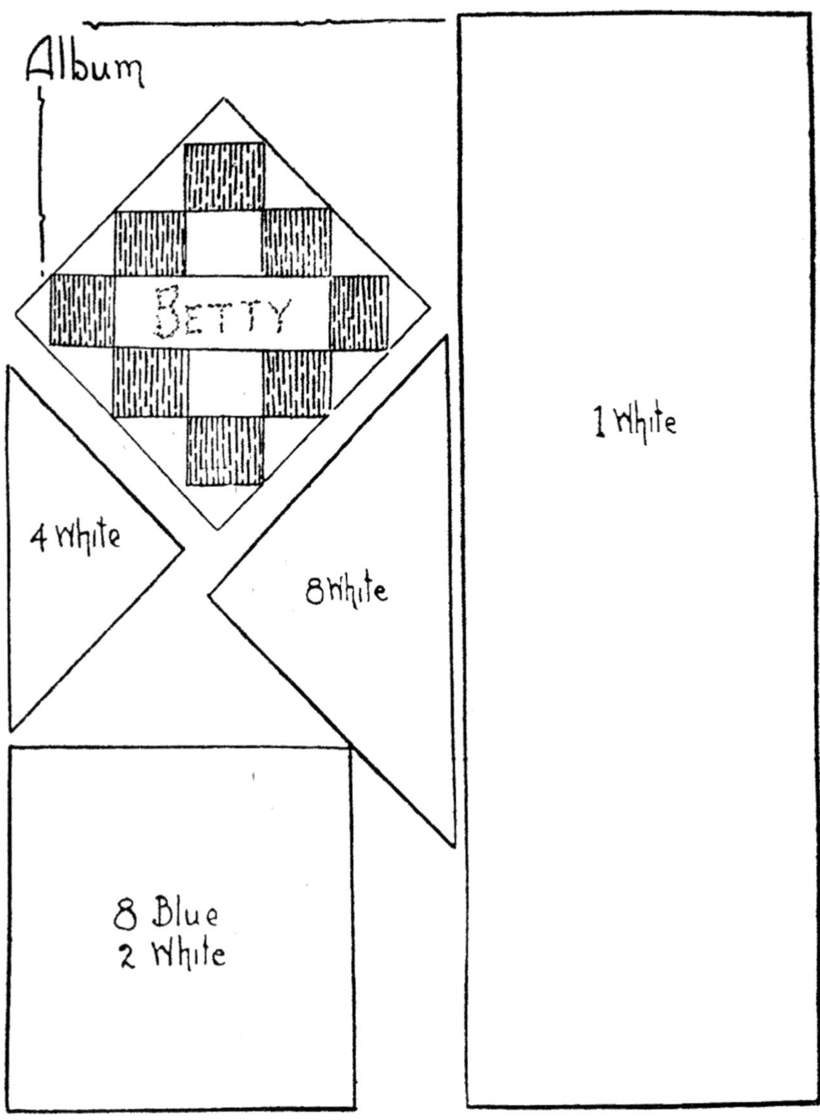

Published Sept. 29, 1928

The album quilt is a real old-timer. Its original purpose was for a gift for a bride-to-be. A group of friends would get together and each would piece a block and embroider her name upon it. Then, of course, they would all come to the quilting bee, and the result, while not exactly a bride's shower, would be something in store for a rainy day.

Make patterns on cardboard exactly the size of the pieces drawn above. Then lay them on the material and mark out with a pencil, making the number of squares of each color as designated above. These patterns do not allow for seams, so after the material is marked cut out each, allowing a seam of the width desired. Then sew on the pencil lines and piece together as indicated in the sketch in the upper left.

One block when completed is ten and one-half inches square. Set the blocks together diagonally with alternate white squares measuring ten and one-half inches. The total number of pieced and white blocks used of course varies according to the size and shape of the quilt desired. But be sure that the names on each block run in the same direction.

Album history

The Album pattern — also known as Odd Fellow's Quilt, Courthouse Square, Arbor Window, the Cross Patch or the Album Patch — is a type of quilt known as a friendship block. Old friendship block quilts are popular collector's items because they feature names of quilters now long gone.

There were more than two dozen friendship or signature block patterns published in *The Kansas City Star.* The Album pattern was the second published, and was produced by McKim Studios in Independence, Mo.

Album quilt No. 364 (1935 pattern) **Quiltmaker unknown** **Owned by Elizabeth A. Wallis**

■ **Block size:** 12"

■ **Fabrics needed:** Two fabrics, a **light** and a **dark.**

Cutting and piecing instructions

■ From **light** fabric, cut:

* Eight squares 3⅜ inches.

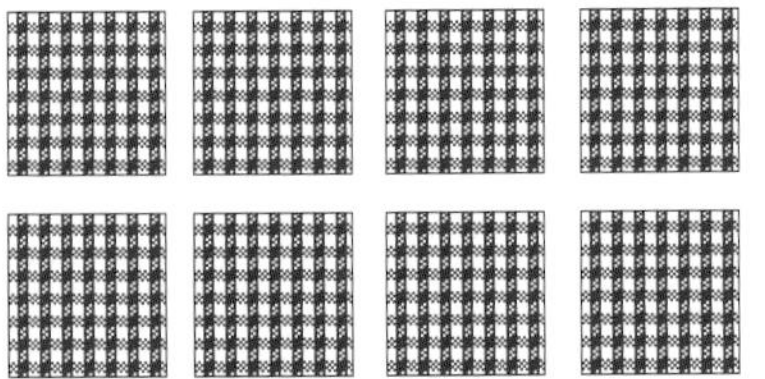

■ From **dark** fabric, cut:

* Two squares 3⅜ inches .

* One strip 3⅜ inches by 9 inches.

* Two squares 5¼ inches.
* Two squares 3 inches.

■ **Subcut** the two 5¼-inch squares into an X, producing 8 triangles .

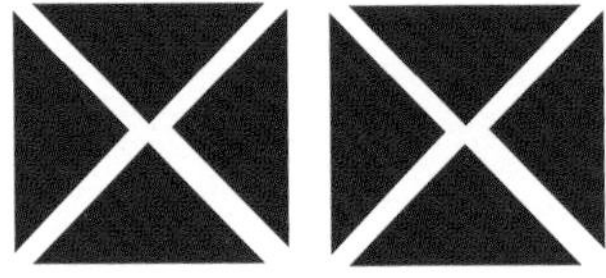

■ **Subcut** the two 3-inch squares diagonally, producing four triangles. These triangles are for the corners of the block.

■ **Assemble** in rows as shown below. Press toward dark fabric squares in each row. Press away from the center strip in the block. Embroider or use a permanent marking pen to put a name on the large center strip.

Templates

See appendix for Sq 3⅜, T 3, T 3¾, P 3⅜ x 9

JACOB'S LADDER IS THE INSPIRATION FOR THIS QUILT PATTERN

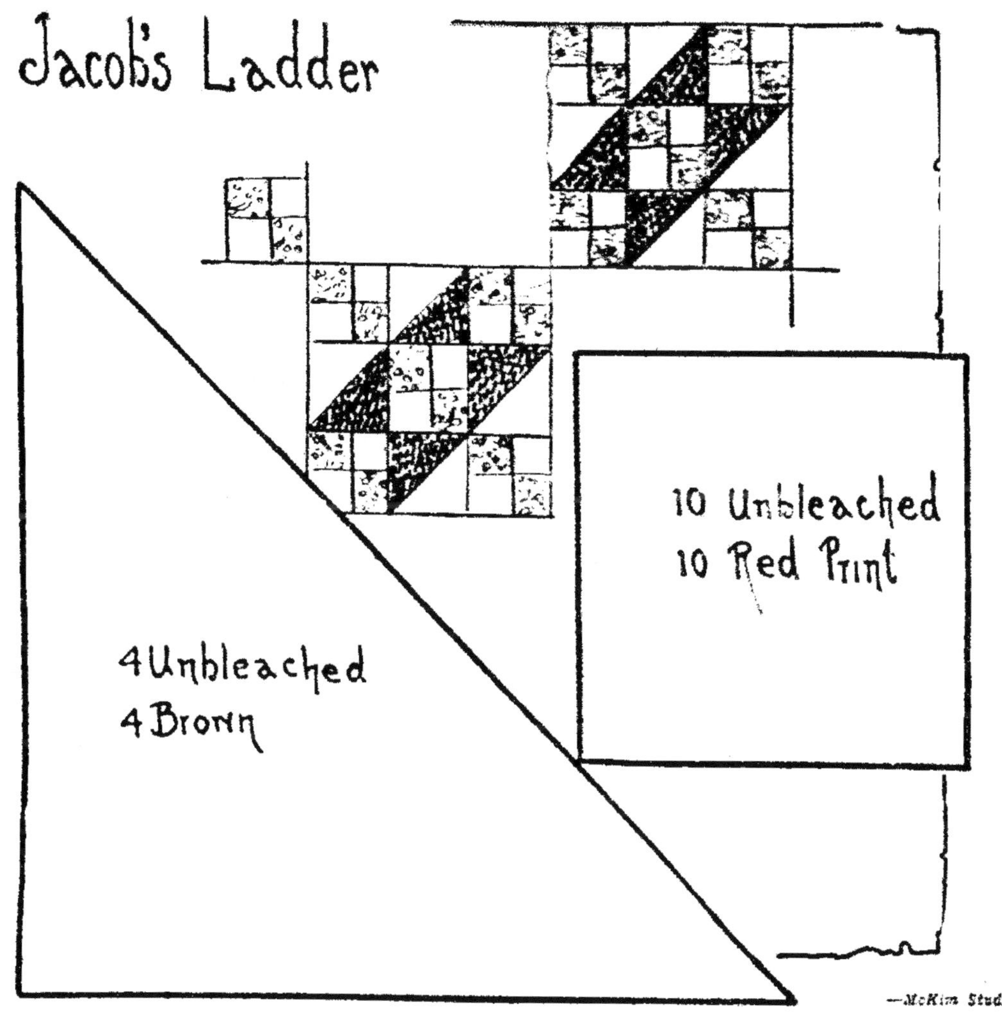

Published Nov. 10, 1928

The names in this old-fashioned quilt series are almost as interesting as the patterns themselves. Today it is the Jacob's Ladder pattern which is given. The blocks are rather large when pieced together, 13 1/2 inches square. Each of these large blocks is composed of nine little pieced blocks. And these little blocks are in turn divided into two groups—five four-patches, and four triangle squares—see the diagram above.

The patterns for the triangle and square are given above. These do not allow for seams. Make the patterns by cutting the square and triangle out of cardboard. Then place the cardboard pattern on your material and draw around it with a pencil. Now when you cut out the pieces, be sure to allow enough extra for a seam, but when you sew it, sew back on the pencil line. Piece the squares and triangles together as shown, alternating dark with light. When the large 13 1/2-inch squares are completed put these together alternately with squares of unbleached material, or whatever light colored fabric is used. Jacob's Ladder is a simple pattern to cut, but, like the others, has to be set together accurately to make perfect patchwork.

A file of these quilt patterns which are published in The Star each week might be kept by putting each set of cardboard patterns into an envelope upon which is pasted the sketch and description.

Jacob's Ladder history

Jacob's Ladder — also known as Stepping Stones, The Tail of Benjamin's Kite, Trail of the Covered Wagon, Wagon Tracks, Underground Railroad, Double Hour Glass, the Railroad, Golden Stair, Pacific Railroad, Foot Prints in the Sands of Time, Blue Chains and Road to California — has pre-Revolutionary origins. Some quilters use two tones, dark and light. Different combinations of fabrics created ladders running in different directions. When a third color was introduced, different patterns emerged, and hence different names. They may have reflected the area the creator came from and the time in which it was produced.

Jacob's Ladder **Made and owned by Martha Schuman**

■ **Block size:** 12"

■ **Fabric:** Three fabrics are used: A **light,** a **medium** and a **dark.**

Cutting and piecing instructions

4-Patch assembly:

■ **Cut** a strip of medium and a strip of light, each 2½ inches by at least 28 inches.

■ **Stitch** with right sides together along the length of the strips. Press toward the medium fabric.

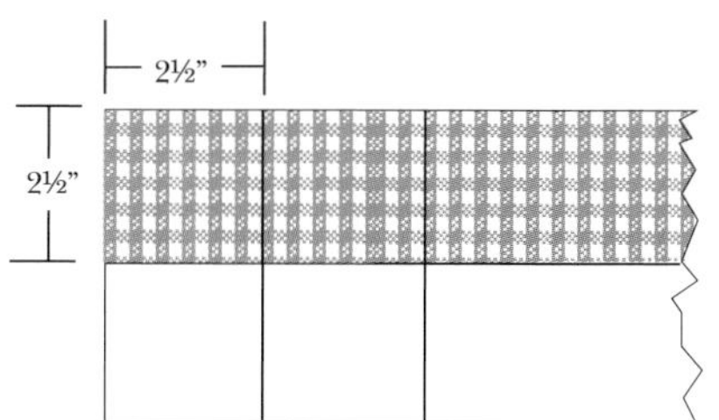

■ **Cut** this strip into 10 pieces, 2½ inches wide. Assemble into the 4-patch as shown below. Five 4-patches are needed.

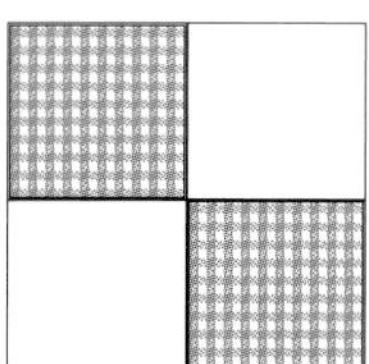

Triangle assembly:

■ **Cut** four 4⅞-inch squares, two of the light and two of the dark fabric. Draw a diagonal line on the wrong side of the light fabric. Place a light square and a dark square together, right sides facing.

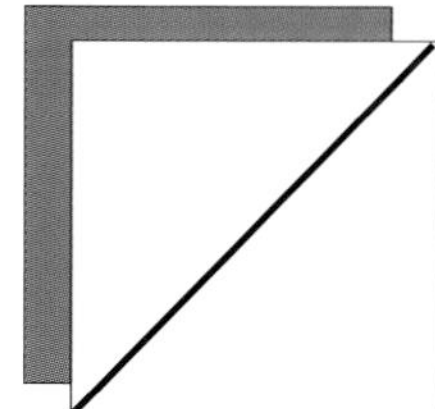

■ **Stitch** together ¼-inch on either side of the line. Cut on the line.

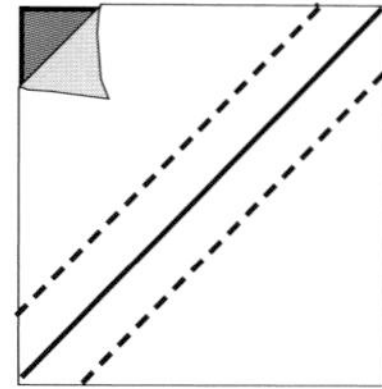

■ **Unfold**, lay flat and press toward the dark fabric

Make three more of these units.

■ **Assemble** the 4-patches and the triangle units in rows as shown.

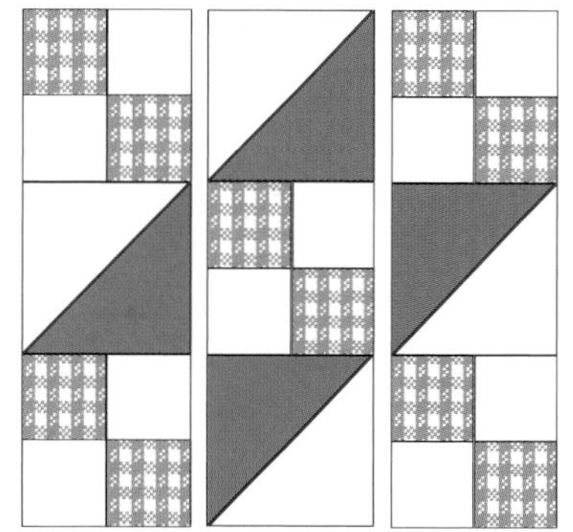

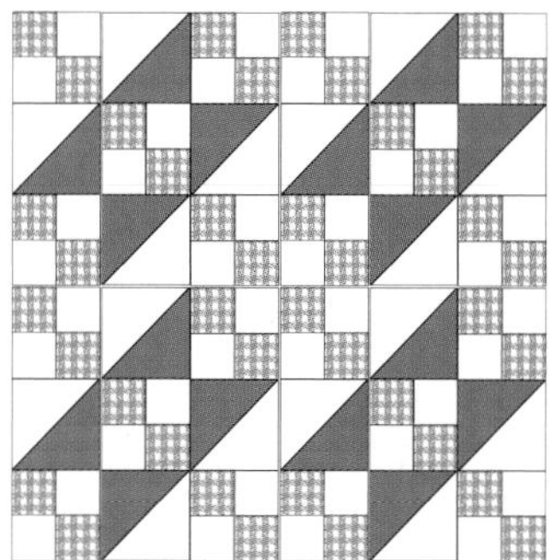

Templates

See appendix for Sq 2½, T 4⅞

USE VARIED COLORS FOR THIS OLD-FASHIONED QUILT BLOCK

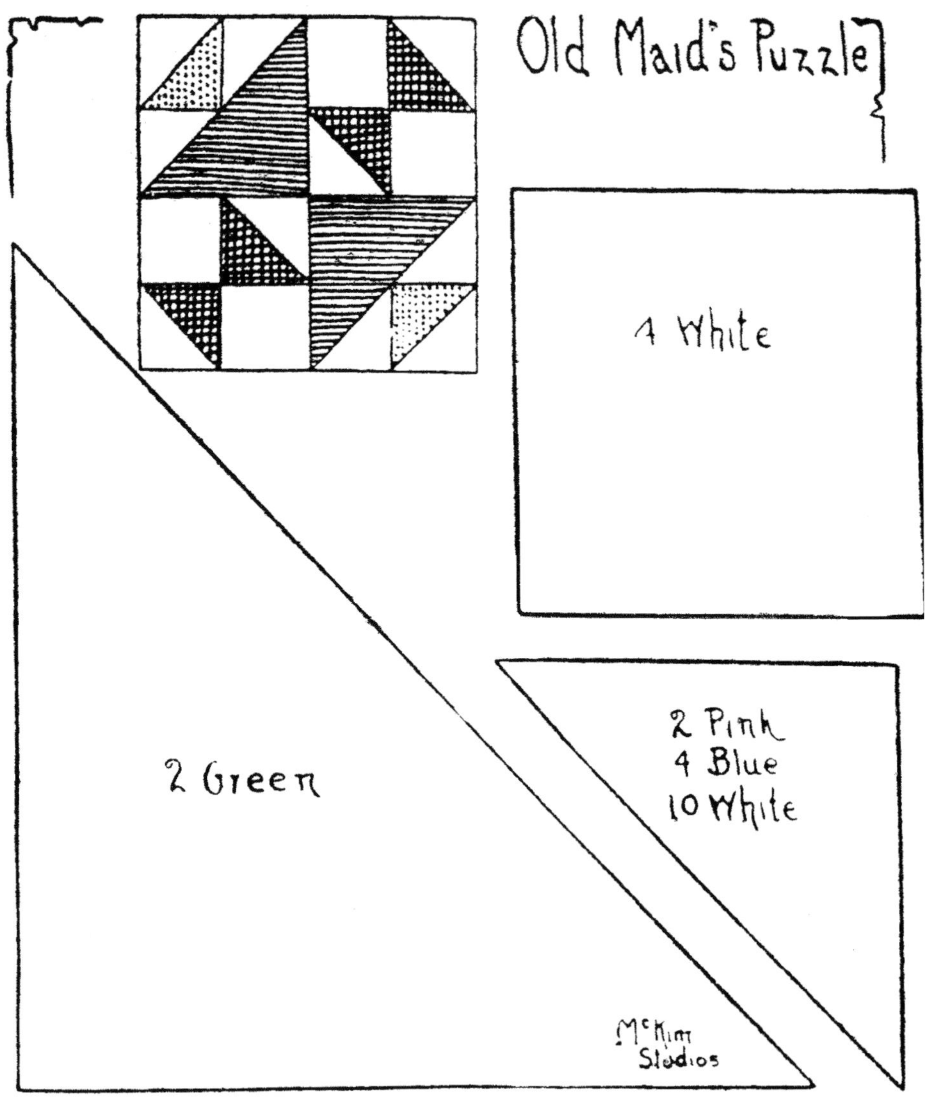

Published Dec. 22, 1928

One may be certain that Old Maid's Puzzle is a genuine antique quilt pattern because there hasn't been an old maid in a generation, and bachelor girls are not so easily puzzled.

With this series of old-time quilt blocks, no additional pattern is needed. The triangles and square here given are the exact size of the finished parts in a block nine inches square. Cut cardboard patterns from these. Then place cardboard patterns on your material and trace around them with a pencil. When you cut the pieces out, allow for a seam and then sew back to the pencil line. (These patterns do not allow for seams.)

This is quite a simple block to piece. There are four pieced squares of two kinds. Just follow the pattern shown in the upper left of the sketch. The color scheme suggested uses odd scraps of pink, blue, and green prints with white, but other color combinations are equally effective.

When the 9-inch blocks are completed set them together, checkerboard style, alternating with plain blocks. Each color then will form a pattern in diagonals across the whole quilt.

1928 Old Maid's Puzzle

Old Maid's Puzzle (also known as Fox and Geese) Made by Christine Husak, Ortonville, Mich. Shown at National Quilting Association Inc. show in Omaha, Neb.

■ **Block size:** 12"

■ **Fabrics needed:** Four fabrics, a **light, medium, medium dark** and **dark.**

Cutting and piecing instructions

■ From **light** fabric, cut:
 * Four squares, 3½ inches
 * Five squares, 3⅞ inches

■ From **medium** fabric, cut:
 * One square, 6⅞ inches

■ From **medium dark** fabric, cut:
 * Two squares, 3⅞ inches

■ From **dark** fabric, cut:
 * One square, 3⅞ inches

■ **Subcut** the five 3⅞-inch light squares diagonally, producing 10 triangles.

■ **Subcut** the medium square diagonally to make two large triangles.

■ **Subcut** the two medium dark squares to make four triangles.

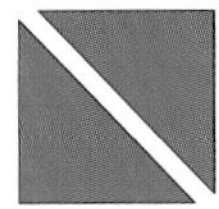

■ **Subcut** the dark square to make two triangles.

■ **Stitch** the dark triangles to the light triangles.

■ **Sew** to a medium triangle. Make two of these blocks.

■ **Stitch** together two light squares, two light triangles and two medium dark triangles.

Make two of these blocks.

■ **Assemble** in rows .

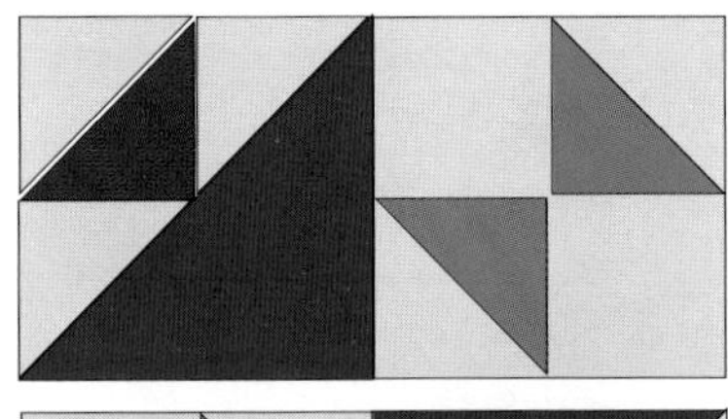

Templates

See appendix for Sq 3½, T 3⅞, T 6⅞

THE WEATHERVANE DESIGN MAKES A STRIKING QUILT

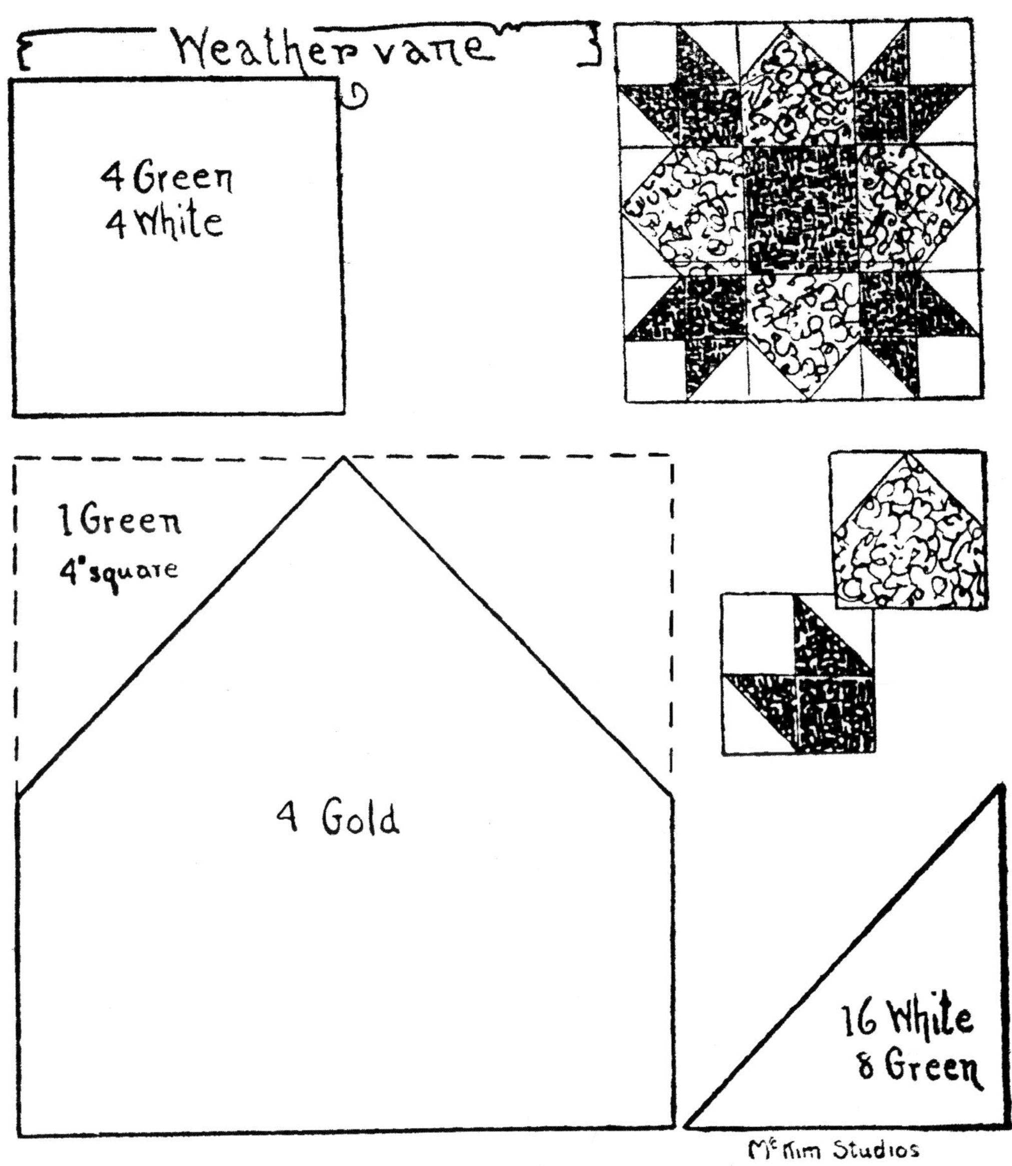

Published Jan. 5, 1929

This patchwork pattern, the Weather Vane, dates back to the time when great-grandmother used that indication to calc'late a change, and is one of the loveliest of the authentic old-time quilt designs.

Cardboard patterns may be cut to the exact size of the units given above (the 4-inch center square and three other pieces used). Trace around these with a lead pencil on your material and then when you cut the cloth allow a seam beyond the pencil line, as these patterns do not allow for seams. Sew on the pencil lines when piecing; the finished block will be twelve inches square.

This block makes up very simply. Small green and white triangles sew into eight squares, two of which combine with a green and white square to make the four corner blocks. White triangles on the four gold pieces make four other blocks. These all set together with the center 4-inch green square to form the Weather Vane block. This is a charming pattern for a quilted pillow of silk scraps or calico, as well as for an entire quilt.

Weathervane block **Made and owned by Jeanne Poore**

■ **Block size:** 12"

■ **Fabrics needed:** Three fabrics, a **light,** a **medium** and a **dark**.

Cutting and piecing instructions

■ From **light** fabric, cut:
* Four 2⅞-inch squares
* Four 2½-inch squares

■ From **medium** fabric, cut:
* Four 4½-inch squares

■ From **dark** fabric, cut:
* Four 2⅞-inch squares
* Four 2½-inch squares
* One 4½-inch square

■ **For the corner units:** Place a 2⅞-inch square of light atop a 2⅞-inch square of dark fabric, right sides facing. Draw a diagonal line on the back of light fabric. Stitch ¼ inch on both sides of line.

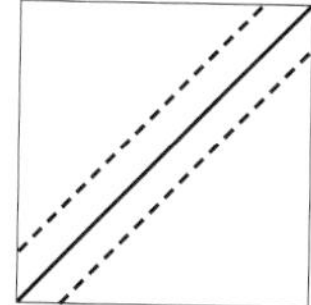

■ **Cut** on the line, unfold, and press to dark fabric. Make eight of these units.

■ **Assemble** each of these with a 2½-inch light square and a 2½-inch dark square as shown.

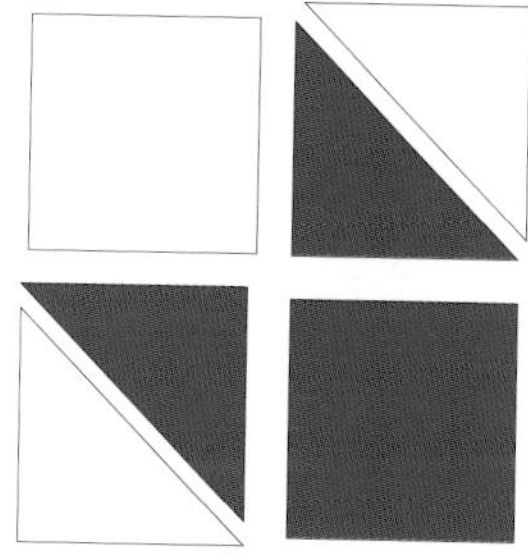

Make four of these units.

For the middle units:

■ **Place** a square of 2½-inch light at the corner of a square of the medium, right sides facing. Draw a line on the light square (dotted line in diagram below).

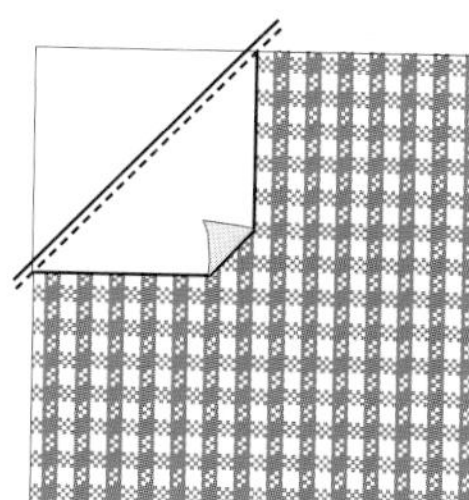

■ **Stitch** on the line. Trim ¼ inch from the seam (solid line in diagram). Repeat the process in the adjacent corner. Press toward the darker fabric. Make four of these units.

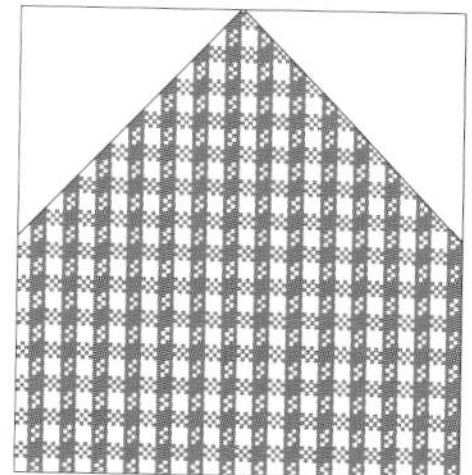

■ **Assemble** in rows as shown. The top and bottom rows contain two corners and a middle unit. The middle row contains two middle units on each side of the center square.

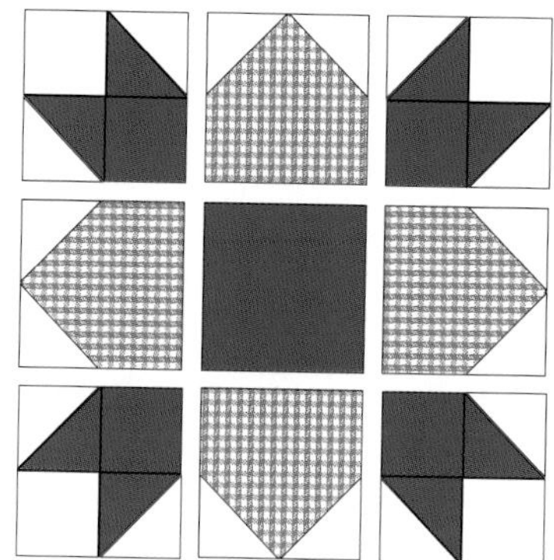

Templates

See appendix for Sq 2½, Sq 4½, T 2⅞, Misc.1

JACK IN THE BOX

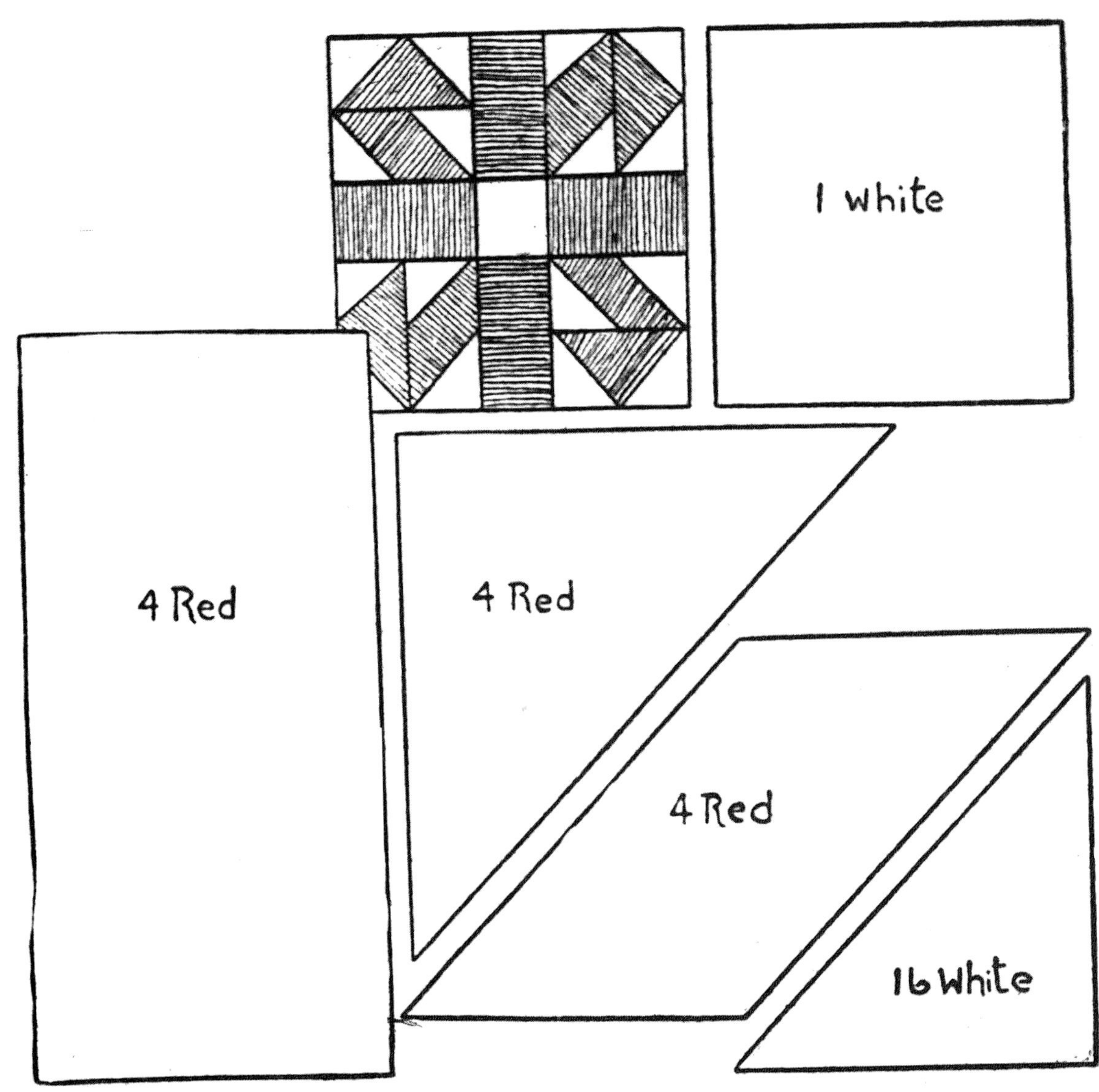

Published July 6, 1929

Jack in the Box is a crisp angular pattern almost as perky as its surprising name. The sketched block shows how easy it is to piece first the white triangles into a diamond, then two white triangles onto a red triangle, then whole making one corner square. Seams are not allowed so should be added to the sizes given.

And right here may we put in a splendid suggestion for those who repeatedly wonder, How much material does it take to make a quilt? By tracing onto brown paper as many patterns of each color as are called for in one block of the design and allowing seams between, quite accurate areas of cloth for one block may be estimated. Then it depends on the size you want the finished quilt and how the blocks are to be set together to determine the number of blocks to be used. Hence if it takes a 6-inch square of pink for one block and the quilt has eighteen blocks you would need half a yard of 36-inch material for that one color.

1929 Jack in the Box

Jack in the Box block **From Susan Jarsulic's sampler quilt**

■ **Block size:** 12"

■ **Fabrics needed:** Two fabrics, a **light** and a **dark.**

Cutting and piecing instructions

Flying Goose unit:

■ From **light** fabric, cut:

* Four 3 ⅜-inch squares

■ From **dark** fabric, cut:

* One 6 ¼-inch square

For strips:

■ From **dark** fabric, cut:

* Two 3 x 23-inch strips

■ From **light** fabric, cut:

* One 3 x 28-inch strip
* One 2 ½-inch square

Flying Goose unit:

■ **Draw** a diagonal line from corner to corner on the wrong side of two light squares.

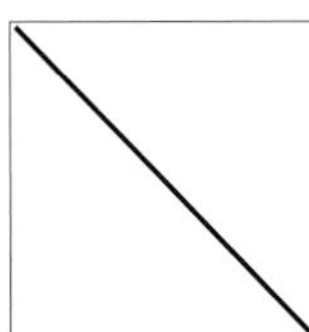

■ **Place** two of these right sides down on top of the dark square.

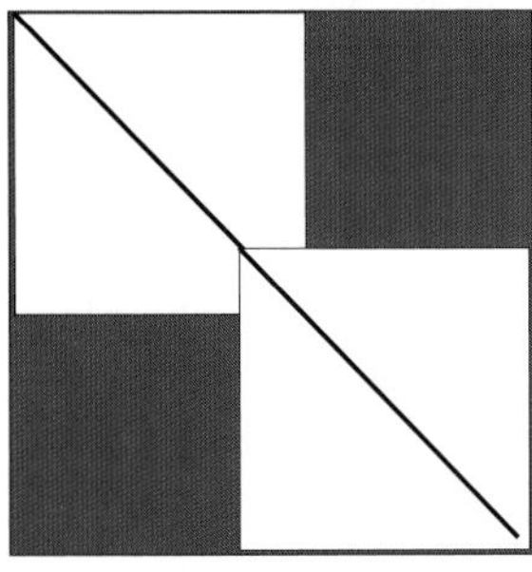

■ **Stitch** ¼ inch on both sides of the line.

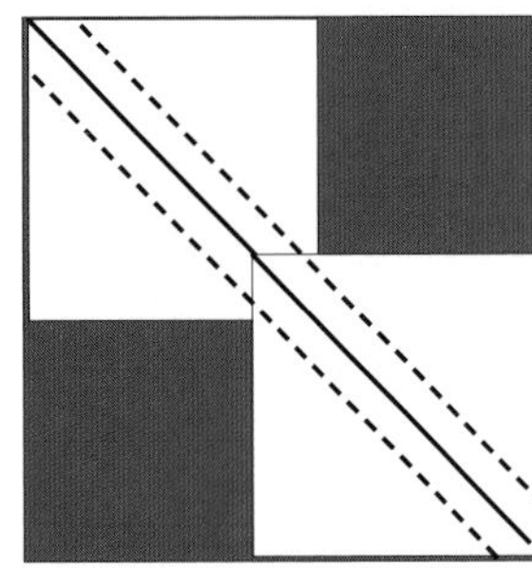

■ **Cut** on the line.

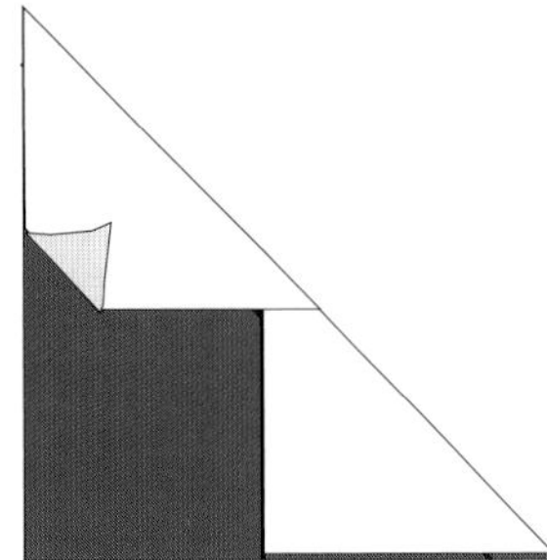

■ **Press** to darker fabric.

■ **Place** a light square in the lower left corner, mark a diagonal as shown and stitch ¼ inch on either side.

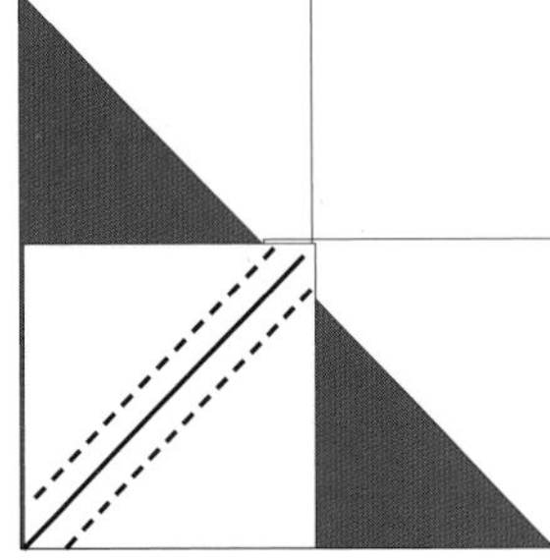

■ **Cut** along the solid line through all layers of fabric.

■ **Press** to dark unit.

You should get these two units. You will need two more like these for the block.

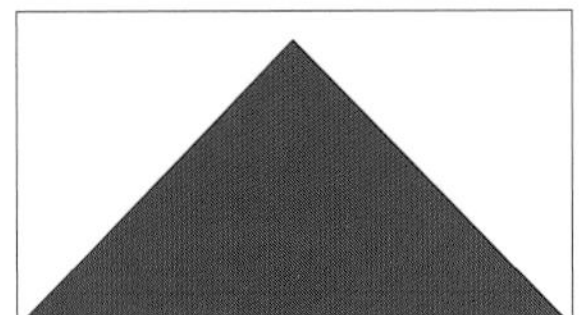

■ **Subcut** one dark 3 x 23-inch strip into four units, 5½ inches wide.

■ **Subcut** the light 3 x 23-inch strip into eight units, 3 inches wide.

5½-inches

3 inches

■ **Draw** a diagonal line on the wrong side of the 3-inch squares. Place one square on the left side of a 5½-inch strip, right sides facing. Stitch on the line. Trim seam to ¼-inch (dotted line).

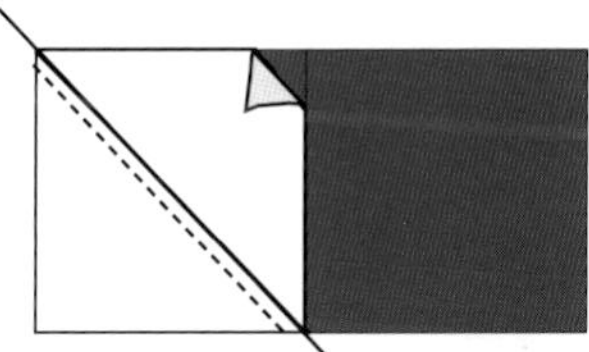

■ **Press** to dark.

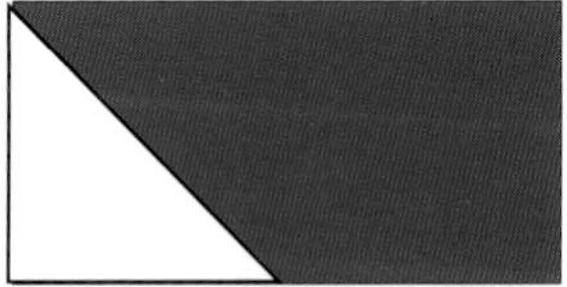

■ **Place** a second light square on the right side of the same 5½-inch dark strip, stitch along the solid line and trim along the dotted line.

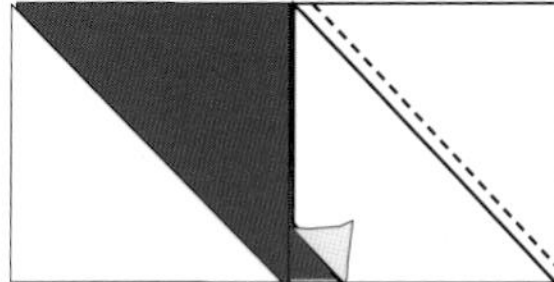

You should now have a unit that looks like this.

You will need four of these.

■ **Assemble** each Flying Goose unit by joining the two units as shown. You will need four of these for the block.

■ **Subcut** the 2½ x 23 inch dark strip into four units, each 5½ inches wide.

5½ " 5½ " 5½ " 5½ "

■ **Put** two Flying Goose units together as shown with the 2½-by-5 ½-inch strip in between.

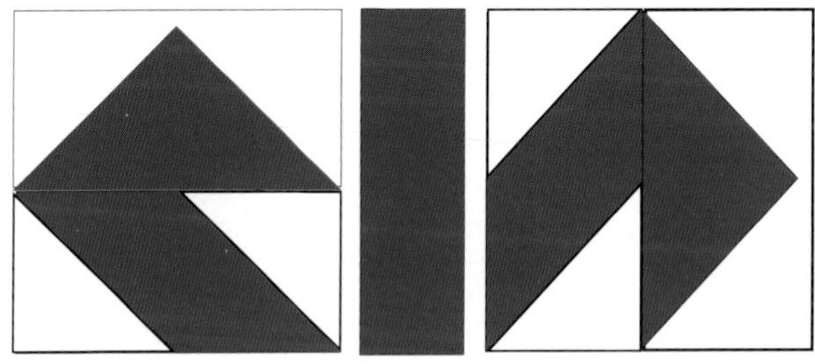

■ **Stitch** together two of the 2½-by-5½-inch strips and a 2½-inch square as shown.

Templates

See appendix for Sq 2½, T 3¼, P 2½ x 5½, T 4⅜, Misc. 2

■ **Assemble** the block as shown.

NECKTIE

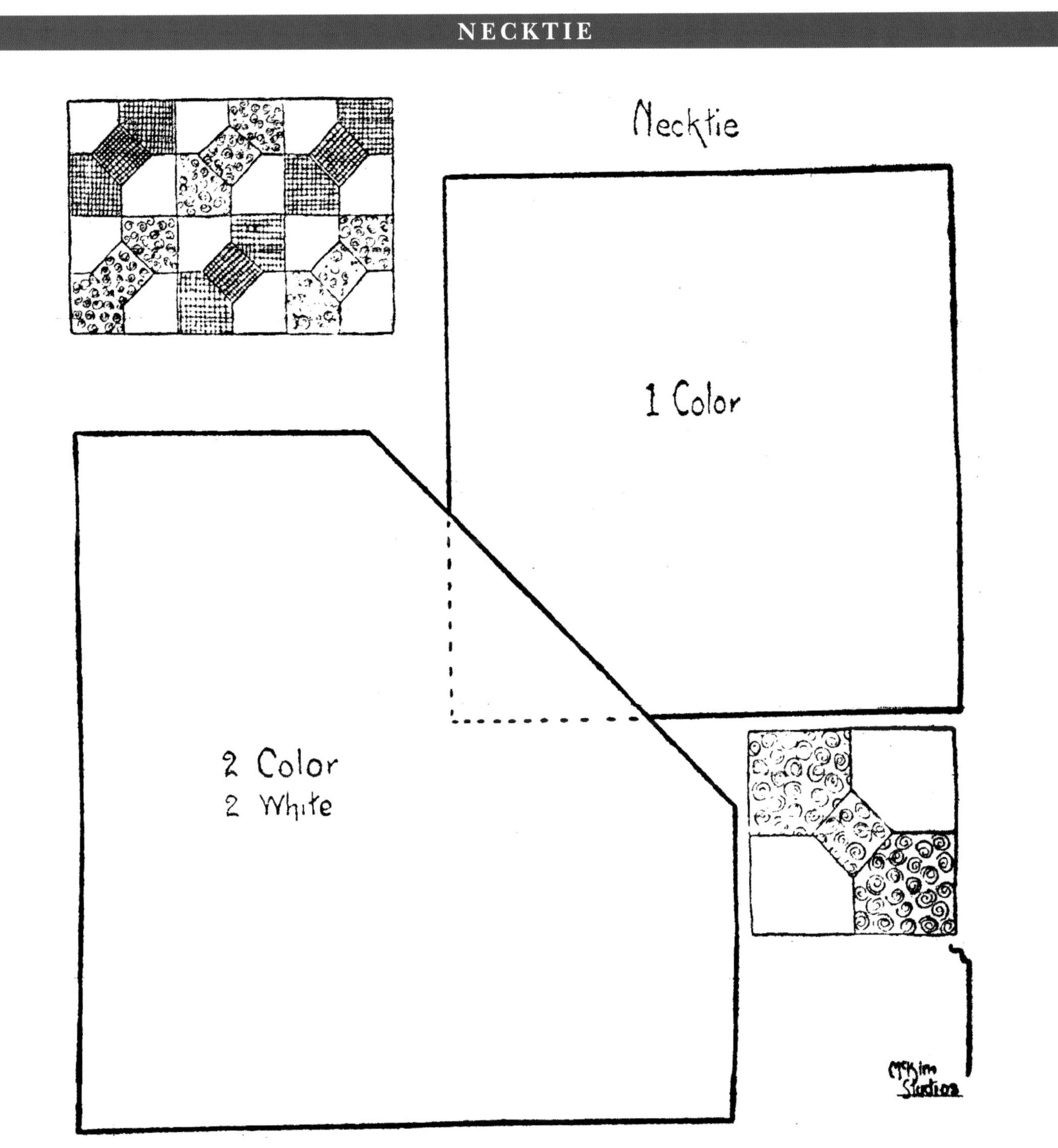

Published April 27, 1929

This design for a quilt block in plain and print scraps has the small bow tie for a motive. The pattern was contributed by Mrs. John Wassman, Boonville, Mo.

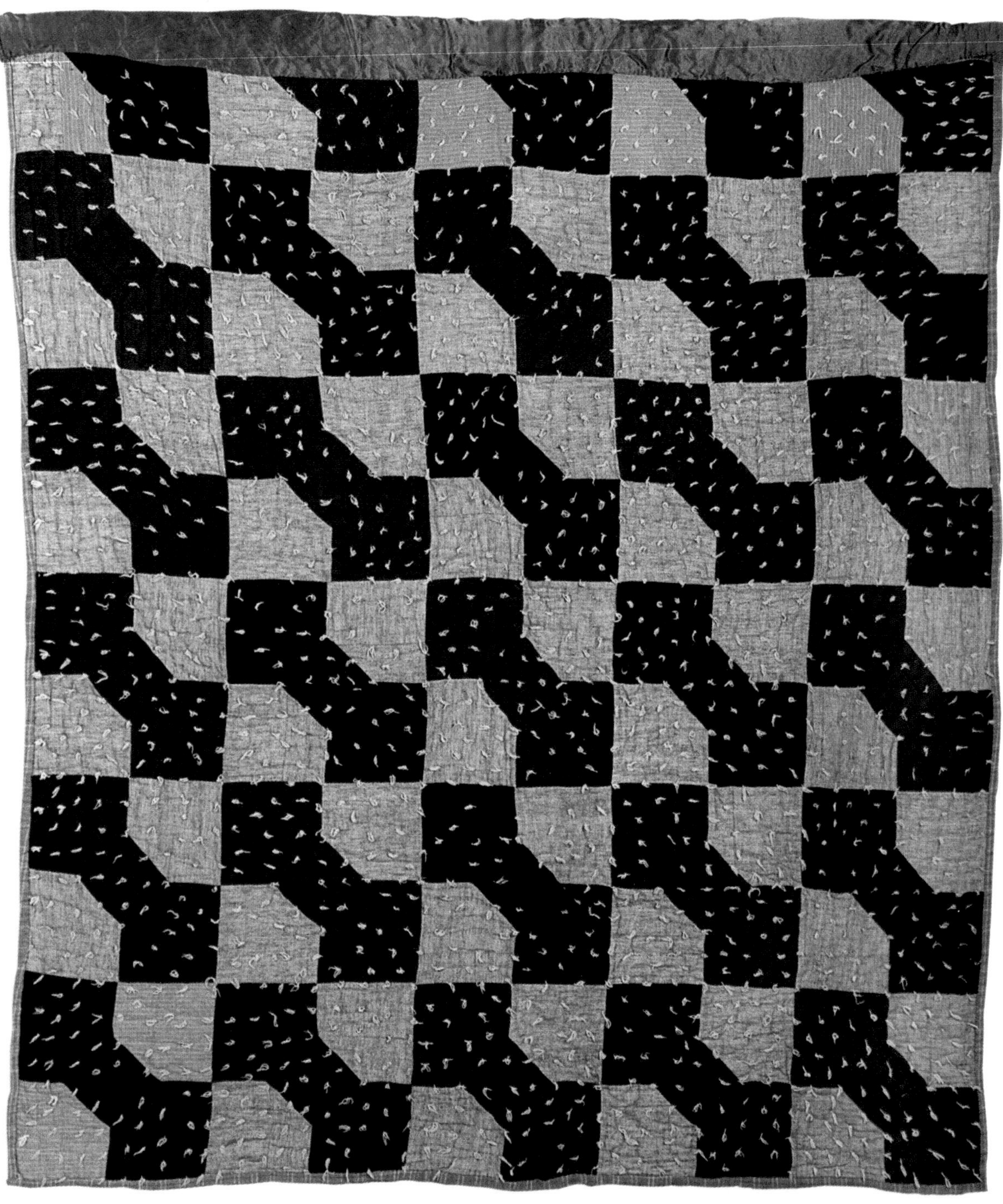

Neck Tie (1929 pattern) **Made in 1904 by Nancy Landess** **Made from wool suit** **Owned by Marilyn Kneale Henderson**

■ **Block size:** 8"

■ **Fabrics needed:** Two fabrics, a **light** and a **medium**

Cutting and piecing instructions

■ From **light** fabric, cut:

* Two 4½-inch squares

■ From **medium** fabric, cut:

* Two 4 ½-inch squares
* Two 2 ½-inch squares

■ **Draw** a diagonal line from corner to corner on the wrong side of a 2½-inch medium square. Place this atop a 4½-inch light square with the top right corners aligned, as shown below.

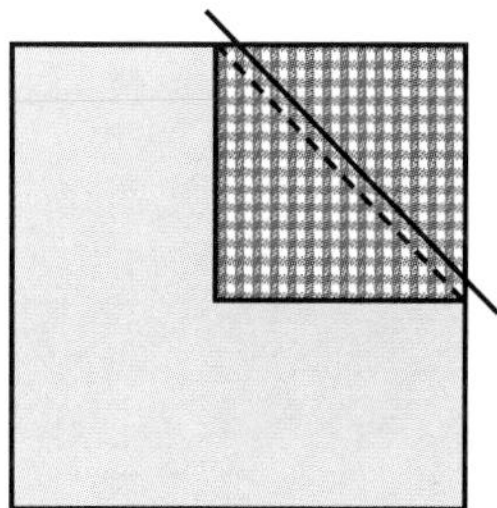

■ **Stitch** on the diagonal line. Trim 1/4 inch from the seam (on the solid line above).

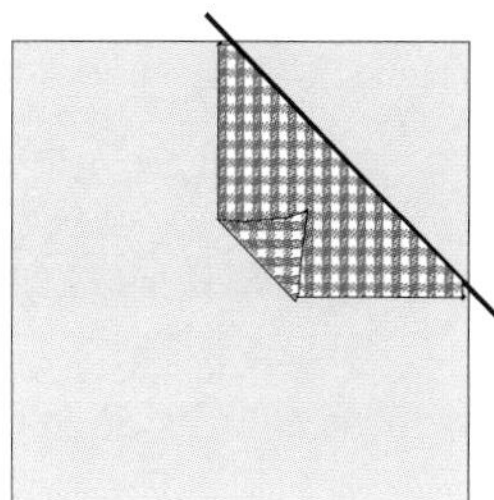

■ **Press** toward the medium square.

Make two of these units.

■ **Stitch** the pieced units together with the 4½-inch medium square, as shown below.

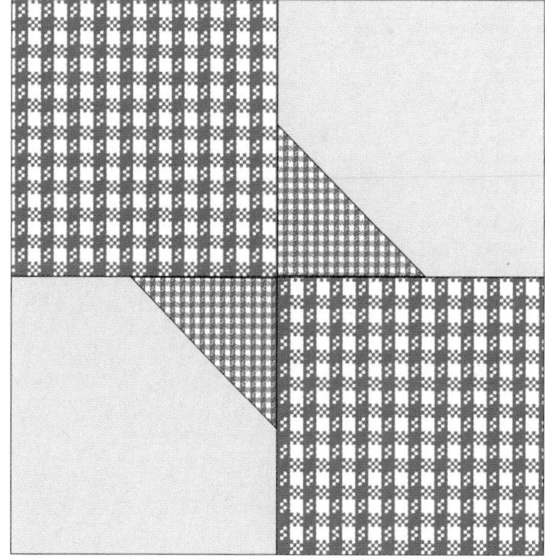

■ **Assemble** in rows.

Templates

See appendix for Sq 2⅞, Sq 4½, Misc 3

Varying the colors can create a strikingly different look for the necktie pattern.

Necktie **Made circa 1910-1915 by Nancy Landess** **Owned by Marilyn Kneale Henderson**
Made of wool dress fabric

THE RAMBLER IS A CHARMING QUILT PATTERN

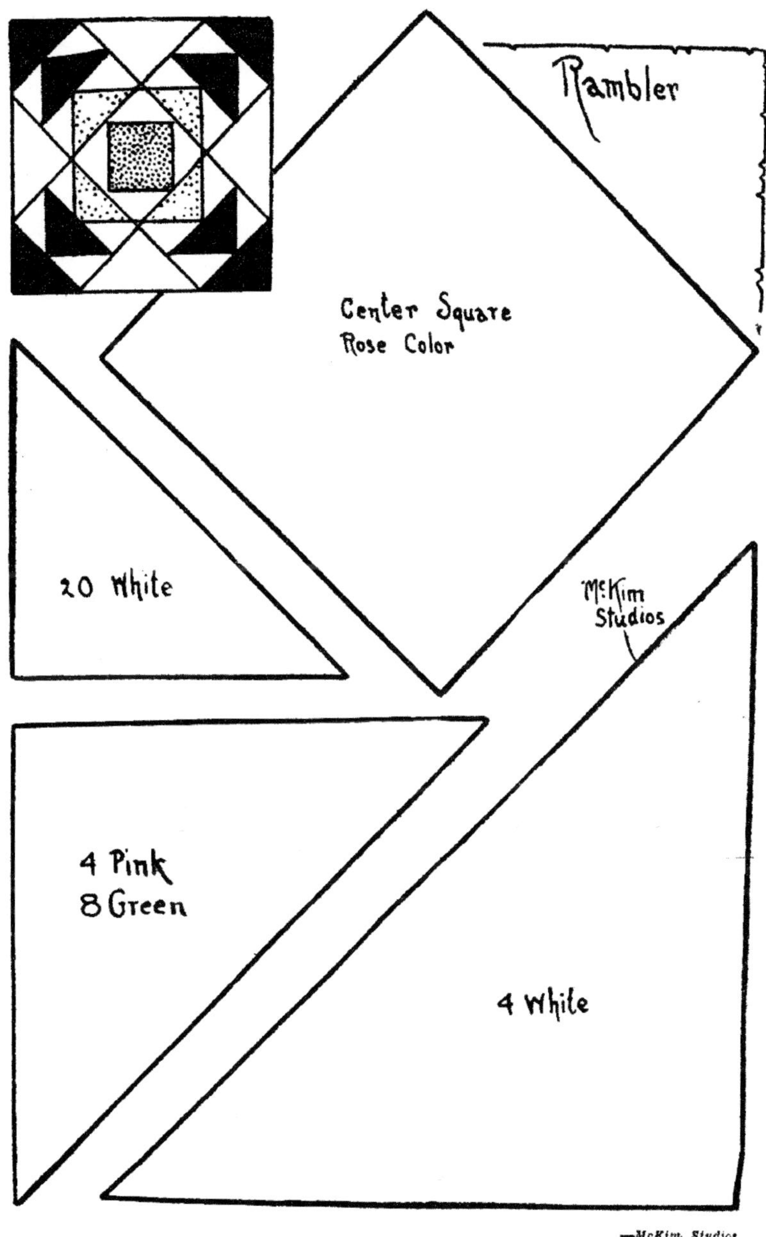

Published Jan. 2, 1929

This is the Rambler, one of the old-fashioned patchwork patterns, which may be used for a pillow, or, set together with alternating white blocks, for a counterpane, the roses spotting color and the triangle leaves rambling in formal pattern diagonally across the quilt. Each block when set together measures approximately twelve and one-half inches.

To piece a block, sew four small white triangles on to the center square of rose. Then piece the four other squares, each consisting of a pink and a green and four small white triangles. Complete by making the diagonal center strip and then the two large corner triangles all of which sewed together will complete the finished square.

1929 Rambler

Rambler block

Made by Jeanne Poore

■ **Block size:** 12"

■ **Fabrics needed:** Three fabrics, a **light**, a **medium,** and a **dark**

Cutting and piecing instructions

■ From **light** fabric, cut:
* One 7½-inch square
* Ten 3-inch squares

■ From **dark** fabric, cut:
* One 3½-inch square
* Two 5½-inch square

■ From **medium** fabric, cut:
* One 5½-inch square

■ **Subcut** the 7½-inch light square into four triangles.

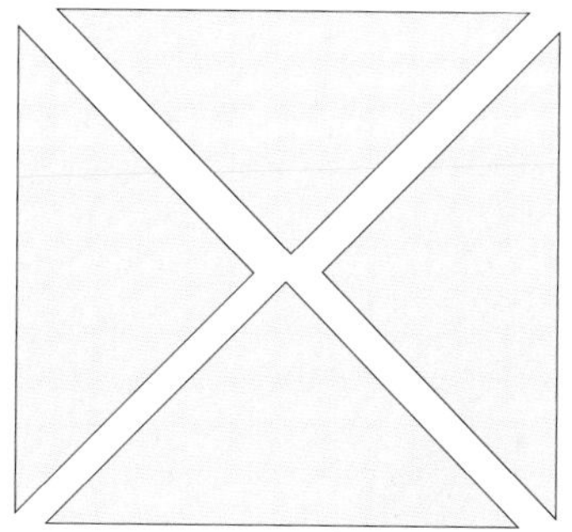

■ **Subcut** two of the 3-inch light squares along a diagonal.

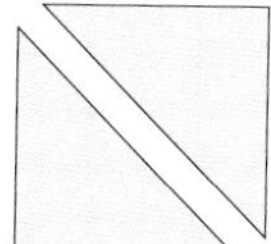
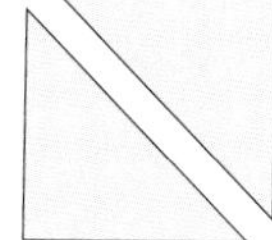

On the remaining eight 3-inch light squares, mark a diagonal line.

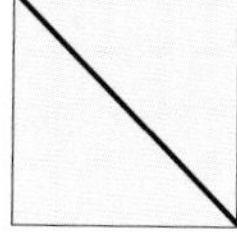

■ Subcut one 5½-inch dark square into four triangles.

■ **Flying Goose units:** Place two of the 3-inch light squares, right sides down, on top of the 5½-inch medium square.

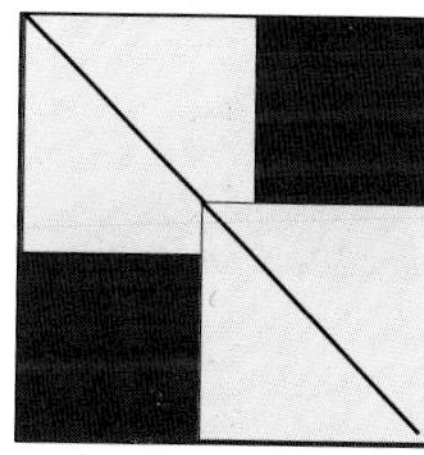

■ **Stitch** ¼-inch on both sides of the line.

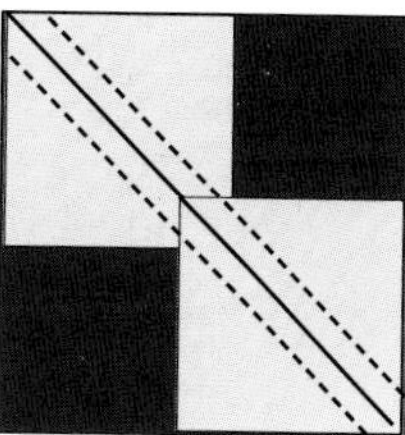

■ **Cut** on the line. Put aside the upper right portion.

■ **Press** to medium units.

■ **Place** a light square in the lower left corner, mark a diagonal as shown and stitch ¼-inch on either side.

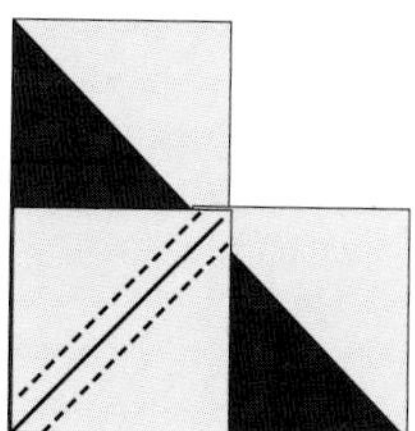

■ **Cut** along the solid line through all layers of fabric.

■ **Press** to medium unit.

You should get these two units. Repeat this process with the upper right portion. You will then have four units like these.

■ **Make** four similar Flying Goose units with the remaining 5½-inch dark square.

■ **Attach** the four small light triangles to the center square.

■ **Sew** together the Flying Goose units (one each color combination), the light triangles and a dark triangle.

■ **Stitch** Flying Goose units and a dark triangle as shown to the opposite sides of the center square. Stitch the large triangle units to this assembled strip.

Templates

See appendix for Sq 3½, T 3, T 4, T 5¼

Here are some interesting ways to assemble the quilt top.

THE CROSS AND CROWN IN PATCHWORK QUILT

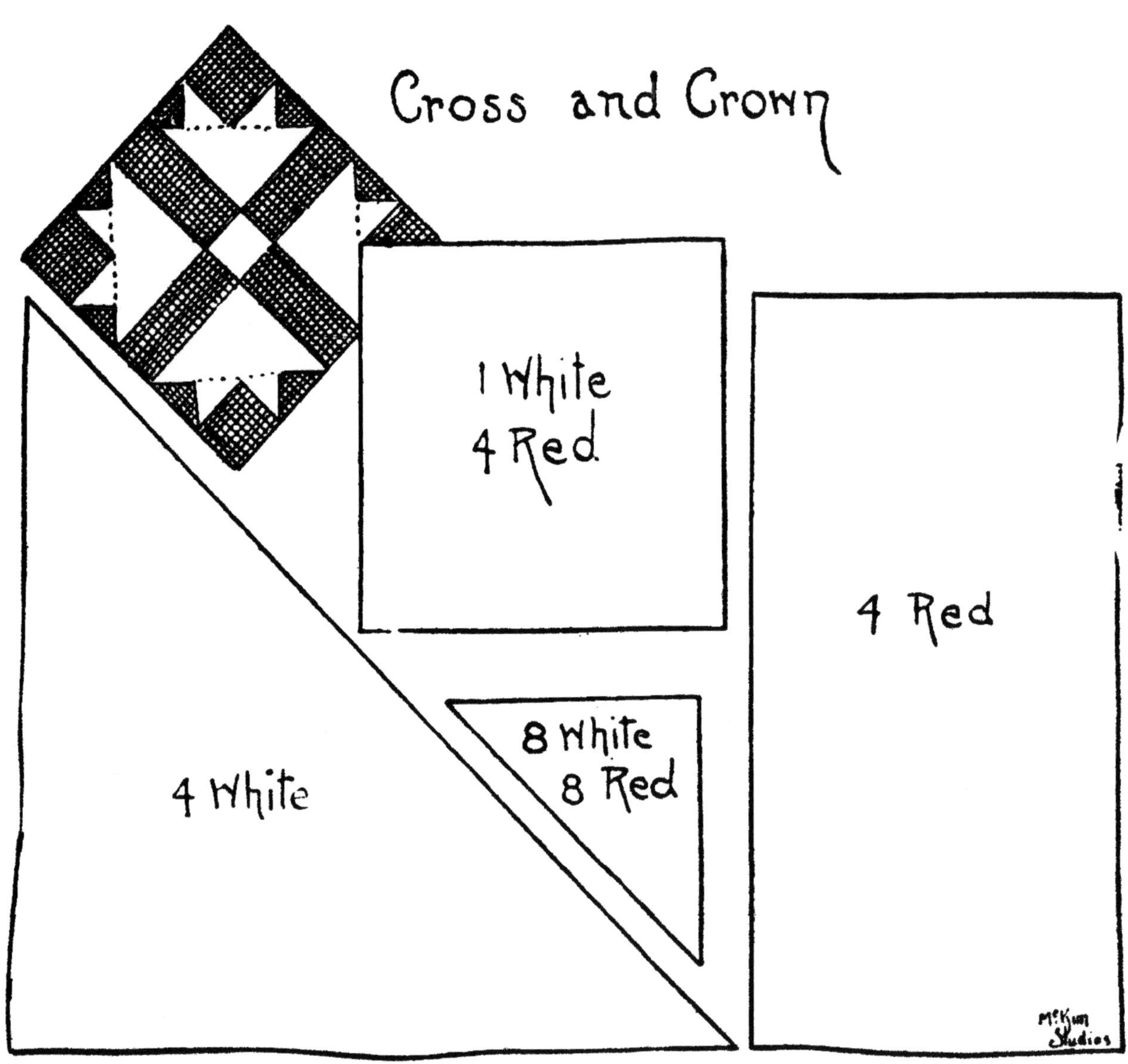

Published April 26, 1930

This quaint old pattern with its "firm-in-the-faith" title is really a variation of the lily blocks which have flowers resembling these "crowns" combined with applique stems, leaves, with perhaps a pieced basket corner as was shown at another time. "Goose tracks" is also quite similar in pattern but of course less dignified in name! This is one of the more simple quilts to piece, the finished effect varying considerably in relation to the way it is set together.

With red lattice strips joining white squares at the corner the pattern stands out entirely different than when white strips or large squares are used, or again the background may be light with darker design. Allow seams extra; about 3-16-inch is right for this

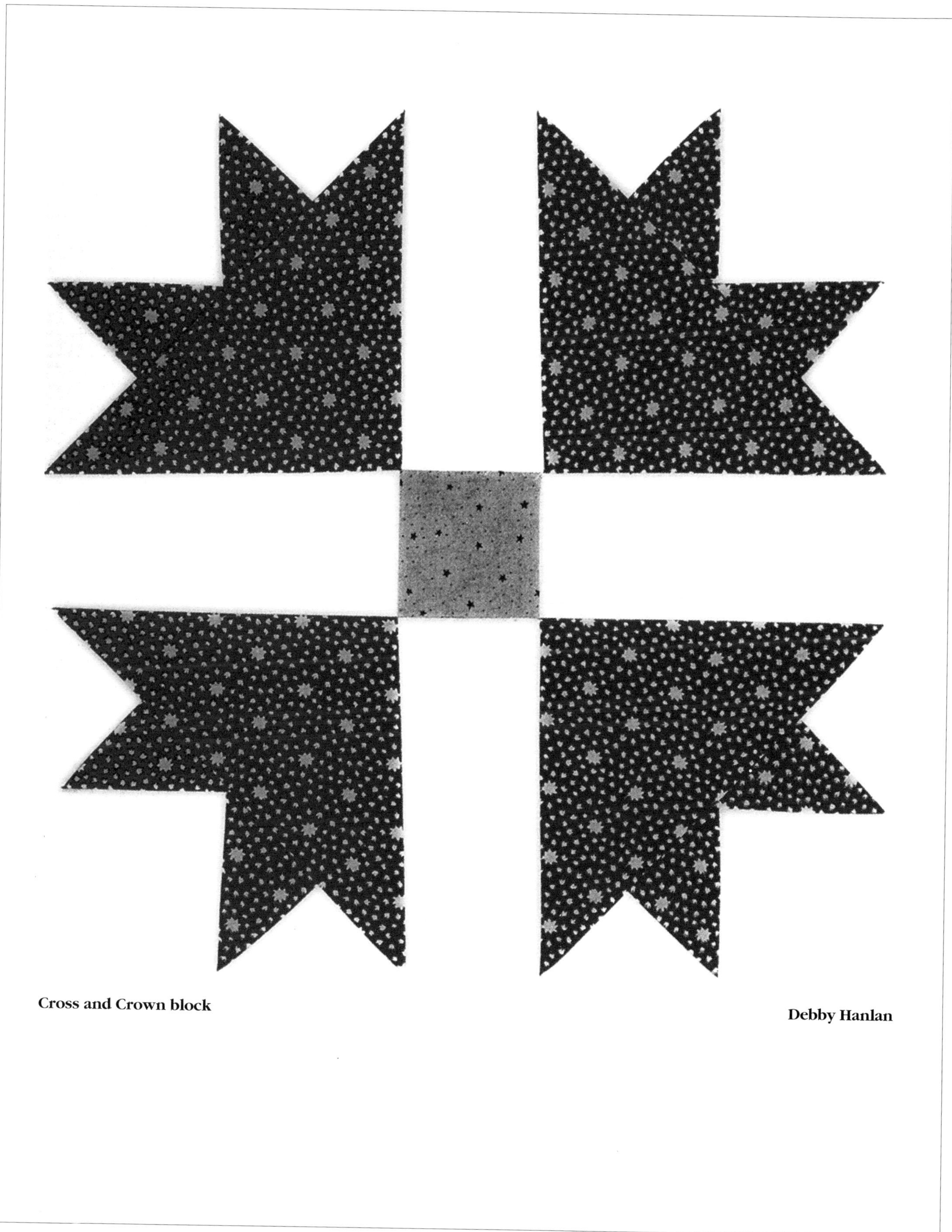

Cross and Crown block

Debby Hanlan

■ **Block size:** 12"

■ **Fabrics needed:** Three fabrics, a **light,** a **medium** and a **dark**.

Cutting and piecing instructions

■ From **light** fabric, cut:
* Six 3¼-inch squares
* Four 2½ x 5½-inch strips

■ From **medium** fabric, cut::
* Two 5⅞-inches squares
* Two 3¼-inch squares

■ From **dark** fabric, cut:
* One 2 ½-inch square.

■ **Subcut** the 5⅞-inch medium squares diagonally to make four triangles.

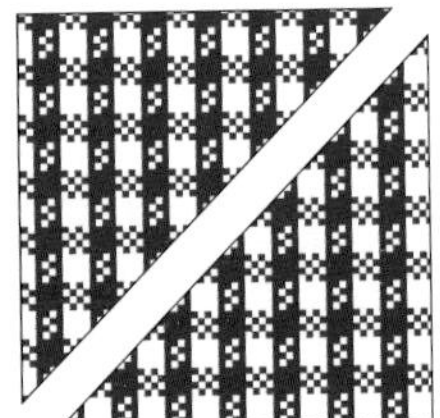

■ **Draw** a diagonal line from corner to corner on the wrong side of the two of the light squares. Place these atop the 3¼-inch medium squares, right sides facing.

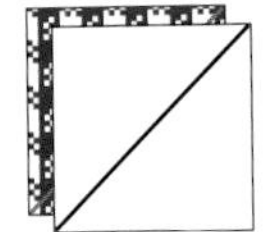
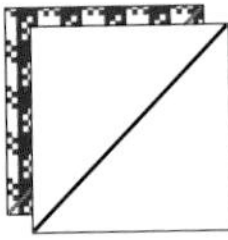

■ **Stitch** ¼-inch on both sides of the solid line. Cut on the line.

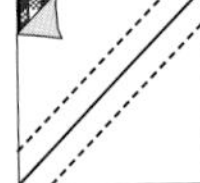
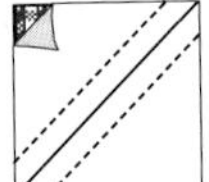

■ **Press** to the print. You will now have four units that look like this.

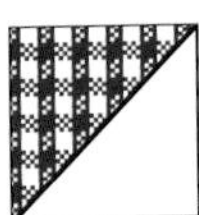
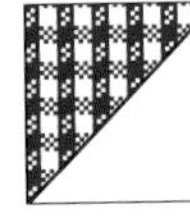
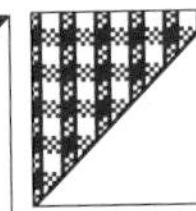
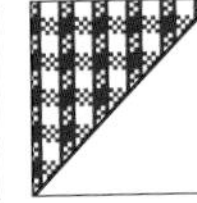

■ **Cut** these diagonally and you will have eight triangles.

■ **Assemble** as shown. Make four of these.

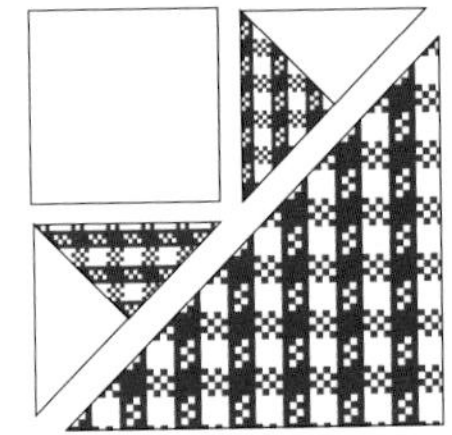

■ **Put** two of these units together as shown with the 2½-by-5½-inch strip between.

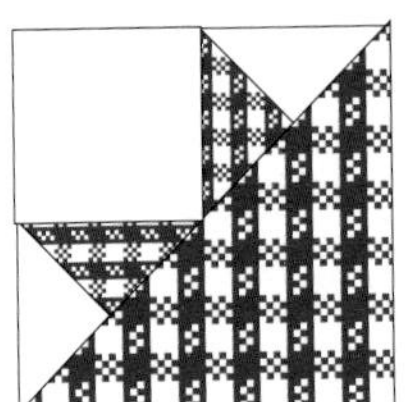

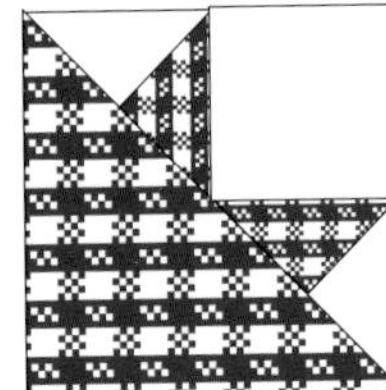

■ **Make** two of these assemblies.

■ **Stitch** together two of the 2½-by-5½-inch strips and the 2½-inch square as shown.

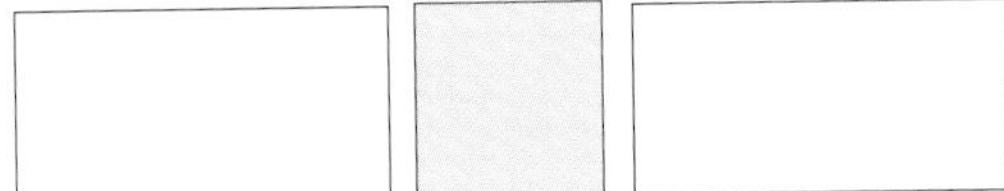

■ **Assemble** the block as shown.

Reversing the use of light and medium fabrics, above right, creates a dramatically different effect when the quilt blocks are assembled.

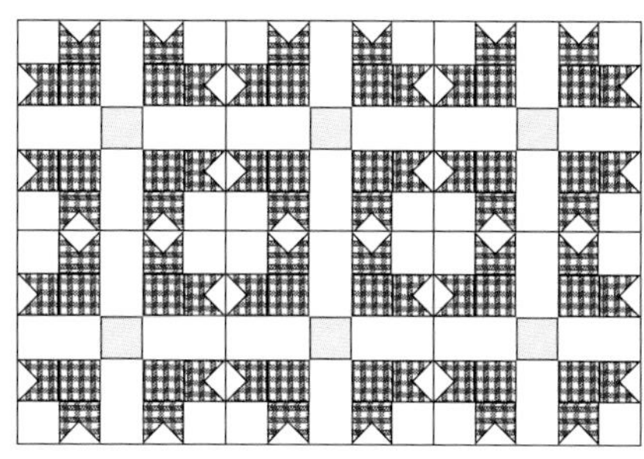

Yet another appearance is created when the blocks are turned 45 degrees.

Templates

See appendix for Sq 2½, Sq 3¼, T 2¾, T 5⅞, P 5½ x 2½

DUTCHMAN'S PUZZLE

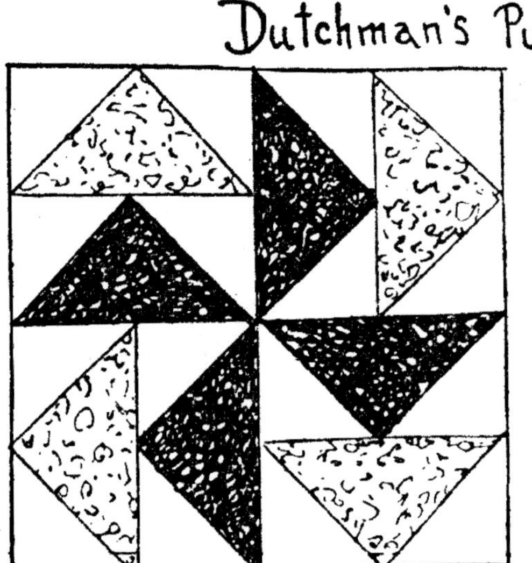

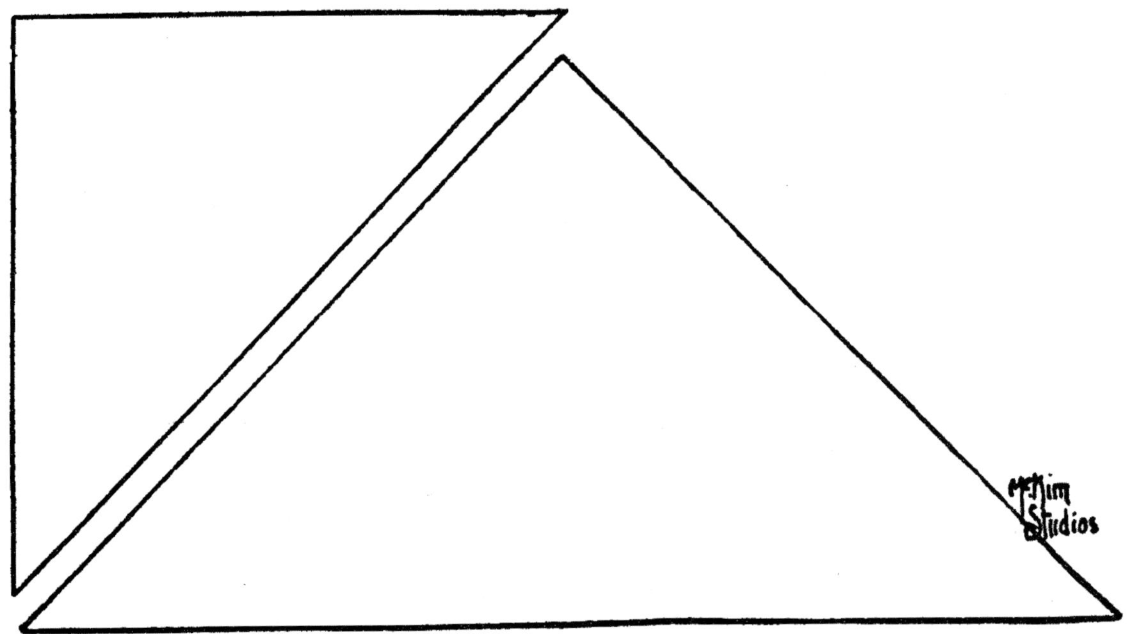

Published March 29, 1930

In Dutchman's Puzzle two smaller triangles add to a larger about like the cutting chart patterns are placed, and this twice done forms a square, one-fourth of the finished block. The darker always points into the lighter and thus the puzzle is solved in a 12-inch block.

Dutchman's Puzzle block

Made by Jeanne Poore

■ **Block size:** 12"

■ **Fabrics needed:** Three are used: a **light,** a **medium,** and a **dark.**

Cutting and piecing instructions

■ From each of the medium and dark fabrics, cut:

* Two 7¼-inch squares

■ From the **light** fabric, cut:

* Eight 3⅞-inch squares

Flying Goose unit:

■ **Draw** a diagonal line from corner to corner on the wrong side of the light squares.

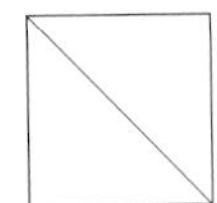

■ **Place** two of these atop a 7¼-inch medium square, right sides facing.

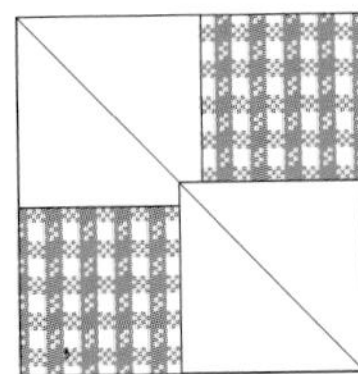

■ **Stitch** ¼-inch on both sides of the line.

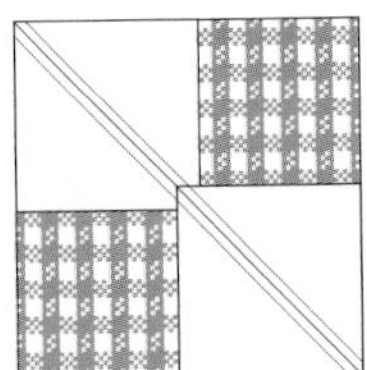

■ **Cut** on the line and set aside remaining fabric.

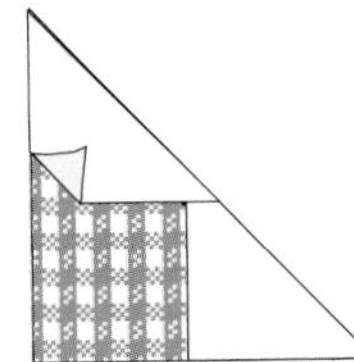

■ **Press** to medium units.

■ **Place** a light square in the lower left corner, mark a diagonal as shown and stitch ¼-inch on either side.

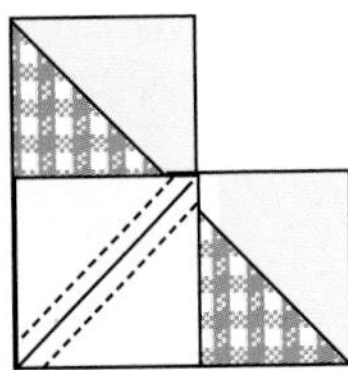

■ **Cut** along the solid line through all layers of fabric.

■ **Press** to medium unit.

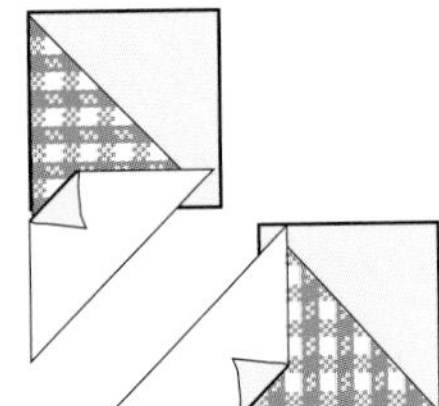

You will get these two units. Make two more like them from the remaining fabric from this square.

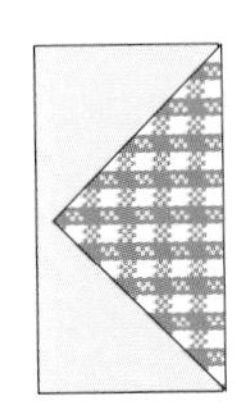

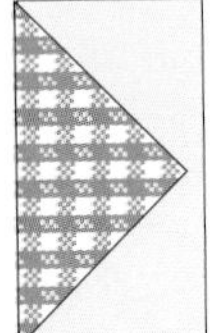

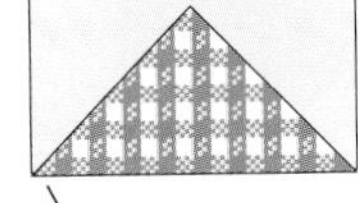

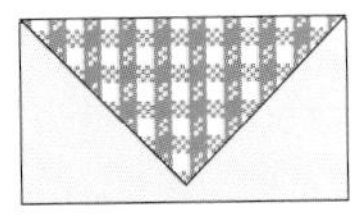

■ **Create** four more Flying Goose units from the dark print.

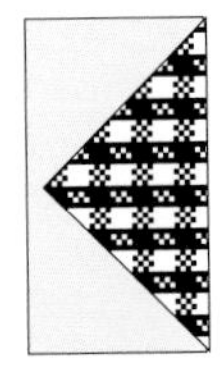

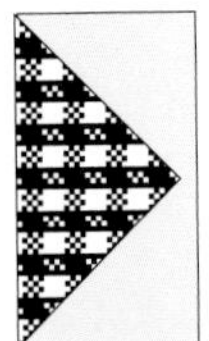

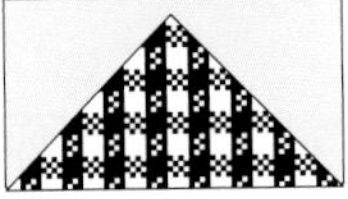

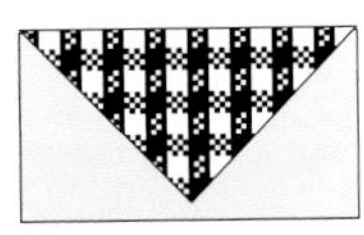

■ Assemble in rows, as shown.

Templates

T 3⅞, T 5

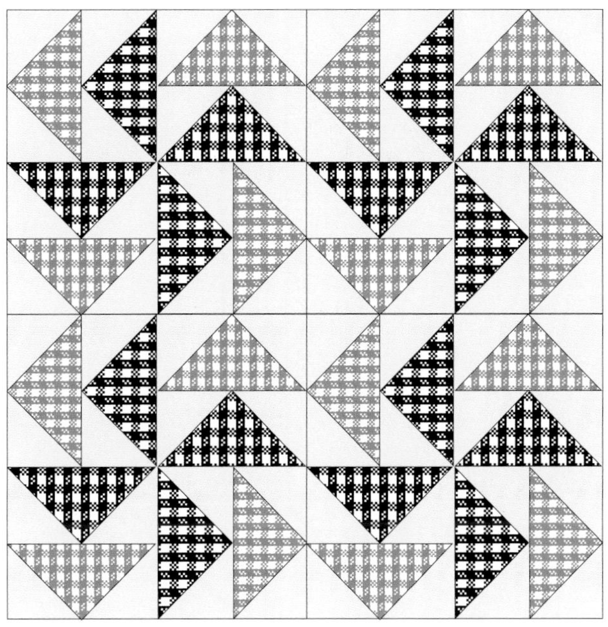

Other fabrics create an interesting variations.

A HISTORICAL BLOCK IS EASILY PIECED

Clay's Choice

4 Darkest (Orange)

4 Medium (Yellow)
4 White

4 White
4 Medium

McKim Studios

Published July 26, 1930

Quilt patterns are ever so much more interesting if one knows their stories. Clay's Choice is a very lovely block in its own right, but when it is traced back to the bitter Calhoun or Clay days one finds it as Harry's Star or Clay's Choice in the soft brown tone prints of pre-war days. Then it becomes Henry of the West as the tide of empire surges westward and another generation forgets Clay entirely and calls it Star of the West. Clay's Choice or Star of the West is easily pieced if developed as shown in the sketch. It might be set together with alternate plain square of either white or yellow.

Clay's Choice

Block from Kansas City Star Sampler Quilt by Jeanne Poore

■ **Block size:** 12"

■ **Fabrics needed:** Three fabrics, a **light,** a **medium**, and a **dark**.

Cutting and piecing instructions

■ From the **light** fabric, cut:
* Two 3⅞-inch squares.
* Four 3½ -inch squares.

■ From the **dark** fabric, cut:
* Two 3⅞-inch squares.
* Four 3½ -inch squares.

■ From the **medium** fabric, cut:
* Four 3⅞-inch squares.

■ **Draw** a diagonal line on the back of the two 3⅞-inch light squares and the two 3⅞-inch dark squares.

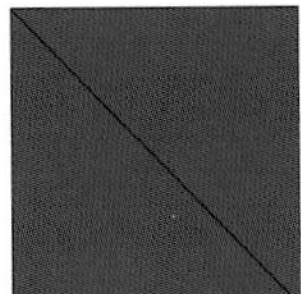
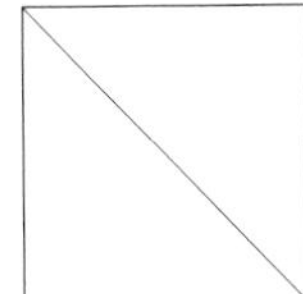

■ **Place** each of these fabrics together with one of the 3⅞-inch medium squares, right sides facing.

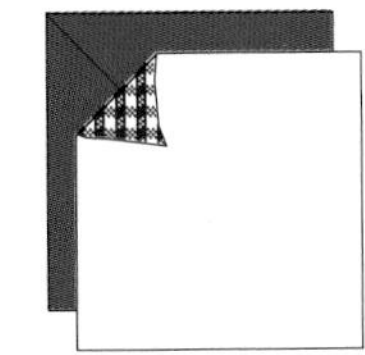
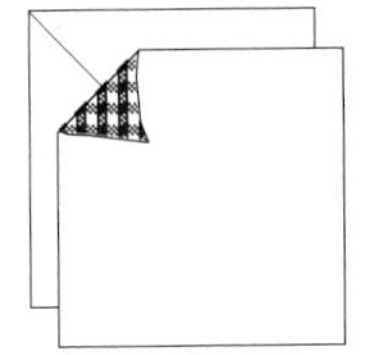

■ **Stitch** ¼-inch from diagonal line along both sides of the line.

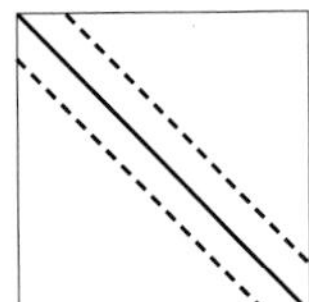

■ **Cut** on the line, unfold, and press to the darker fabric.

You should have units that look like this:

■ **Assemble** these units with the four 3½-inch light squares and four 3½ -inch dark squares in rows as shown.

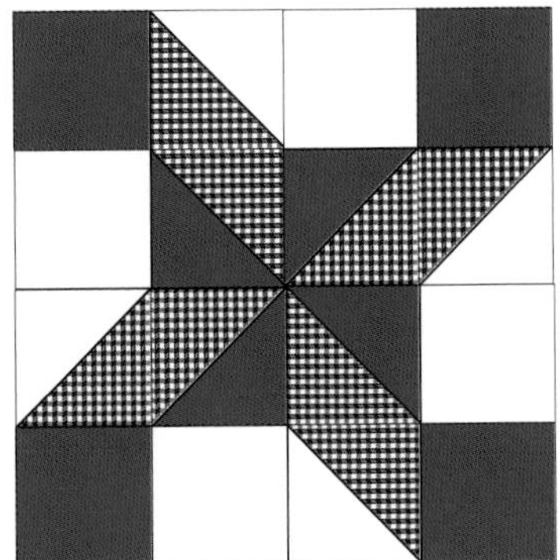

Templates

See appendix for Sq 3½, T 3⅞

The quilt's overall pattern begins to appear as blocks are assembled.

GREEN MAKES A PRETTY MAPLE LEAF QUILT

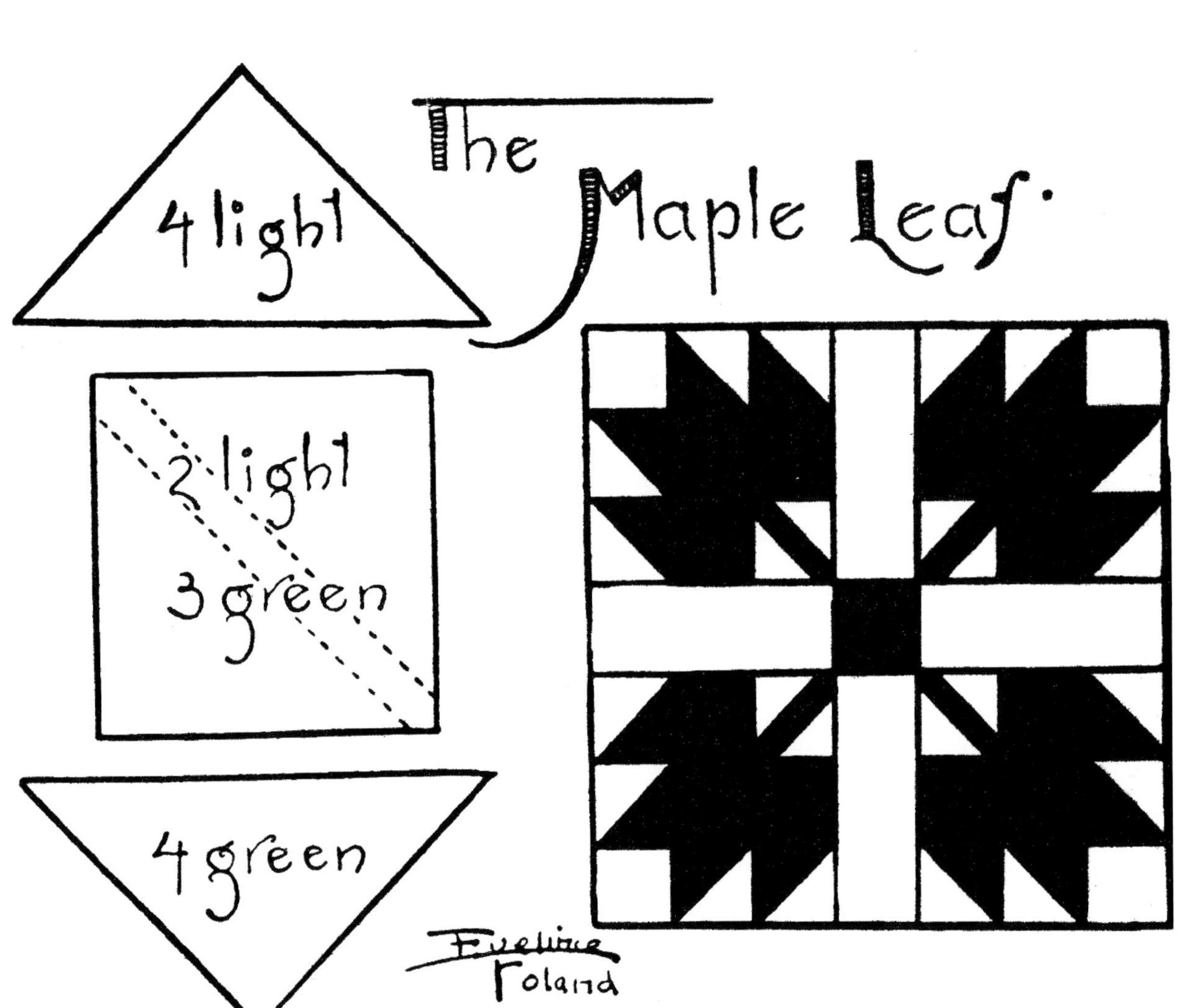

Published August 2, 1930

Surely this pretty little Maple Leaf quilt pattern will have a special appeal to any Canadian quilters who happen to be in the States. While green seems to be the most natural color to use, pastel colors would be effective also. It is quite a small block, only five and a half inches square — four blocks being shown above. The separate blocks are stripped together with plain fabric, the width of the square patch, and a colored one used at each corner. These patches, being small, must be very carefully cut, allowing a narrow seam.

Maple Leaf on Point (1938 version) **Made by Miriam G. Eads** **Lougene Eads Geary, owner**

■ **Block size:** 12"

■ **Fabrics needed:** Two fabrics: A **light**, and a **dark**.

Cutting and piecing instructions

■ From the **light** fabric, cut:
* Sixteen 2¼-inch squares.
* Four 2 x 5¾-inch strips

■ From the **dark** fabric, cut:
* Twenty 2¼-inch squares.
* One 2x2-inch square.
* Four ¾ x 4-inch strips

■ **Press** the raw edges of the four ¾ x 4-inch dark strips under. Applique diagonally from corner to corner on four of the 2¼-inch squares.

■ **Triangle assembly:**

Draw a diagonal line on the wrong side of four of the 2¼-inch dark squares. Place a dark square and a 2¼-inch light square together, right sides facing.

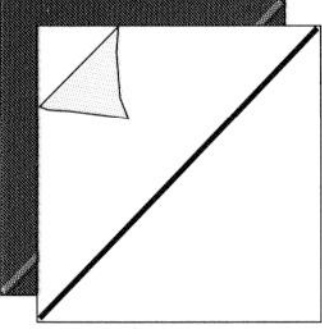

■ **Stitch** together ¼ inch on either side of the line. Cut on the line.

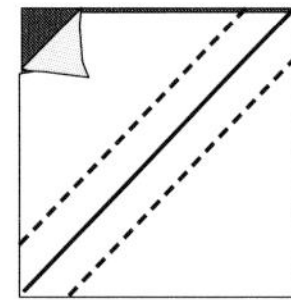

■ **Unfold**, lay flat and press toward the dark fabric

Make 15 more of these units.

■ **Maple Leaf assembly:**

With a 2¼-inch light square and three 2¼-inch dark squares, assemble the Maple Leaf unit as shown:

■ **Put** two Maple Leaf units together as shown with one of the 2 x 5¾-inch strips in between.

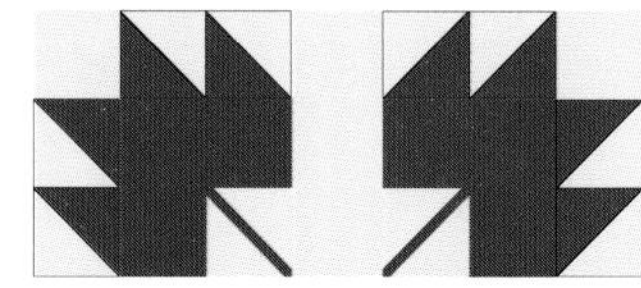

■ **Make** two of these units, with the second one upside down.

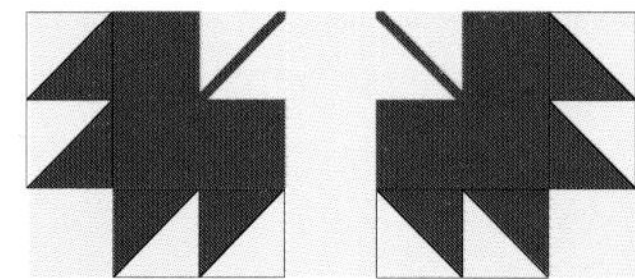

■ **Stitch** together two more of the 2 x 5¾-inch strips and the 2 x 2-inch accent square as shown.

■ **Assemble** block as shown.

Templates

See appendix for Sq 2, Sq 2¼, T 2¼, P 5¾ x 2, P 4 x ¾

"MILKY WAY" BLOCK MAY BE MADE WITH OR WITHOUT BORDERS

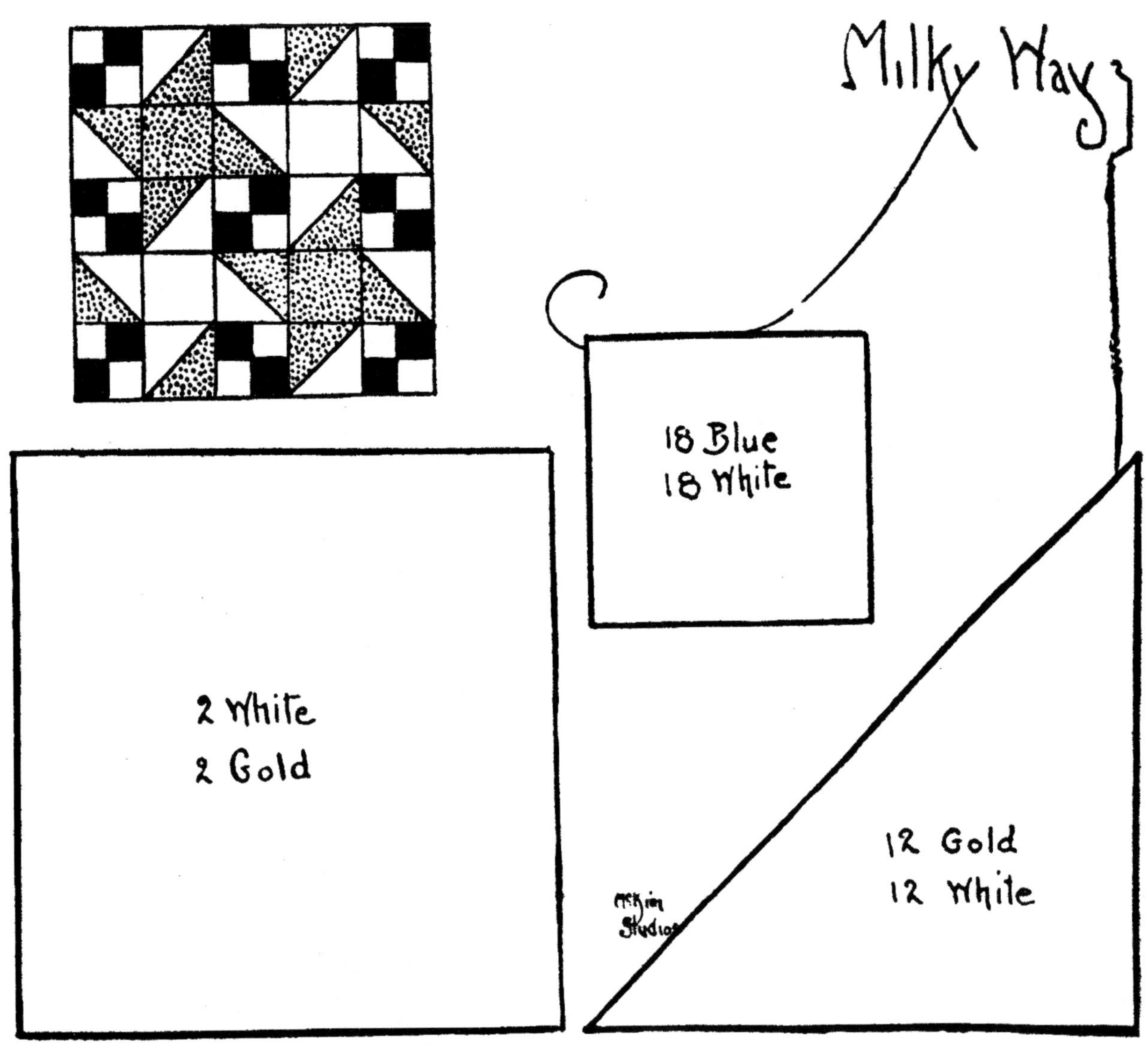

Published Jan. 25, 1930

Milky Way is a large block fifteen inches square, or by continuing two more rows top and side it could be made twenty-one inches square. It would make an unusual counterpane by piecing a border all around nine inches wide, which completes the dark and light stars to use with a large continuing block either square or oblong as the quilt's center. This would leave a wide plain space of blue or white for quilting between the pieced center and the pieced border.

Milky Way **Made and owned by Martha Schuman**

■ **Block size:** 12"

■ **Fabrics needed:** Three fabrics, a **light,** a **medium** and a **dark.**

Cutting and piecing instructions

■ From **light** fabric, cut:
* Two 4⅞-inch squares
* One 2½ x 22-inch strip

■ From **medium** fabric, cut:
* Two 4⅞-inch squares
* One 4½-inch square

■ From **dark** fabric, cut:
* One 2½ x 22-inch strip

■ **Draw** a line from corner to corner on the wrong side of a 4⅞-inch light square. Place together with a 4⅞-inch medium square, right sides facing.

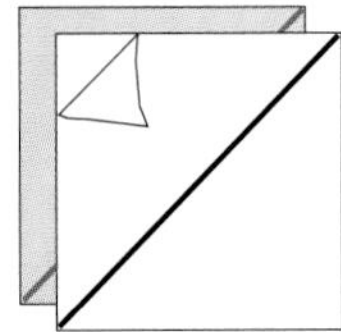

■ **Stitch** ¼-inch on both sides of the diagonal line.

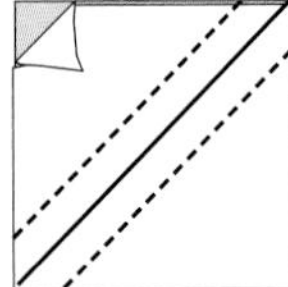

■ **Cut** on the solid line, unfold, and press both to darker fabric. Repeat with the remaining 4⅞-inch squares. You should now have four units that look like this:

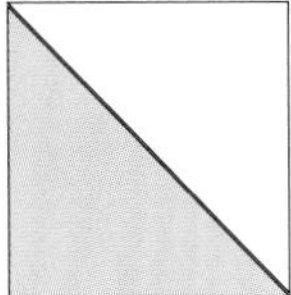

4-patch assembly:

■ **Stitch** with right sides together the 2½ x 22-inch light and dark fabric strips along their lengths.

■ **Press** toward the background.

■ **Cut** this strip into 2½-inch units.

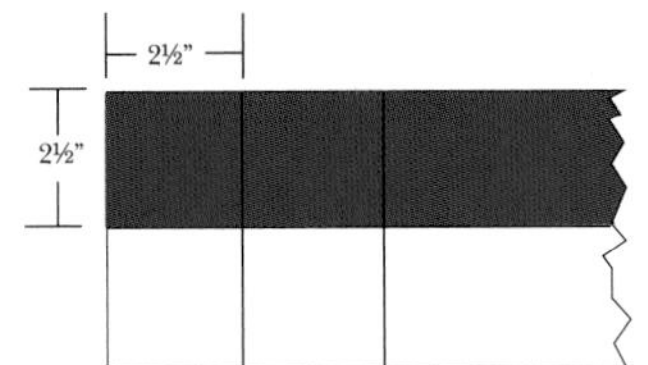

■ **Assemble** into a 4-patch as shown below. Four 4-patches are needed.

■ **Stitch** together two 4-patch units with a triangle unit between. Two of these units are needed for the block.

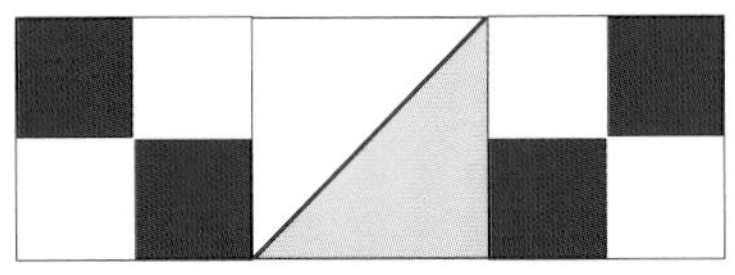

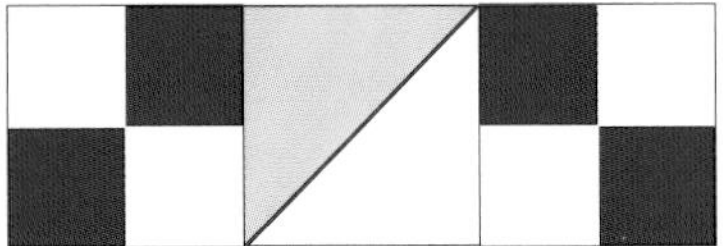

■ **Stitch** together two of the triangle units with the remaining medium square between.

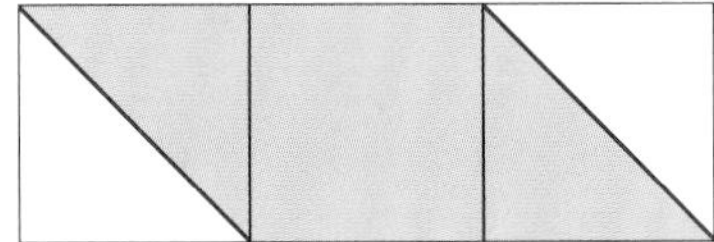

■ **Assemble** the three units like this.

Templates

See appendix for Sq 2½, Sq 4½ and T 4⅞

A PUZZLE FOR MISSOURI QUILT FANS

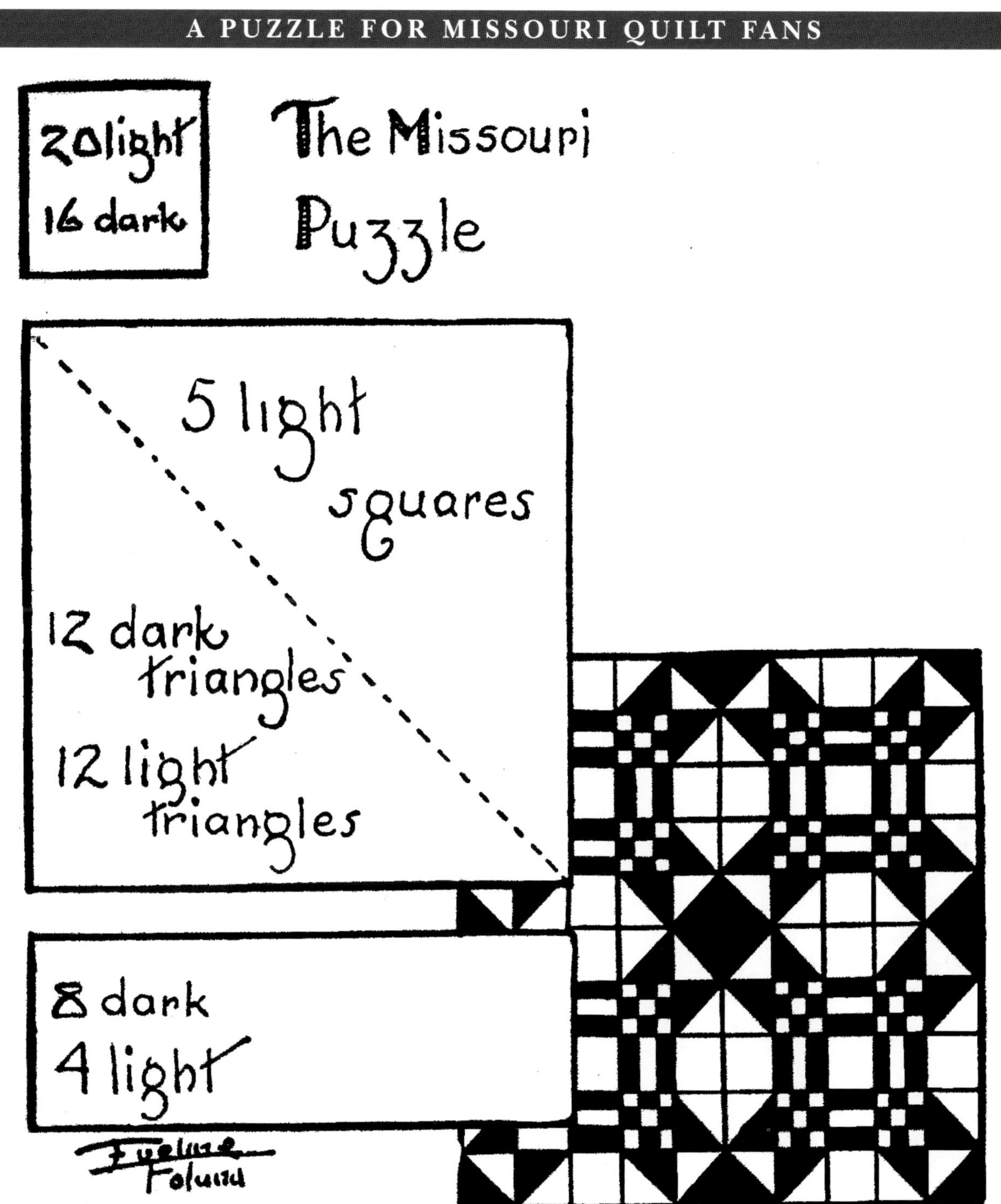

Published May 3, 1930

From Ellington, Mo., comes the Missouri Puzzle block which is quite as effective as the Indiana Puzzle and very attractive. The light, inner pieces should be made first and then the block pieced in rows which are then joined together. This pattern makes a lovely quilt when developed in pastel shades, particularly rose and lavender and set together with white.

The finished block measures fifteen inches square. No seams are allowed.

Missouri Puzzle block

By Jeanne Poore

■ **Block size:** 12"
■ **Fabrics needed:** Two fabrics, a **light** and a **dark color**

Cutting and piecing instructions

■ From **light** fabric, cut:
* Six 3¼-inch squares
* Five 2⅞-inch squares
* Two 1⅜ x 12-inch strips
* One 1⅜ x 18-inch strip

■ From **dark** fabric, cut
* Six 3¼-inch squares
* One 1⅜ x 12-inch strip
* Two 1⅜ x 18-inch strips

■ **Draw** a solid diagonal line from corner to corner on the wrong side of a 3¼-inch light square. Place together with a 3¼-inch dark square, right sides facing.

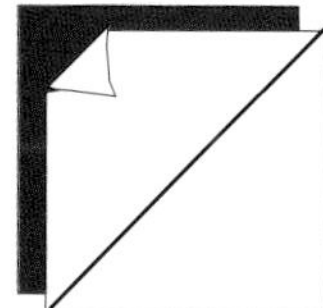

■ **Stitch** ¼-inch on both sides of the diagonal line.

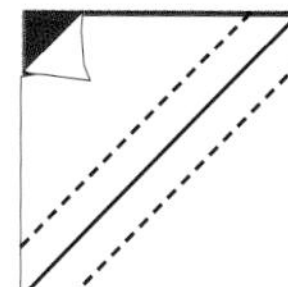

■ **Cut** on the solid line, unfold, and press to dark. Repeat this process with all six 3¼-inch light and dark squares to create 12 units that look like this:

9-patch assembly:
■ **Stitch** together the two 1⅜ x 12-inch strips of light fabric and the 1⅜ x 12-inch strip of dark fabric along their lengths, as shown:

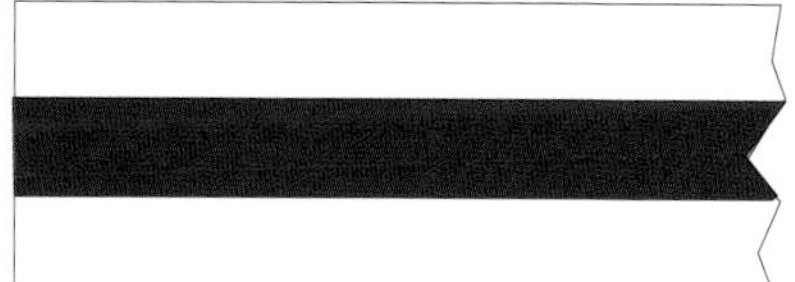

■ **Subcut** the 12-inch strips into eight units, each 1⅜-inches wide.

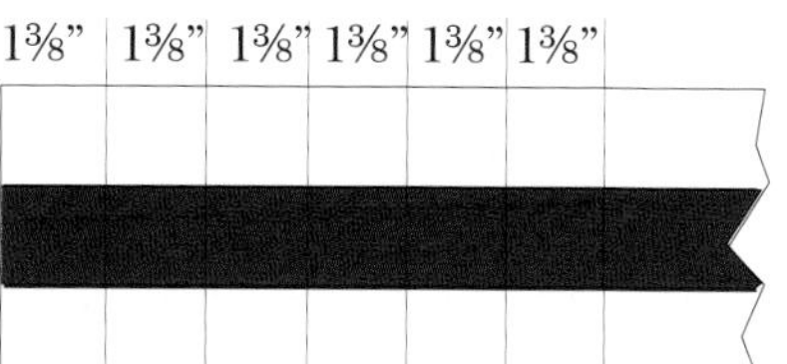

■ **Stitch** together the two 1⅜ x 18-inch strips of dark fabric and the 1⅜ x 18-inch strip of light fabric along the lengths, as shown:

■ **Subcut** the 18-inch strips into four units, each 2⅞-inches wide, and four units, each 1⅜-inches wide.

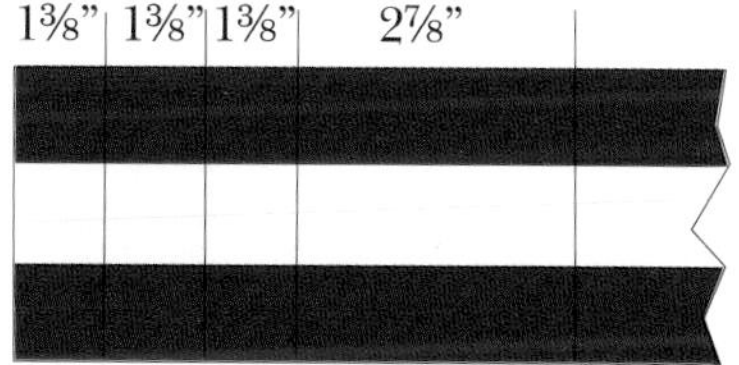

■ **Assemble** the 9-patch block as shown.

(Instructions continued on next page)

Templates

See appendix for templates Sq 1⅜, Sq 2⅞, T 3¼, P 2⅞ x 1⅜

■ **Assemble** the block as shown below.

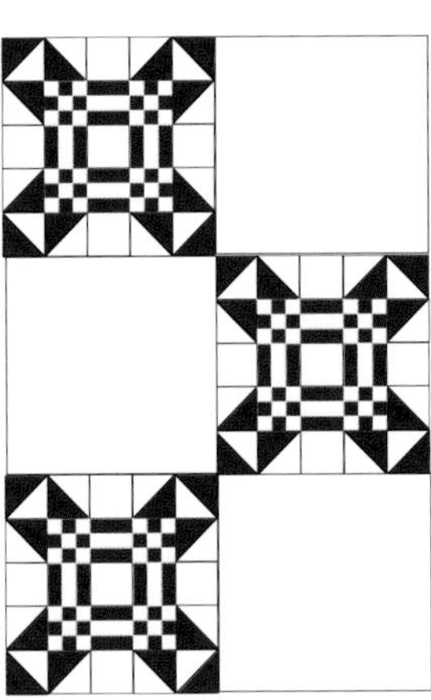

SIMPLICITY RECOMMENDS THIS QUILT BLOCK

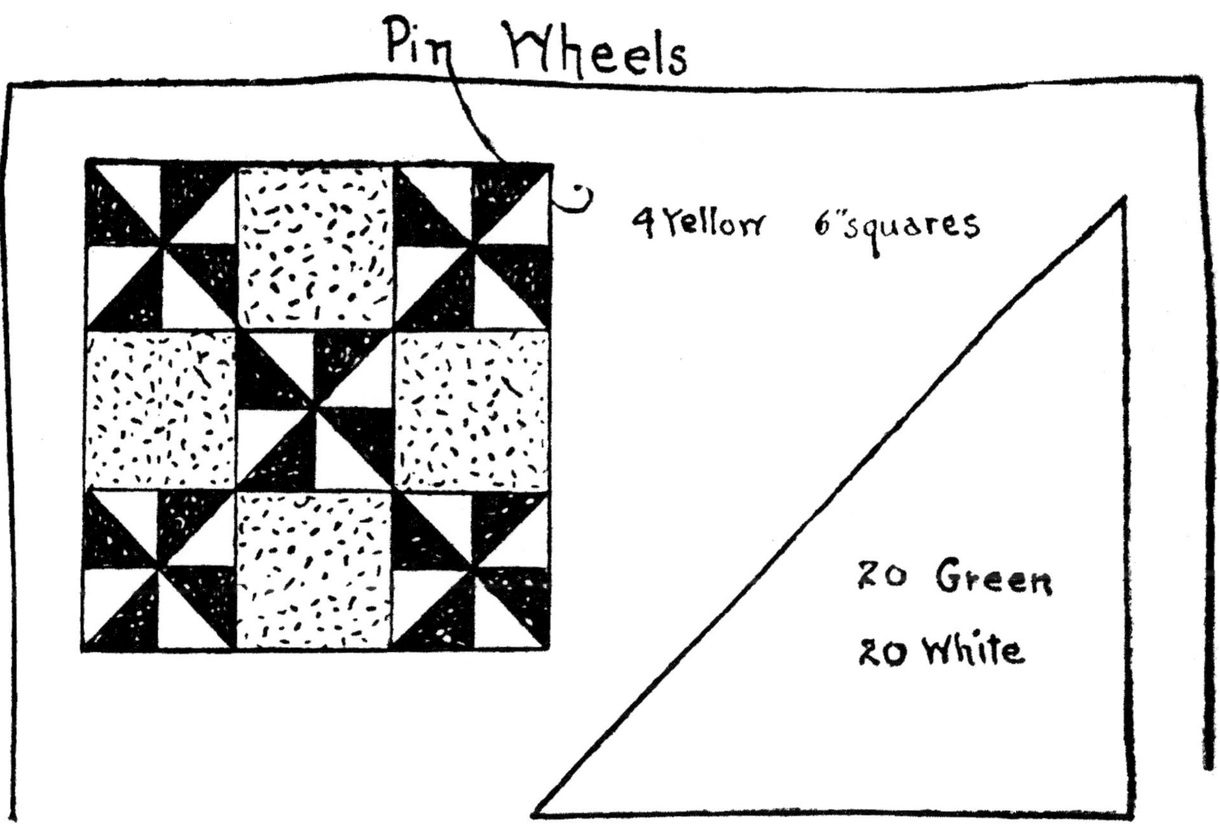

Published April 19, 1930

Pin Wheels, with an ancestral name older yet — Flutter Wheels — is one of the easiest of all patchworks to make. The only bit of wisdom offered on making this pattern is to cut all triangles on the true diagonal, that is with threads parallel to the two shorter sides each time, and then not to stretch the bias edges in seaming them together. This may be an all-over pattern or the 9-patch unit here shown may be used as a block and set together with lattice strips or plain squares. This is a good design for using scrap material of the children's frocks and rompers-dainty bits of print and plain to commemorate happy days. Seams may or may not be allowed extra.

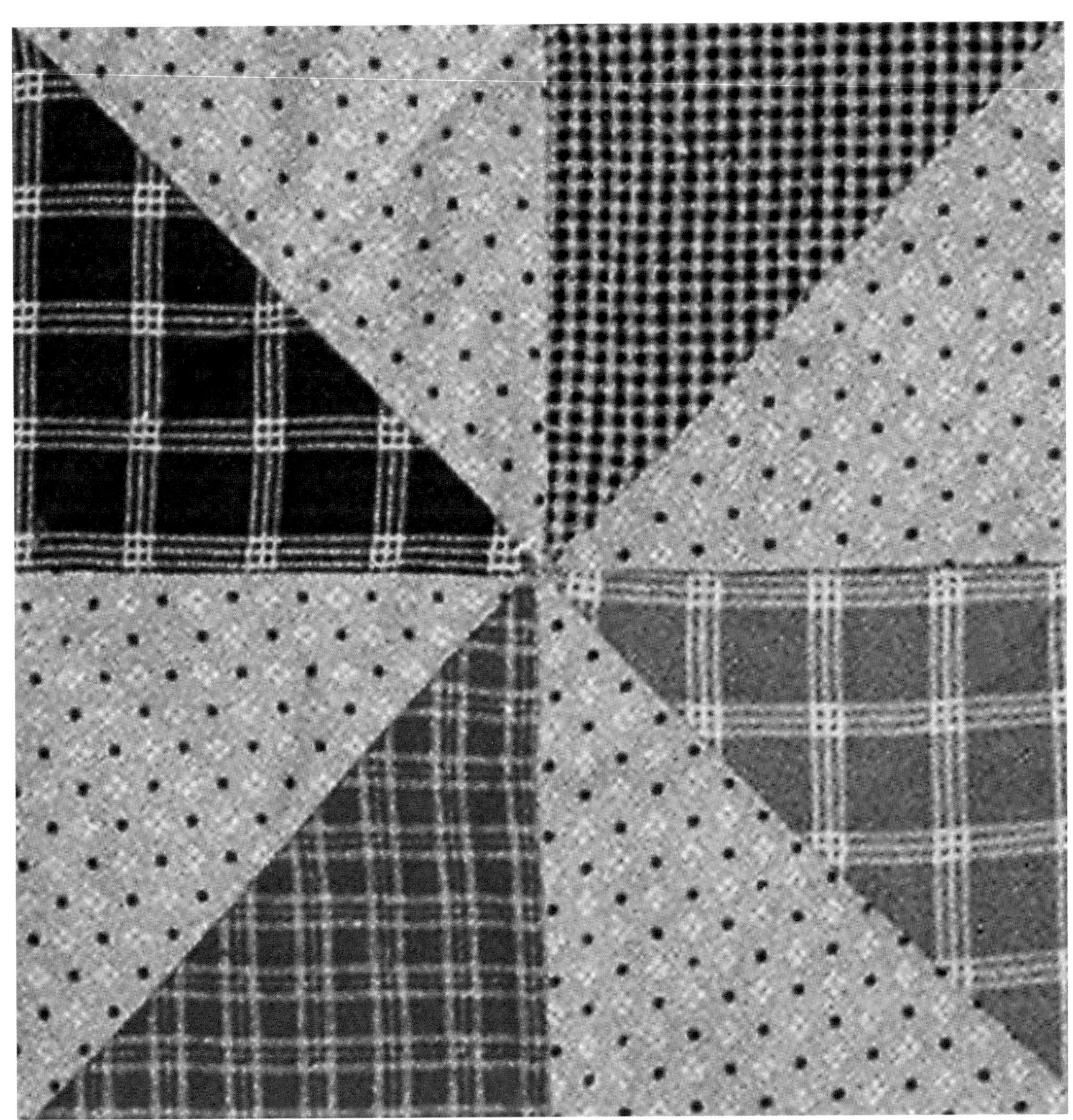

Pin Wheel block (1930 pattern)

From sampler quilt by D. Thomas

■ **Block size:** 12”

■ **Fabrics needed:** Three fabrics, a **light**, a **medium** and a **dark**.

Cutting and piecing instructions

■ From the **dark** fabric, cut:
* Ten 2⅞-inch squares

■ From the **medium** fabric, cut:
* Ten 2⅞-inch squares

■ From the **light** fabric, cut:
* Four 4½-inch squares

■ **Draw** a solid diagonal line from corner to corner on the wrong side of a 2⅞-inch dark square. Place together with a 2⅞-inch medium square, right sides facing.

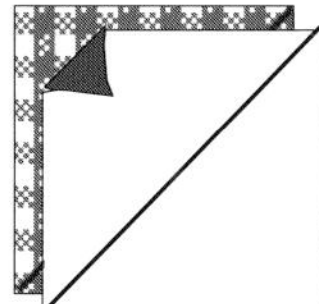

■ **Stitch** ¼-inch on both sides of the diagonal line.

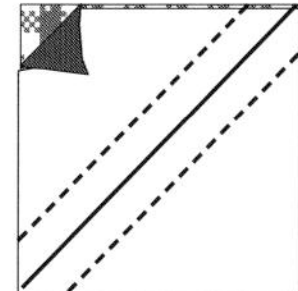

■ **Cut** on the solid line, unfold, and press to dark. Repeat this process with all 2⅞-inch medium and dark squares to create 20 units that look like this:

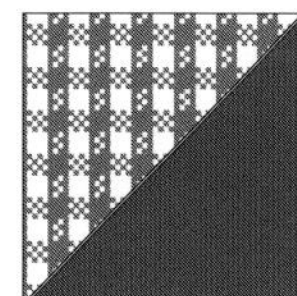

■ **Stitch** together the triangle units as shown:

■ **Stitch** together two of the triangle units with a 4½-inch light fabric square between. Make two of these units.

■ **Stitch** together two of the 4½-inch dark fabric squares with a triangle unit in between.

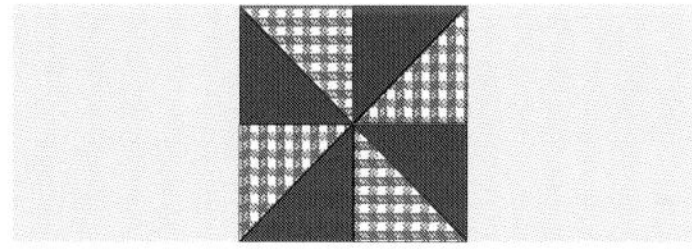

■ **Assemble** the 9-patch by sewing the rows together as shown:

Templates

See appendix for templates T 2⅞, and Sq 4½

1930 Pin Wheels: The Redraft

CRAZY ANNE IS AN OLD-TIME PATTERN

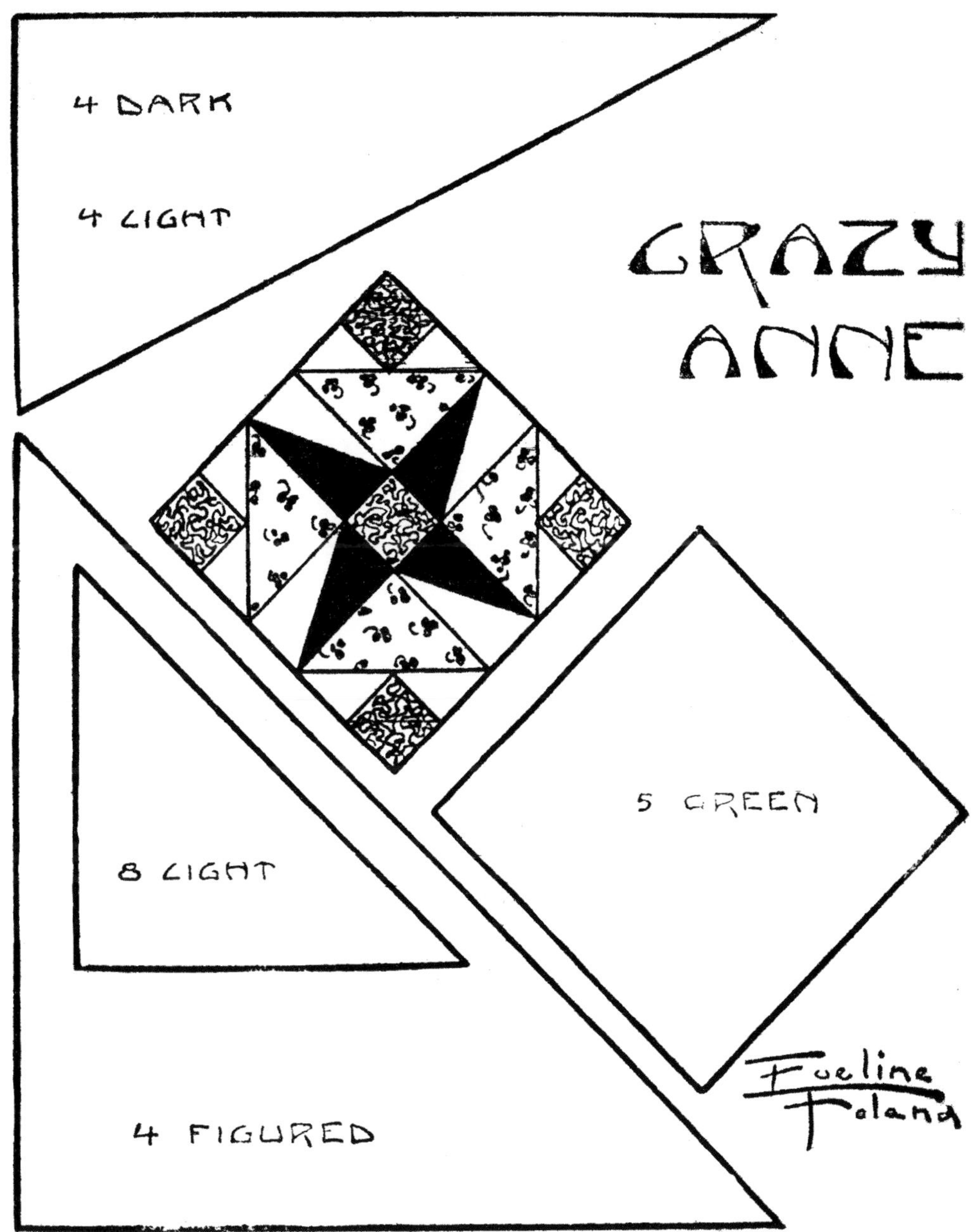

Published Oct. 15, 1932

This futuristic pattern is so prophetic of the latest trend in decorative design as to be quite startling, yet it is one of our great-grandmother's favorites. While three colors are shown above, two are equally interesting and give an entirely different effect. This is not a difficult block to piece as the rows are so well defined and the edges straight. It is twelve inches square and will be alternated with plain blocks of the same size. No seams are allowed.

Crazy Anne block **Jeanne Poore**

■ **Block size:** 12"

■ **Fabrics needed:** Four fabrics, a **light,** a **medium light,** a **medium** and a **dark.**

Cutting and piecing instructions

■ From the **light** fabric, cut:
 * Four 3¼-inch squares.
 * Two 3 ¼ x 6-inch strips.

■ From **medium** fabric, cut:
 * Four 2⅞-inch squares
 * Two 3¼x 6-inch strips.

■ From **dark** fabric, cut:
 * Two 5⅝-inch squares.

■ From **medium light** fabric, cut:
 * One 3-inch center square

■ **Subcut** the four 3¼-inch light squares diagonally to create eight triangles.

■ **Subcut** the two 5⅝-inch squares diagonally to create four large triangles.

■ **Place together** a 3¼ x 6-inch light strip with a 3¼ x 6-inch medium strip, right sides up.

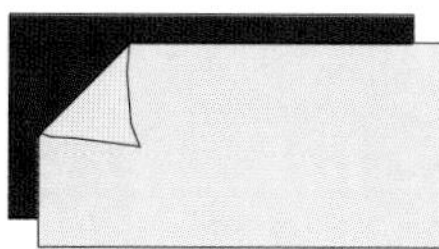

■ **Subcut** diagonally to create four triangles.

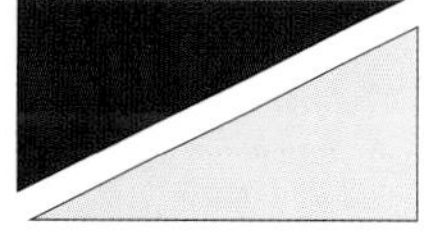

■ **Trim** off ¾-inch of the narrow tip. Stitch together diagonally.

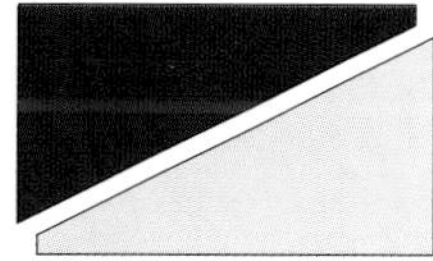

■ **Repeat** this process to create three similar units.

■ **Sew together** one of the 2⅞-inch medium squares with two of the 3¼-inch triangles, as shown.

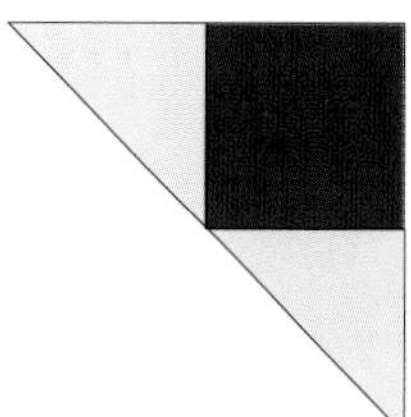

■ **Sew** this unit to one of the big 5⅝-inch triangles, as shown. Four of these units are needed.

■ **Assemble** the units this way. Repeat until you have two units that look like this.

■ **Assemble** these with the middle strip as shown (next page).

Templates

See appendix for templates Sq 2⅞, Sq 3, T 3¼, T 5⅝, Misc. 4

Some variations

KANSAS TROUBLE ORIGINATED IN CIVIL WAR DAYS

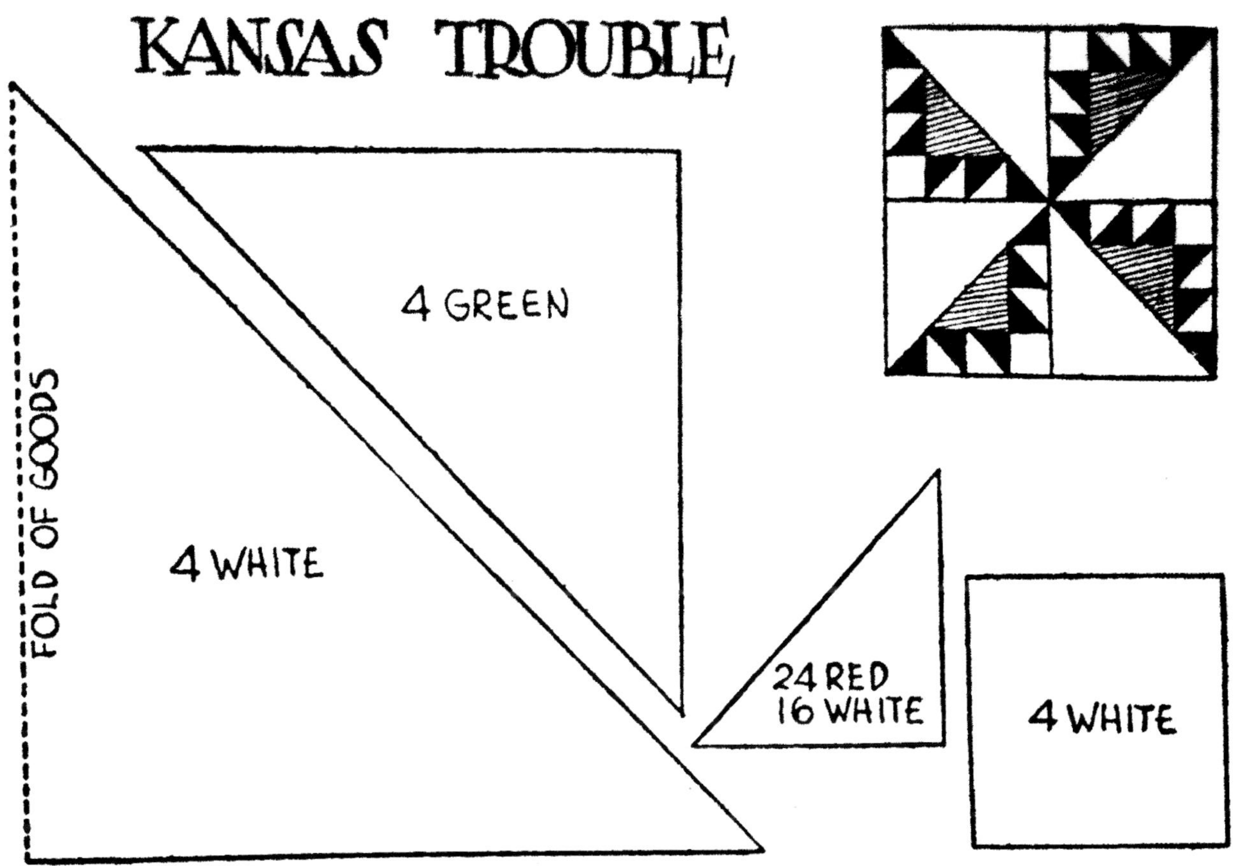

Published March 3, 1934

This quilt takes its name from the troubled days of early Kansas history, when a pioneer woman pieced this block and sent it to her New England home. The contributor states that the quilt may be in odd scraps or in solid colors. Allow for seams.

1934 Kansas Trouble

Kansas Trouble block **Jeanne Poore**

■ **Block size:** 12"

■ **Fabrics needed:** Three fabrics, a **light,** a **medium ,** and a **dark**.

Cutting and piecing instructions

■ From the **light** fabric, cut:

* Four 2-inch squares. These are the corner squares.
* Eight 2 ⅜-inch squares.

■ From the **medium** fabric, cut:

* Two 3⅞-inch squares.
* Twelve 2⅜-inch squares.

■ From the **dark** fabric, cut:

* Two 6⅞-inch squares.

■ **Subcut** the two 6⅞-inch dark squares diagonally to create four triangles.

■ **Subcut** the two 3⅞-inch medium squares to create four triangles.

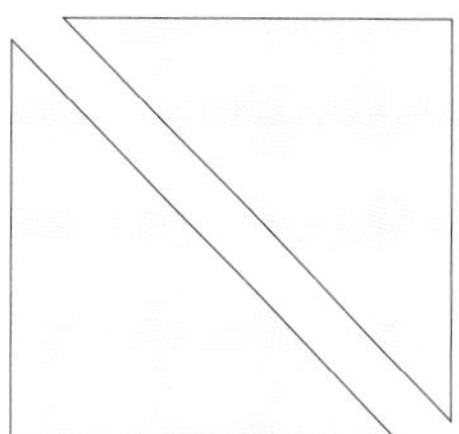

■ **Draw** a solid diagonal line from corner to corner on the wrong sides of the 2⅜-inch light squares. Place those squares together with the 2⅜-inch medium squares, right sides facing.

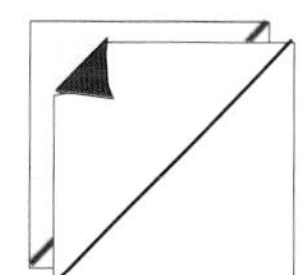

■ **Stitch** ¼ -inch on both sides of the diagonal line.

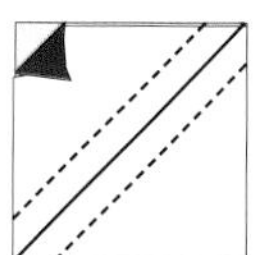

■ **Cut** on the solid line. Repeat this process with seven other 2⅜-inch light and medium squares. You should have 16 units like this:

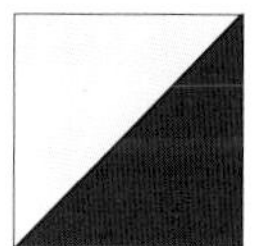

■ **Subcut** the remaining four 2⅜-inch medium squares diagonally to create eight triangles.

■ **Assemble** a unit as shown.

■ **Assemble** the block as shown (next page).

Templates

See appendix for templates Sq 2, T 2⅜, T 3⅞, T 6⅞

1934 Kansas Trouble:The Redraft

THE RED CROSS LIVES IN ITS TRUE COLORS

10 RED
8 WHITE

THE
RED
CROSS

Published July 21, 1934

A Kansas City quilt fan who worked for the Red Cross during the World War knitting and wrapping bandages sent this attractive block which may be done in red and white and set together with white squares which may be quilted with patriotic emblems – the flag, the eagle, the crossed swords, the outline of the Liberty Memorial. Many quilt fans will think of others as they plan the plain blocks.

Red Cross history

The Red Cross quilt was inspired by the famous international charity. The symbol of the Red Cross, the Swiss flag with the colors reversed, is recognized around the world as an emblem of aid in the midst of crisis.

The Red Cross was founded by Henri Dunant, a young Swiss. In 1859 Dunant was traveling in Castiglione in northern Italy when he came upon a battlefield. The day before, armies of France and Italy had waged a bloody battle against the Austrians in which some 40,000 soldiers had been wounded. Surgeons were working nonstop but could not attend to all the victims; Dunant did what he could to help. Soon housewives, townsmen and strangers were bandaging wounds, providing water and offering whatever comfort they could.

When Henri returned to Switzerland he formed societies in every country in Europe to organize and train volunteers to aid the wounded of war.

For nearly five years he traveled until he had lobbied each of Europe's governments to formalize his idea. Finally, in 1864, representatives of 16 nations drew up the world's first treaty to care for the wounded — whether friend or enemy — during wartime. The convention adopted a red cross on a white background as an emblem so that hospitals, doctors and nurses could be recognized during battle.

Red Cross (1934 pattern) **Jeanne Poore**

The American Red Cross was organized in 1881, largely through the effort of Clara Barton, who had done relief work during the Civil War. In 1905 the society was chartered by Congress.

Six Red Cross quilt patterns ran in *The Kansas City Star* — in 1932, 1934, 1939, 1941, 1942 and 1947. Included here is a redraft of a version from 1934.

■ **Block size:** 8"

■ **Fabrics needed:** Two fabrics, a **light** (preferably white) and a **dark** (preferably red).

Cutting and piecing instructions

■ From the **light,** cut:

* Two 4½-inch squares.
* Eight 1⅞-inch squares.

■ From the **dark** fabric, cut:

* Four 1⅞-inch squares.
* Two 1⅞ x 4½-inch strips

■ **Put** two 1⅞-inch light squares together as shown with one of the 1⅞-inch dark squares between. Four of these units are needed.

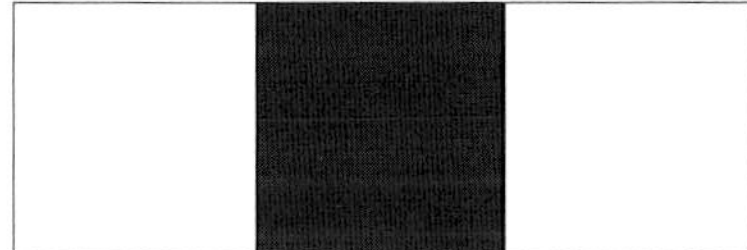

■ **Stitch** these units together as shown with one of the 1⅞ x 4½-inch dark strips between. Two of these units are needed.

■ **Assemble** as a 4-patch as shown.

Templates

See appendix for Sq 1⅞, Sq 4½, P 1⅞ x 4½

THE BEAUTY OF THIS QUILT DEPENDS ON YOUR COLOR SELECTION

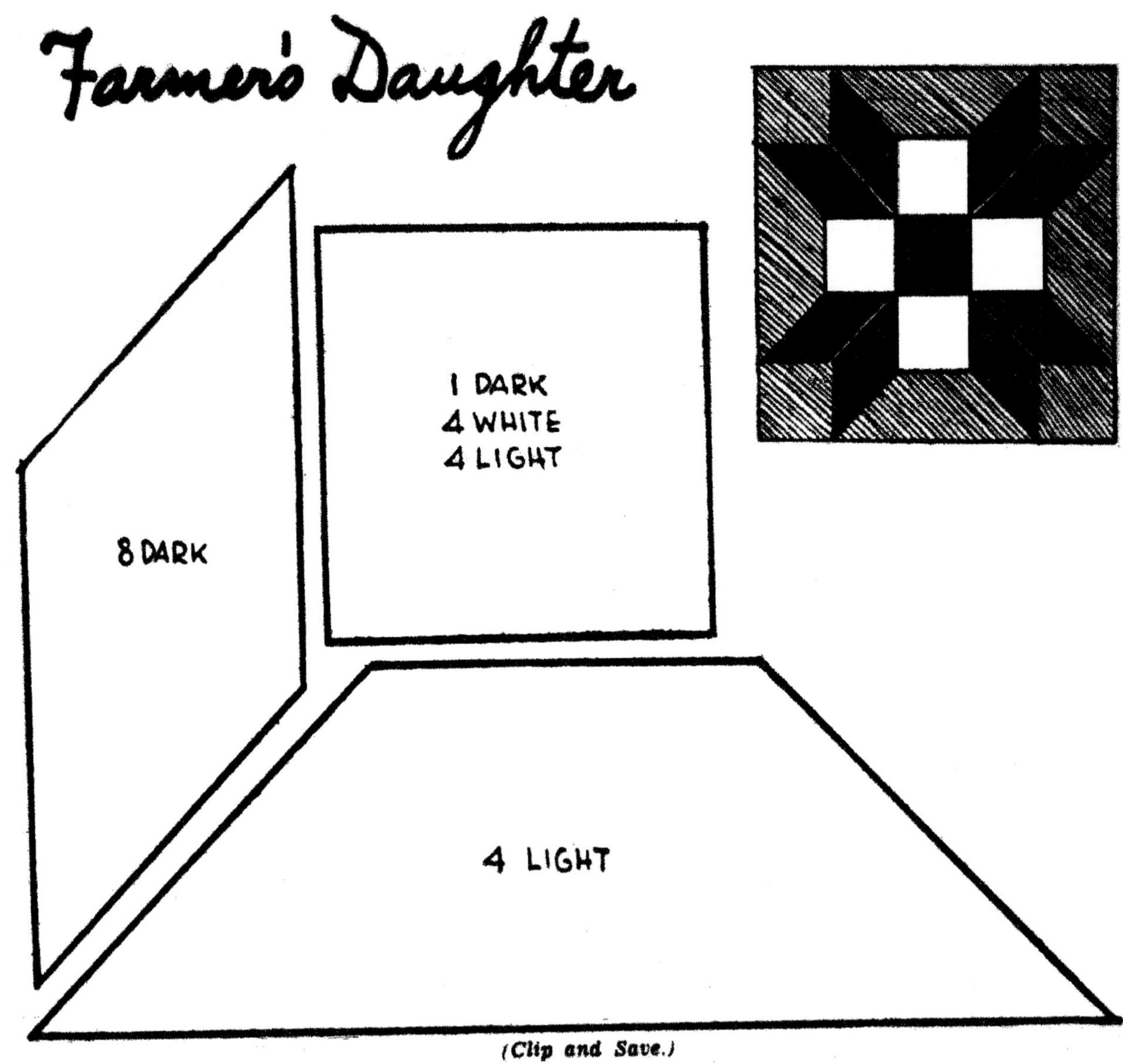

Published March 16, 1935

The Farmer's Daughter is an old pattern. The favorite of Mrs. Wiley Barks, Doniphan, Mo. Allow for seams. The blocks are large, a modification of the Dove in the Window pattern.

1935 Farmer's Daughter

Farmer's Daughter block — Jeanne Poore

■ **Block size:** 12"

■ **Fabrics needed:** Three fabrics, a **light,** a **medium** and a **dark.**

Cutting and piecing instructions

■ From **light** fabric, cut:
 * Four rectangles, 7¾ by 2$^{15}/_{16}$ inches
 * Four 2$^{15}/_{16}$-inch squares

■ From **dark fabric,** cut:
 * Thirteen 2$^{15}/_{16}$-inch squares

■ From **medium** fabric, cut:
 * Four 2$^{15}/_{16}$-inch squares

For the 9-Patch

■ **Assemble** five dark and four medium squares as shown.

■ **Draw** a diagonal line on the wrong side of the remaining eight dark squares. Place the squares on the ends of the light rectangle, right sides facing.

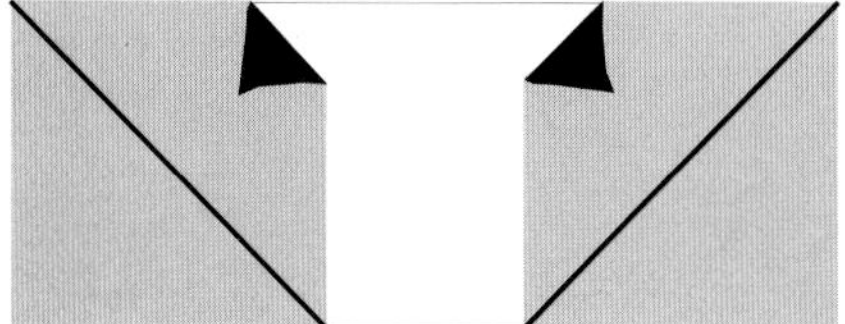

■ **Stitch** on line. Trim ¼-inch from seam line on side closest to the corner and fold over square and press toward dark fabric.

■ **Stitch** the four light squares to the ends of two of the rectangle units.

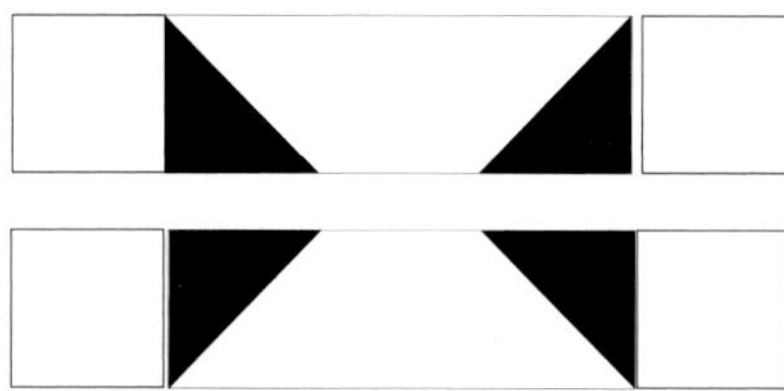

■ **Sew** the two other rectangles to the 9-patch.

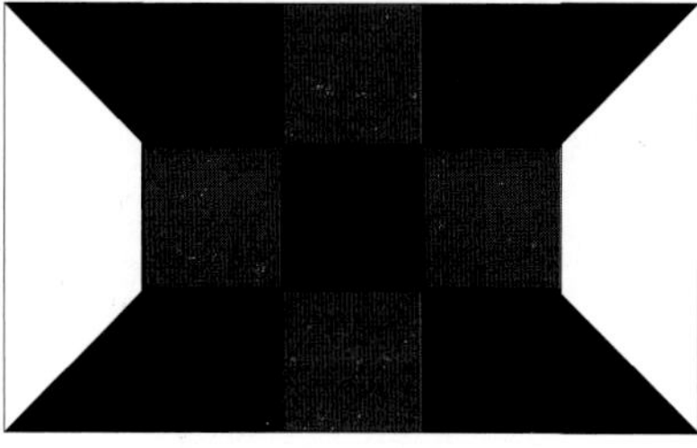

■ **Sew** longer rectangles (with the background squares) to the assembled 9-patch/rectangle unit (opposite page).

Templates

See appendix for Sq 2$^{15}/_{16}$, T 2$^{15}/_{16}$, Misc. 5

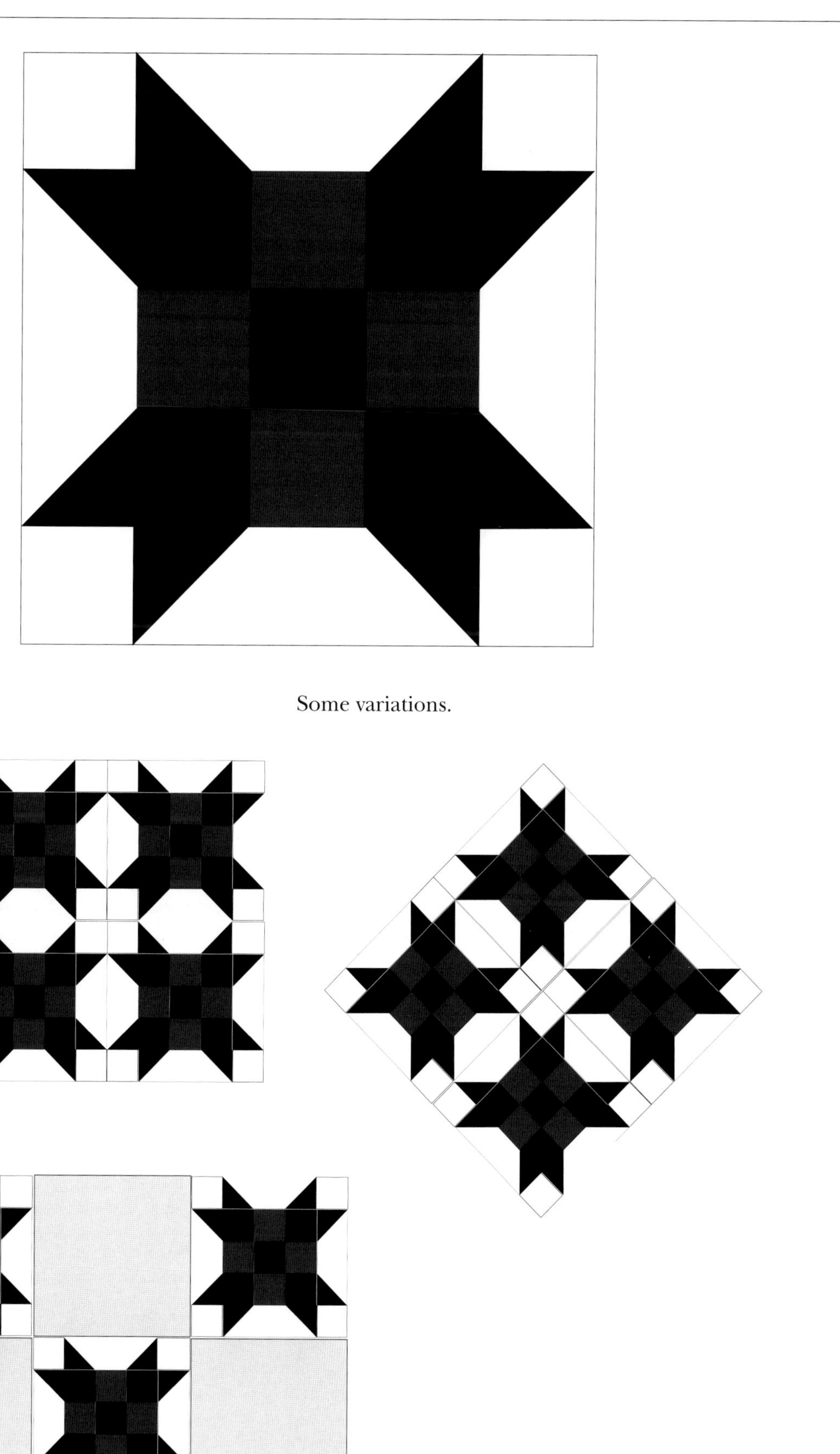

Some variations.

AN EFFECTIVE PATTERN IN ANY COLOR

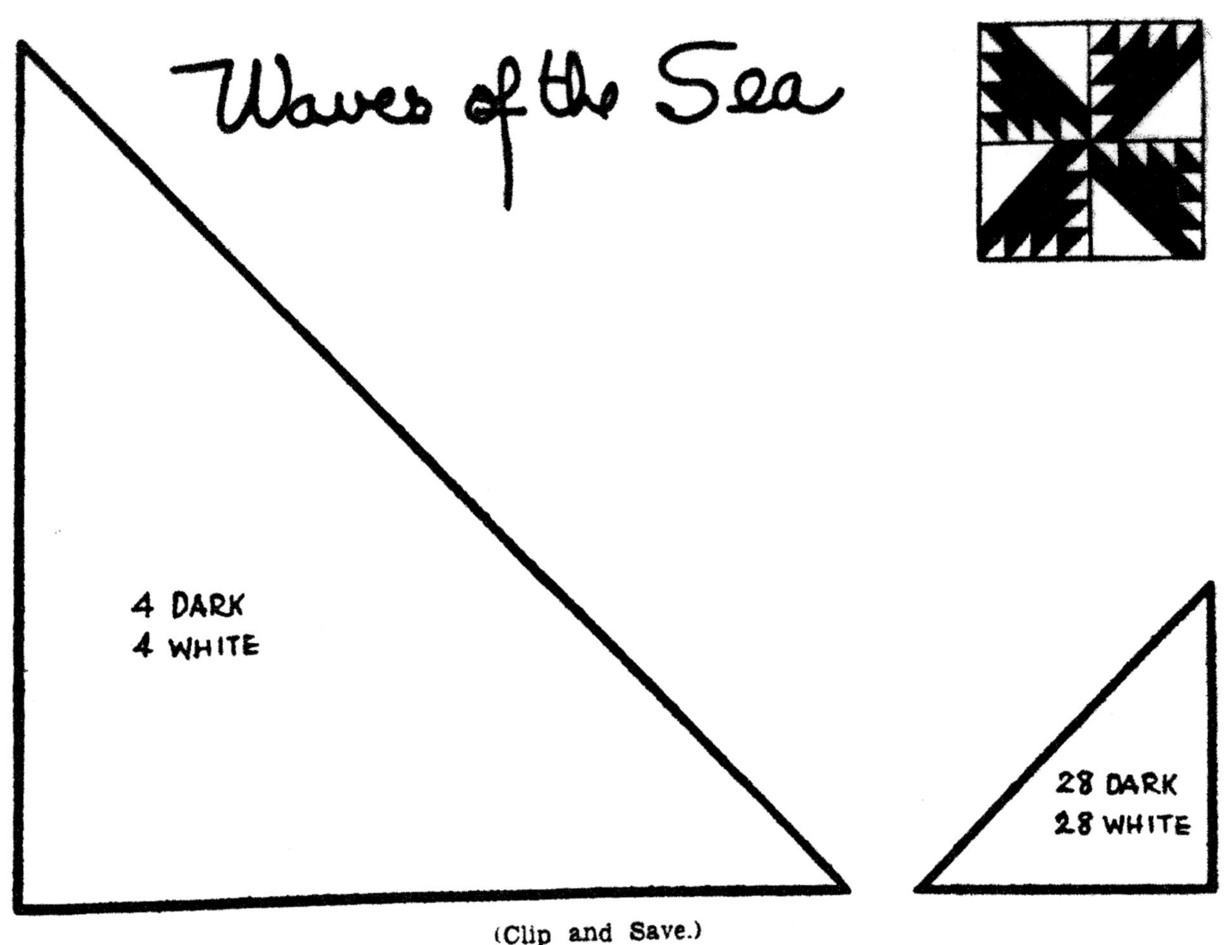

Published March 6, 1937

Here is a quilt that can be made quickly in any colors desired. Allow for seams. This design is an old one contributed to The Star's quilt fans by Lora Stevens, Springfield, Mo. Thank you very much.

1937 Waves of the Sea

Waves of the Sea block **Jeanne Poore**

■ **Block size:** 12"

■ **Fabrics needed:** Two fabrics, a **light** and a **dark.**

Cutting and piecing instructions

■ From **light** fabric, cut:
- * One 4⅝ -inch square
- * Fourteen 2⅛ -inch squares

■ From **dark** fabric, cut:
- * One 4⅝ -inch square
- * Fourteen 2⅛ -inch squares

■ **Draw** a diagonal line on the back of a 2⅛-inch dark square. Place together with a 2⅛-inch light square, right sides facing.

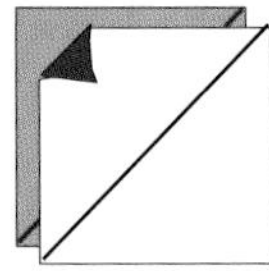

■ **Stitch** ¼-inch on both sides of the diagonal line.

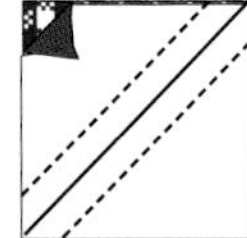

■ **Cut** on the solid line, unfold, and press to dark. Repeat this process with all six 2⅛-inch light and dark squares to create 28 small units that look like this:

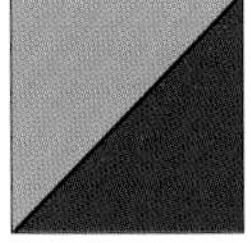

■ **Repeat this process** with the 4⅝-inch light and dark squares to create four large units that look like this:

■ **Stitch** three of the small units together, and stitch this unit to one side of the dark half of the larger square as shown.

Stitch four of the small units together and stitch to the other dark side of larger square as shown. Create four units like this.

■ **Assemble** the four units into a block as shown (opposite page).

Templates

See appendix for T 2⅛, T 4⅝

1937 Waves of the Sea: The Redraft

"A FLYING KITE" FOR PORCH WORK SEWING

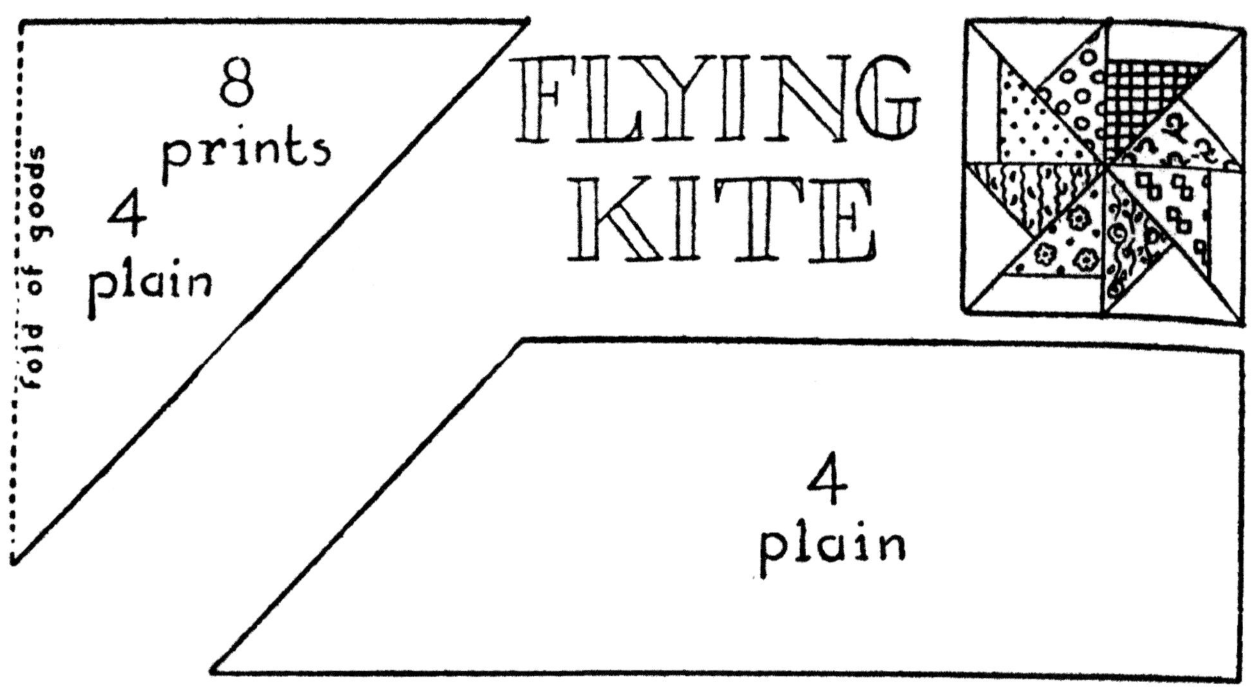

Published July 7, 1937

This simple and effective quilt pattern was contributed to The Star by Mrs. Everett Royster, Silex, Mo. Thank you.

Flying Kite block **Jeanne Poore**

■ **Block size:** 12"

■ **Fabrics needed:** Three fabrics, a **light,** a **medium** fabric, and a **dark** fabric.

Cutting and piecing instructions

■ From **light** fabric, cut:

* Four rectangles, 2¼ inches by 7 ⅜ inches

* One 7⅜-inch square

■ From **medium** fabric, cut:

* One 7⅜-inch square

■ From **dark** fabric, cut:

* One 7⅜-inch square

■ **Cut** the three 7⅜-inch squares as shown. You will have four triangles of each color.

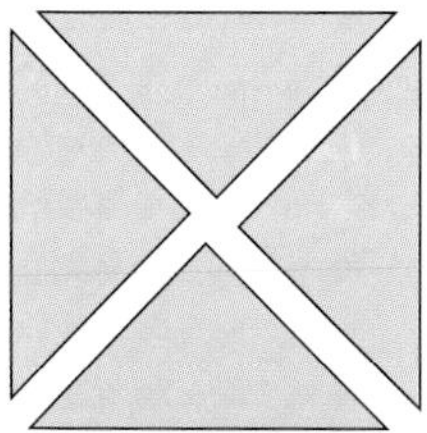

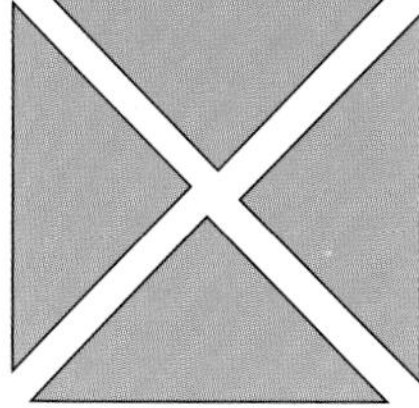

■ **Stitch** together a dark triangle and a light triangle as shown. Press toward the dark.

■ **Stitch** together a medium triangle and a light rectangle, right sides facing, as shown.

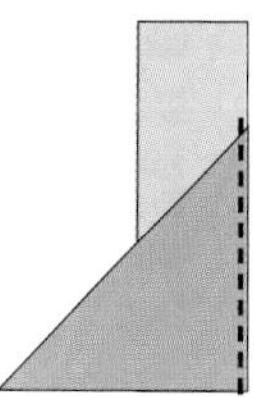

■ **Unfold** triangle away from rectangle. Place rule along edge of triangle and cut off corner of rectangle.

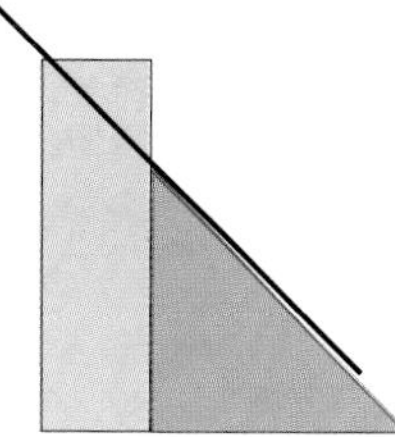

The light fabric now forms a trapezoid. Press toward the medium.

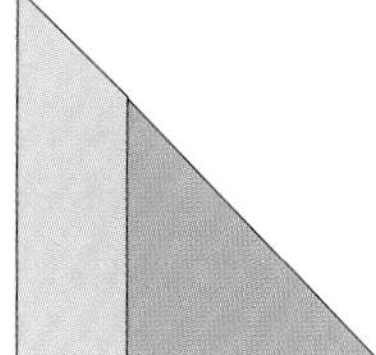

■ **Stitch** together these two units to create one-quarter of your block as shown.

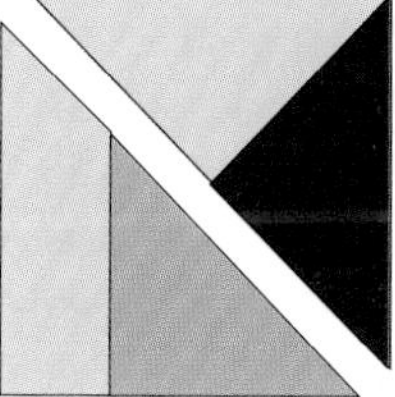

■ **Join** the four squares to complete the block as shown (next page).

Templates

See appendix for T 5¼, Misc. 6

1937 Flying Kite: The Redraft

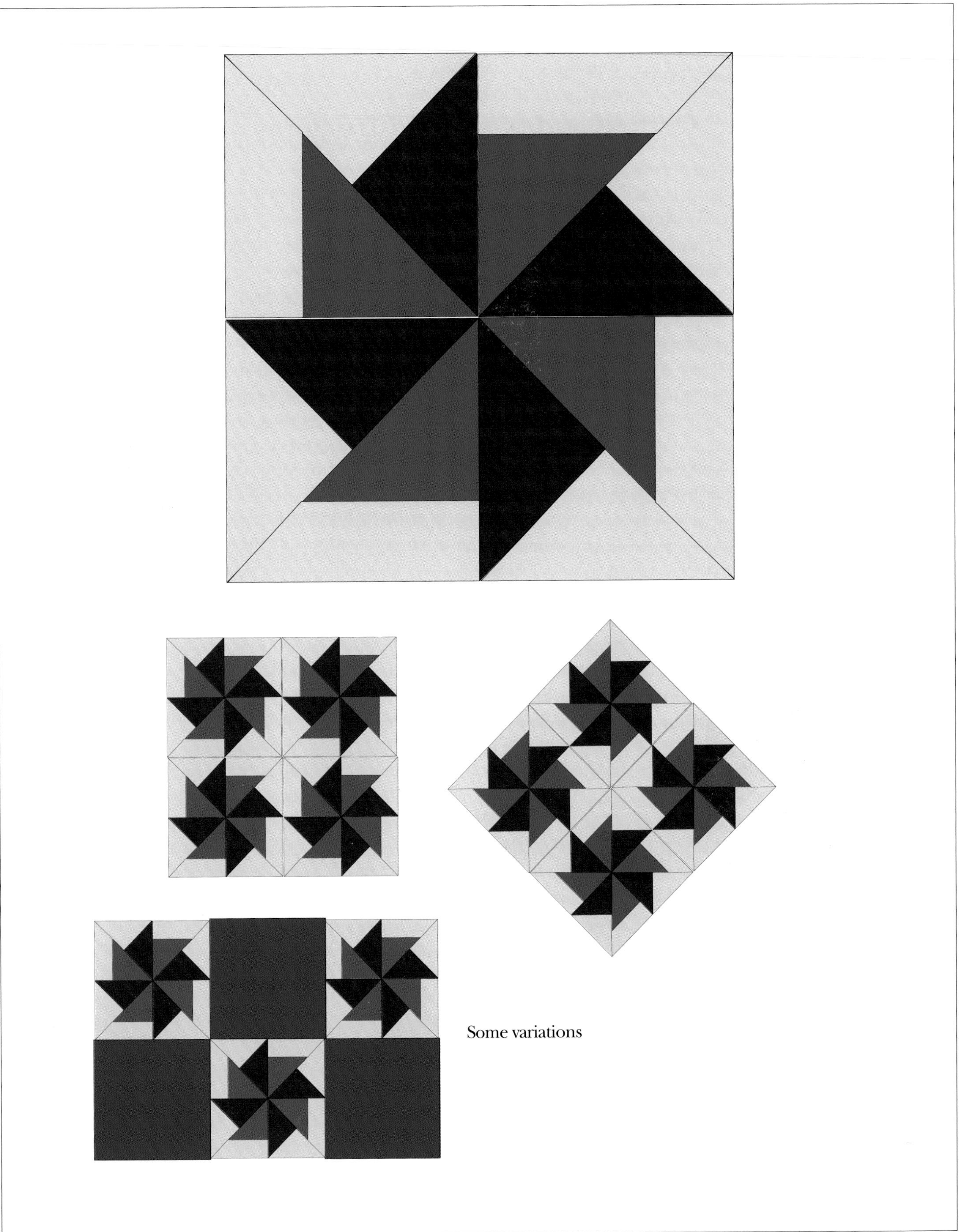

Some variations

BEAR'S PAW IS A GAY DESIGN

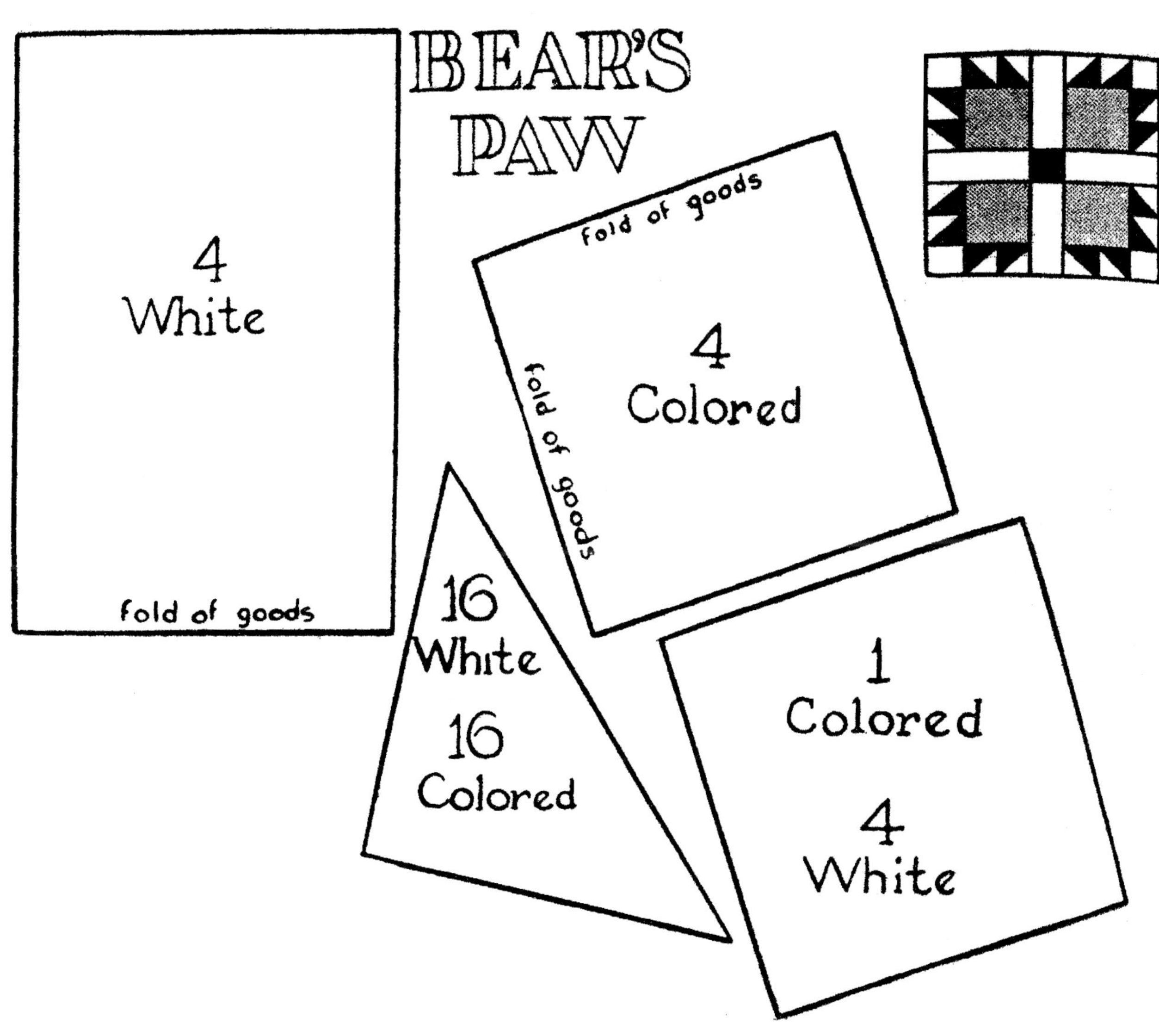

Published Sept. 15, 1937

This is a welcome pattern because it can be used to make small scraps into a lovely quilt.

1937 Bear's Paw

Bear's Paw **Pieced and quilted by Elizabeth Leding Evans** **Owned by Susan Jarsulic**

■ **Block size:** 12"

■ **Fabrics needed:** Three fabrics, a **light,** a **dark** and a **medium**.

Cutting and piecing instructions

■ From **light** fabric, cut:
* Four 2½-inch x 6½-inch strips
* Four 2½-inch squares
* Eight 2⅞-inch squares

■ From **dark** fabric, cut:
* One 2½-inch square for the center square of block
* Eight 2⅞-inch squares

■ From **medium** fabric, cut:
* Four 4½-inch squares

■ **Draw** a solid diagonal line from corner to corner on the wrong side of a 2⅞-inch light square. Place together with a 2⅞-inch dark square, right sides facing.

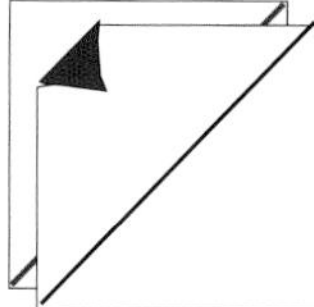

■ **Stitch** ¼-inch on both sides of the diagonal line.

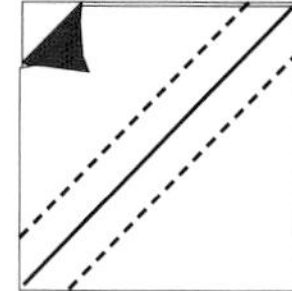

■ **Cut** on the solid line, unfold, and press to dark. Repeat this process with all eight 2⅞-inch light and dark squares to create 16 units that look like this:

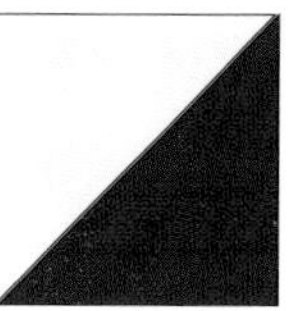

■ **Stitch** two of these units together as shown

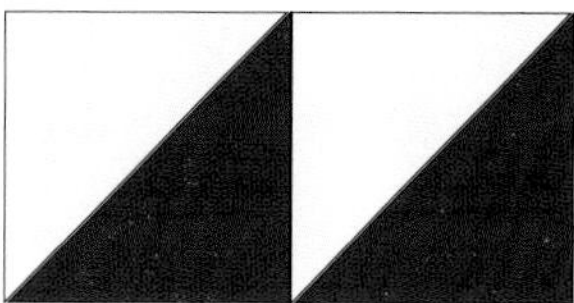

■ **Stitch** two more of these units together the same way and attach a 2½-inch light square to one end.

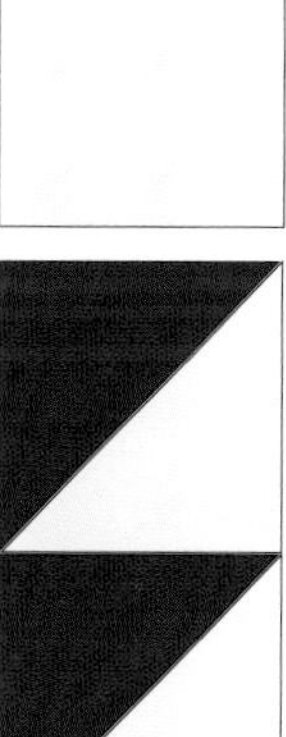

■ **Stitch** the set of two units to the 4½-inch medium fabric square.

■ **Stitch** the set of three small squares to the side of 4½-inch medium fabric square as shown.

■ **Join** two of these units together with a strip between them. Repeat this process.

Templates

See appendix for Sq 2½, Sq 4½, T 2⅞, P 2½ x 6½

Sew two background strips to the 2½-inch center square. Assemble the three sections as shown.

Some variations.

1938 Six Pointed Star

Six Pointed Star **Made and owned by Peggy and Francis Hutinett**

Garden Patch (1940 pattern)
Quilted and owned by Edie McGinnis

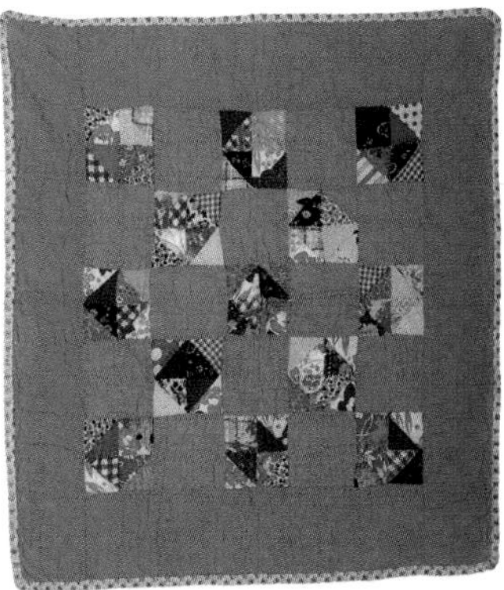

Small Triangle (1945 pattern)
Made in 1945 by Addah Menzies
Owned by Jeanne Poore

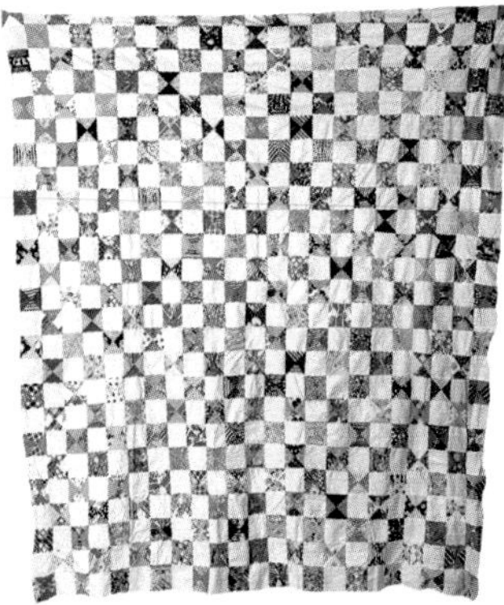

Envelope Quilt (1943 pattern)
Made in 1945, maker unknown
Owned by Bonnie Ingram

Broken Star (1939 pattern)
Made by Amanda Brazea
Owned by Madelyn Goode

Lone Star (1930 pattern) **Made of 1940 feed sacks by Pauline Loffler in 1990** **Owned by Dorothymae Groves**

1939-1945

The patriotic quilts

As their men fought World War II overseas, women back home took over factory jobs and tended to their families. Time for quilting was scarce.

The war effort also drained their resources. Fabric rationing forced women to return to feed sacks for quilts, which had been used extensively in the Depression. Paper shortages cut back on the number of patterns in magazines and newspapers. In 1937, *The Star* ran 50 patterns, most in the daily as well as its weekly editions; in 1939 that fell to 36.

In 1939 *The Star* also switched to running the patterns in its weekly newspapers only.

But readers kept right on submitting their favorite designs, which often reflected fervent public interest in the war. One design, "The Army Star," was contributed by two soldiers in an Army training camp.

Victory quilts were popular throughout the country during World War II. Here, Blanche Preston Jones and a friend display a variation of the pattern outside a cabin in the mountains of eastern Kentucky.

THE PATTERN THAT WILL CAUSE DISCUSSION

Published Nov. 9, 1938

The name of this pattern Contrary Husband, will provoke conversation. It is an attractive pattern in two colors. This was sent by quilt fan, Mrs. Cassie Rundel, Old Mines, Mo. Thank you.

1938 Contrary Husband

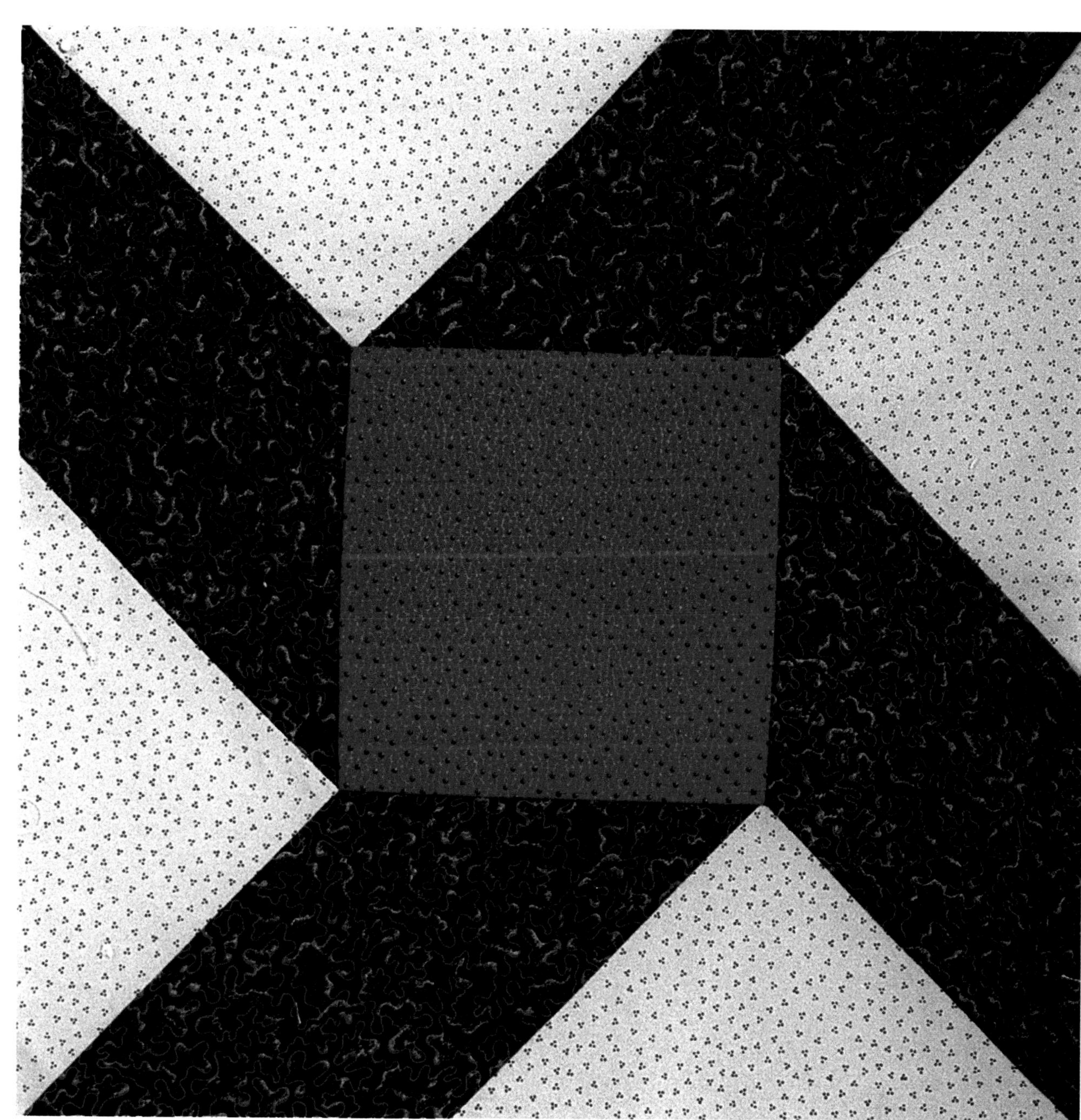

Contrary Husband block **Jeanne Poore**

■ **Block size:** 12"

■ **Fabrics needed:** Three fabrics, a **light,** a **medium** and a **dark.**

Cutting and piecing instructions

■ From **light** fabric, cut:
* One 8¼-inch square.

■ From **medium** fabric, cut:
* A 4-inch wide strip, 40 inches long.

■ From **dark** fabric, cut:
* One center 5½-inch square.

■ **Subcut** the 4-inch wide strip into four parallelograms with side angles of (45) degrees. Each subsection should measure 5½ inches lengthwise along the two longer sides.

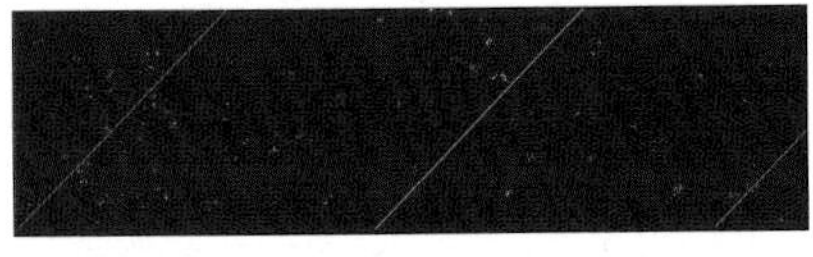

■ **Cut** the 8¼-inch light square twice diagonally into four triangles.

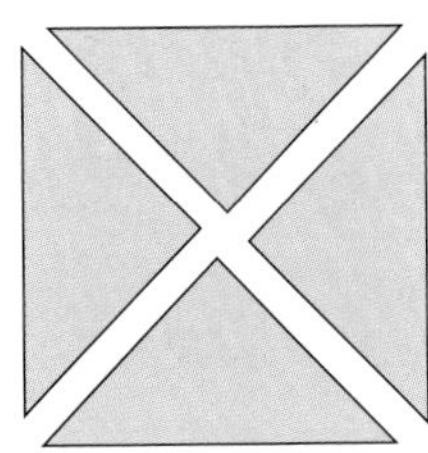

■ **Stitch** one parallelogram and one light triangle as shown. Repeat three more times for a total of the four sides.

■ **Stitch** the four side units to the center square, one at a time (put the two opposite sides on, then fill in the two remaining sides) starting and stopping at the ¼-inch seam allowance.

■ **Starting** at the center, match the diagonal seam on the corners between the side units and stitch to the outer edge (as if you were stitching a mitered corner). Repeat for all four corners.

Templates

See appendix for Sq 5½, T 5⅞, Misc. 7

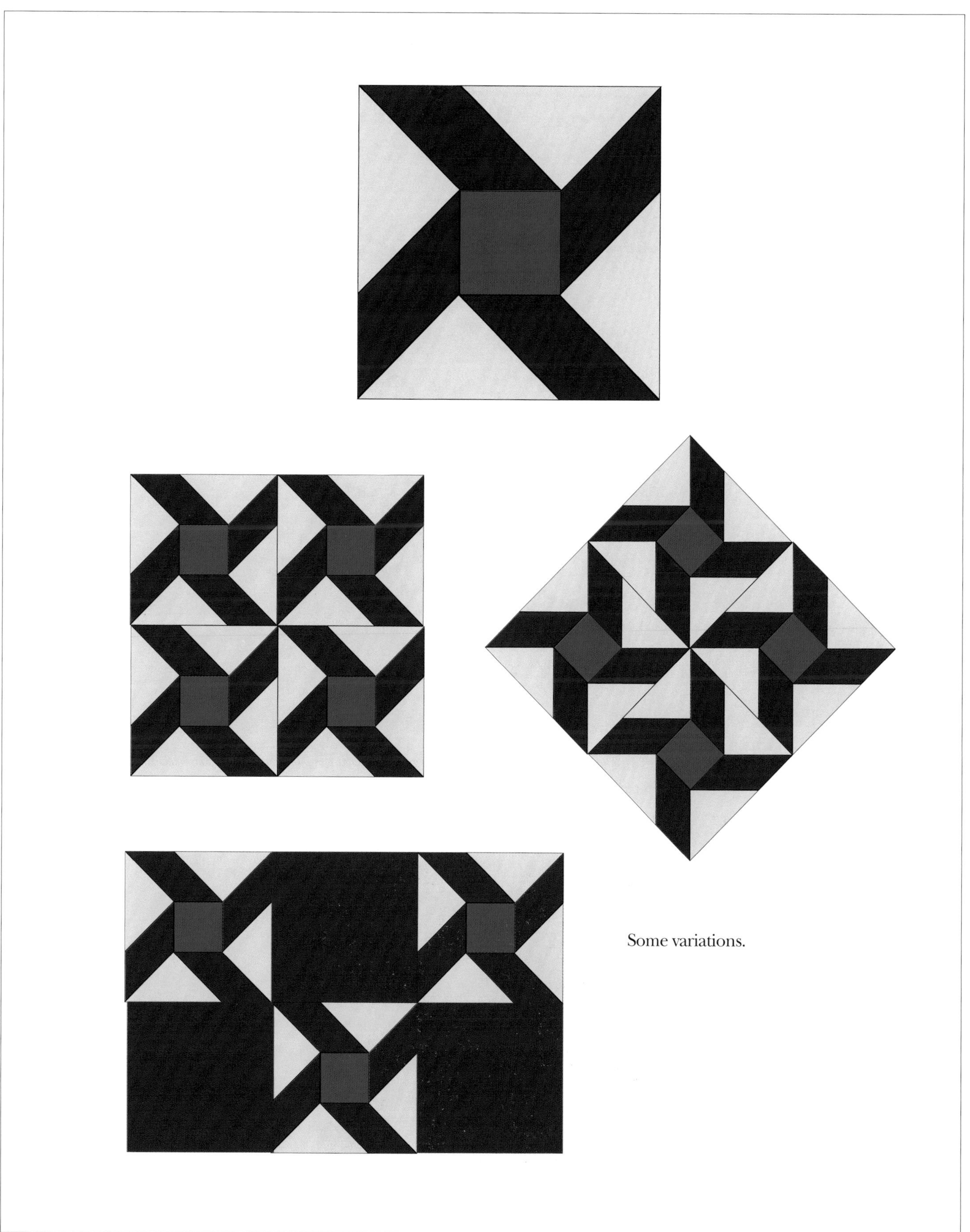

Some variations.

STEPPING STONES AMONG THE FLOWERS

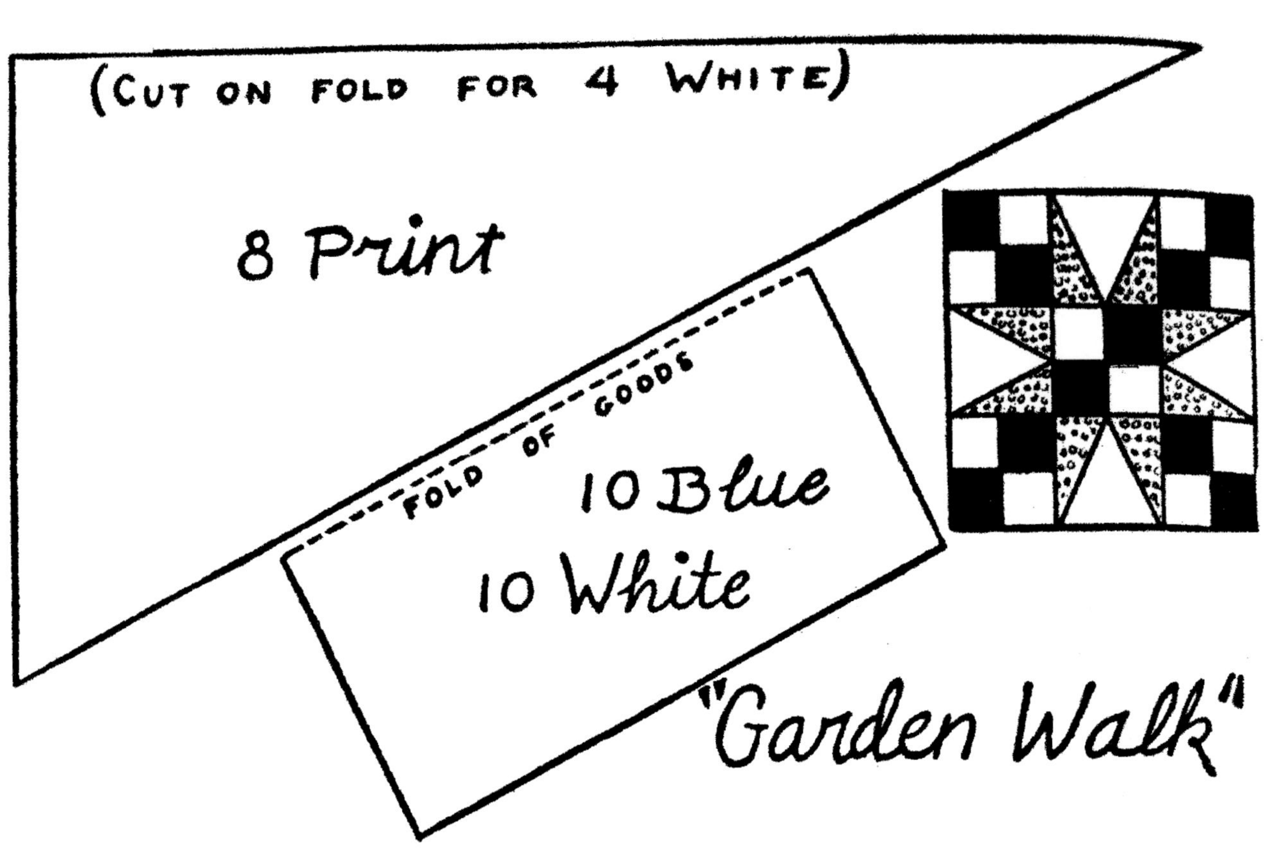

Published June 19, 1940

"This quilt is lovely," says Mrs. George M. Kennedy of Hutner, Ark., the contributor, "if the 'stepping' blocks are made of blue and the triangular pieces of print in a mixture of pink, lavendar and yellow."

■ **Block size:** 12"

■ **Fabrics needed:** Four fabrics, a **light,** a **medium light,** a **medium** and a **dark.**

Cutting and piecing instructions

■ From **light** fabric, cut:

* One strip, 4½ inches by at least 13 inches.

■ From **medium light** fabric, cut:

* One strip, 2½ inches by at least 27 inches.

■ From **medium** fabric, cut:

* One strip, 2½ inches by at least 27 inches.

■ From **dark** fabric, cut:

* Four 2¾-inch x 5¼-inch rectangles.

4-patch assembly:

■ Stitch the medium light and medium strips together along their lengths. Press toward the medium. Subcut them into 2½-inch-wide units.

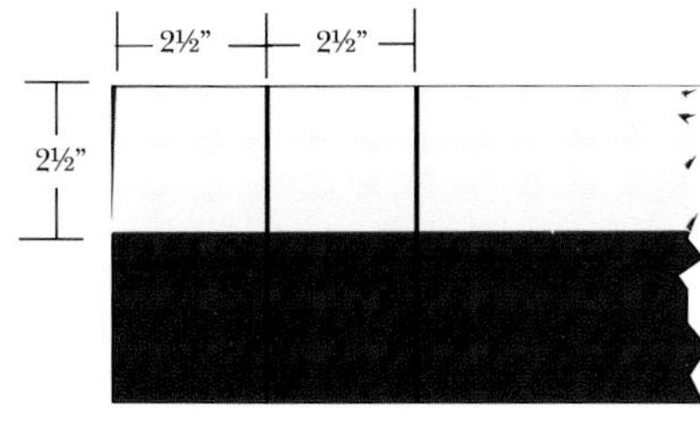

■ **Assemble** into the 4-patch as shown below. Five 4-patches are needed.

Triangle assembly:

■ **Subcut** the 4½-inch light strip into four triangles using Misc. 9 template.

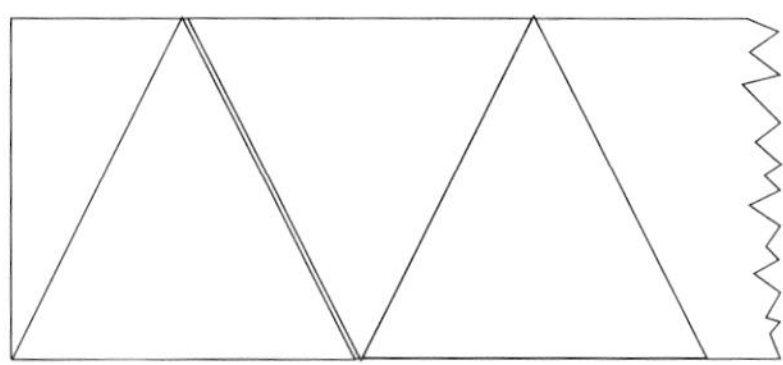

■ **Stack** two of the dark rectangles. Cut through them on a line from corner to corner. Stack the other two rectangles and cut them from the opposite corner to the opposite corner. You will have eight triangles.

■ **Stitch** two triangles of dark fabric to the sides of each light triangle. Make four of these units.

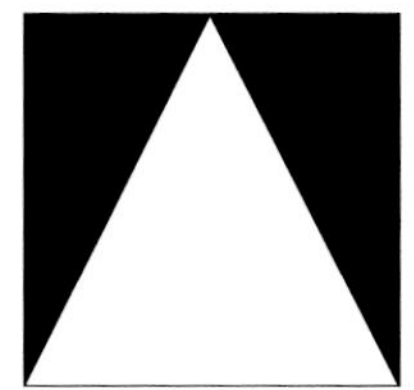

■ **Stitch** the units together in rows.

Templates

See appendix for Sq 2½, Misc. 8, Misc. 9

Some variations

CONTRARY WIFE QUILT

5 PRINT

4 RED
4 BLUE

Published Aug. 27, 1941

The Contrary Wife was originated by Mrs. Bertha Oglesby, R.R. 2, Arkinda, Ark.

Contrary Wife block **Jeanne Poore**

■ **Block size:** 12"

■ **Fabrics needed:** A **light, medium** and **dark.**

Cutting and piecing instructions

■ From **light** cut:

* Two 4⅞-inch squares.

■ From **medium,** cut:

* Five 4½-inch squares.

■ From **dark,** cut:

* Two 4⅞-inch squares.

■ **Place** a light square atop a dark square, right sides facing.

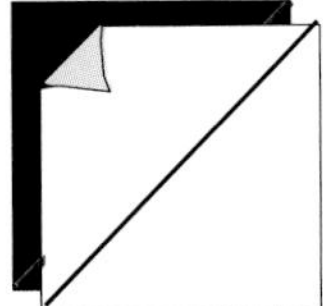

■ **Draw** a diagonal line between corners (solid line.) Stitch ¼-inch on either side (dotted line) and cut on solid line.

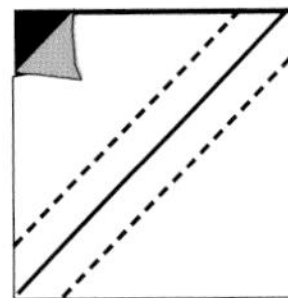

■ **Press** to dark.

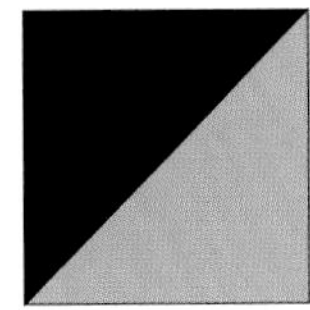

Make four units like this.

■ **Assemble** these units with the medium units as shown.

Templates

See appendix for T 4⅞, Sq 4½.

Contrary Wife **Made in 1987 by Sharon McMillan, Marquette Heights, Ill.**

1941 Contrary Wife: The Redraft

Some variations.

A SALUTE TO THE COLORS

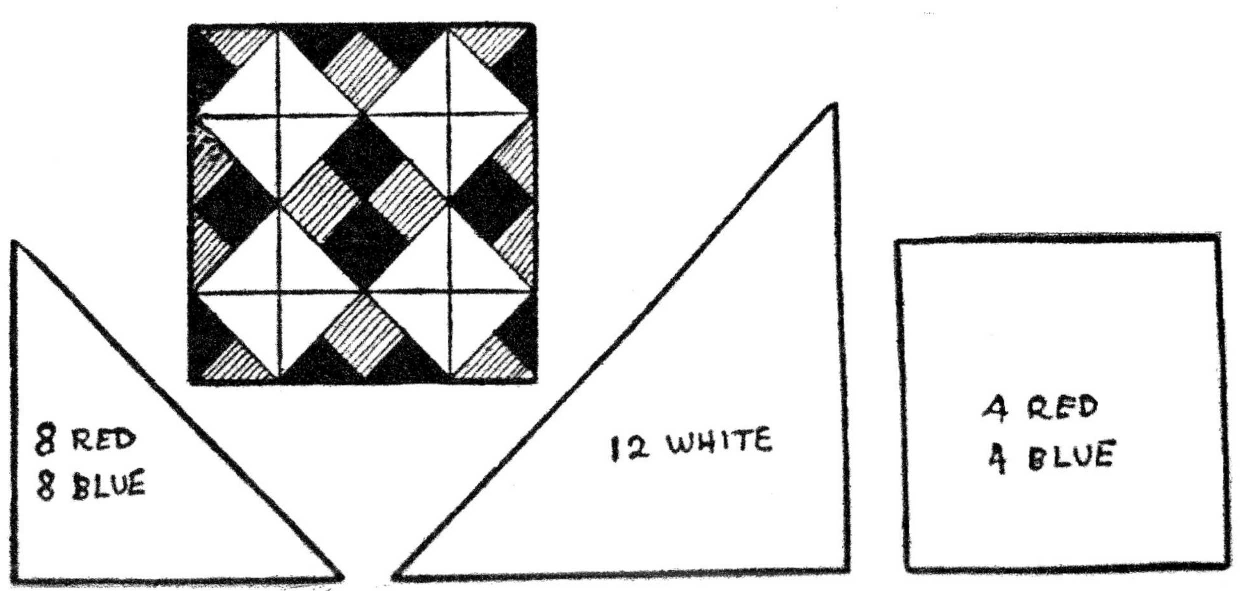

Published May 6, 1942

Listening to daily talk by our soldiers on national loyalty inspired Miss Adelia Meyer, Chester, Neb., to design the "Salute to the Colors."

Salute to the Colors **Jeanne Poore**

1942 Salute to the Colors

■ **Block size:** 12"

■ **Fabrics needed:** Three fabrics, a **light** (preferably white), a **medium** (preferably red), and a **dark** (preferably blue).

Cutting and piecing instructions

■ From **white** fabric, cut:
  * Eight 2⅞-inch squares.

■ From **medium** fabric, cut:
  * One 3¼-inch square.
  * Two 2¼-inch squares.
  * Four 1⅞-inch squares.

■ From **dark** fabric, cut:
  * One 3¼-inch square.
  * Two 2¼-inch squares.
  * Four 1⅞-inch squares.

■ **Stitch** together two medium 1⅞-inch squares and two dark 1⅞-inch squares to form the center of the block as shown.

■ **Cut** two white squares diagonally and stitch them to the edges of the center unit as shown.

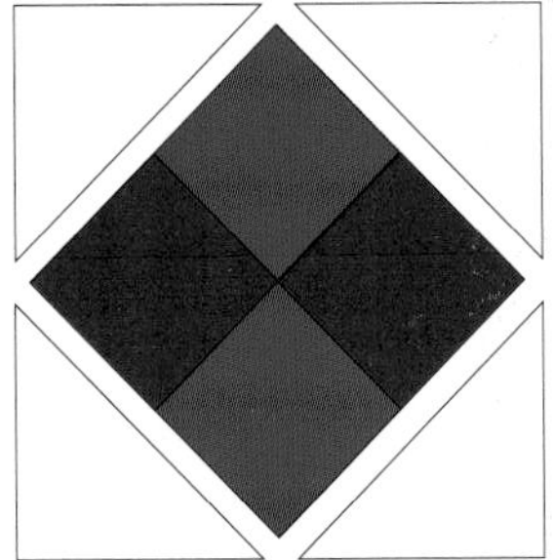

■ **Place** the medium 3¼-inch square atop the dark 3¼-inch square, right sides facing.

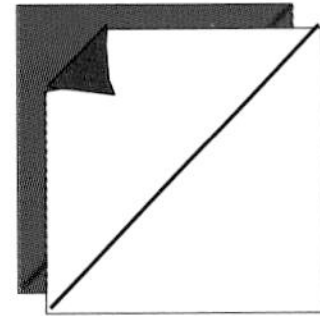

■ Draw a line from corner to corner (solid line), stitch ¼-inch on either side of the line.

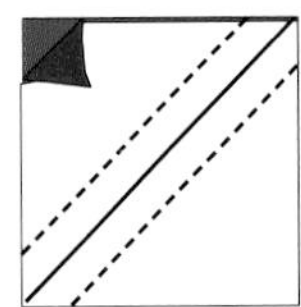

■ **Cut** on the solid line, unfold, and press to dark

■ Make two of these units.

■ Atop each of these units, place a 2⅞-inch white square, centered. Draw a diagonal across the light square as shown.

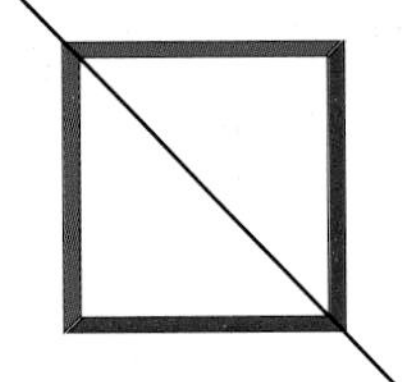

■ **Stitch** ¼-inch on either side of this line.

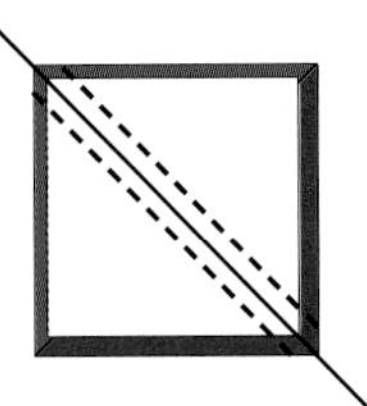

■ **Cut** along the line. Unfold.

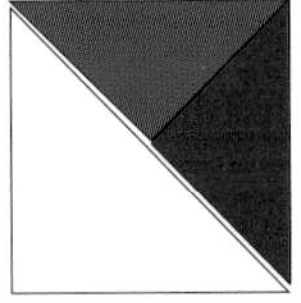

■ **Make** four of these units.

■ **Cut** two medium 2¼-inch squares and two dark 2¼-inch squares diagonally.

■ **Attach** two triangles of the same color to adjacent sides of a 1⅞-inch square of the other color — two dark triangles to one medium square, two medium triangles to one dark square.
■ **Subcut** four white squares into triangles and attch to the color units as shown.

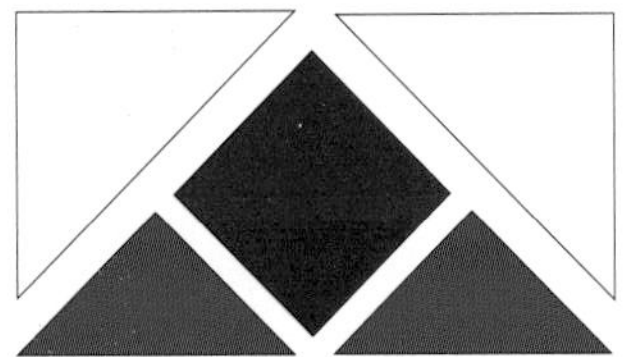

■ **Make** four of these units.

Templates

See appendix for Sq 1⅞, T 2¼, T 2⅞, T 3¼

■ **Cut** the remaining 2⅞-inch light squares diagonally and stitch their long sides to the just-completed medium-and-dark (or red-and-blue) units as shown.

ENVELOPE MOTIF

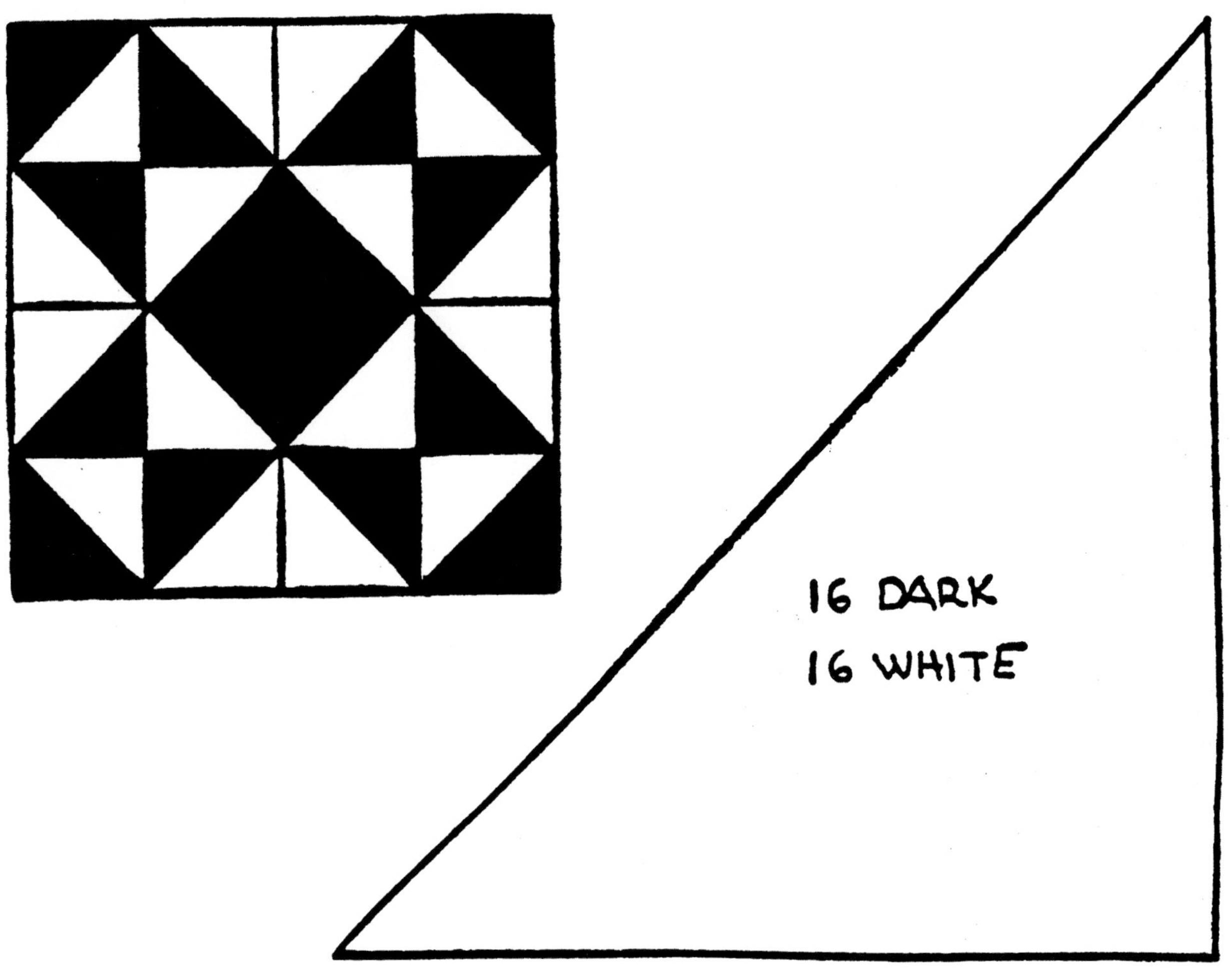

Published August 19, 1942

One has a choice of contrasting 1-tone pieces in putting together this quilt which has its inspiration in the envelope, or one may choose two pieces of print and two pieces of 1-tone material for a block. Miss Dorothy Lallak, Haddam, Kan., contributor of the design, offers Half a Square as another name for it.

Envelope Motif block **Jeanne Poore**

■ **Block size:** 12"

■ **Fabrics needed:** Two fabrics, a **medium** and a **dark.**

Cutting and piecing instructions

■ From **medium** fabric, cut:

* Eight 4⅞-inch squares.

■ From **dark** fabric, cut:

* Eight 4⅞-inch squares.

■ **Draw** a diagonal line on the back of each dark square. Place each atop a medium square, right sides facing.

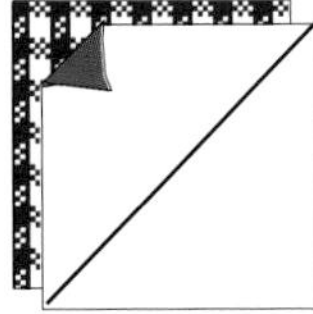

■ **Stitch** ¼-inch on either side of the line.

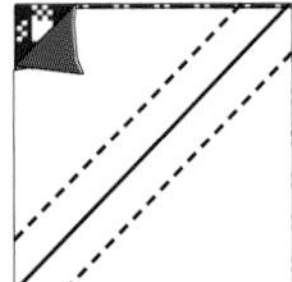

■ **Cut** along the line. Press to dark.

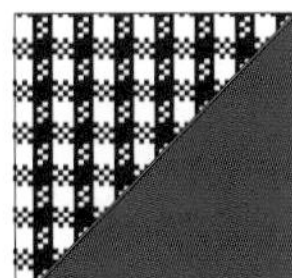

Now, you have 16 units.

■ Assemble in rows as shown.

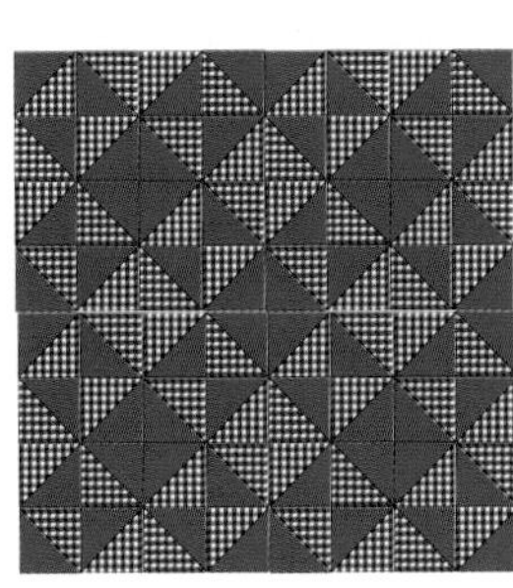

Templates

See appendix for T 4⅞

Women put the finishes touches on a quilt at a bee in 1948 in Francestown, N.H.

Four Leaf Clover (1935 pattern)
Made by Lula Tucker
Owned by Susan Gandy

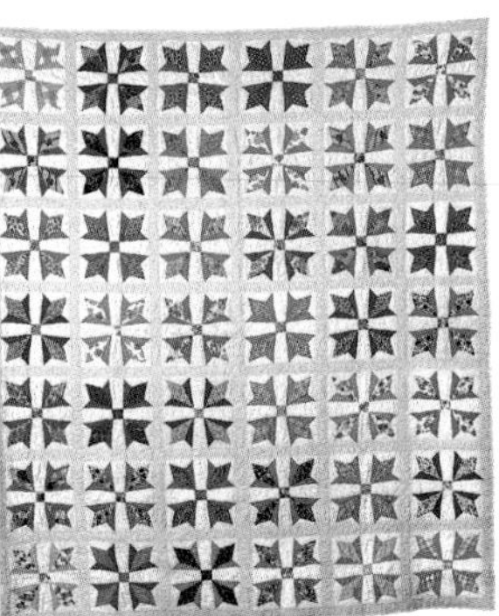

Tulip quilt (1935 pattern)
Made in 1950
by Anna Morrow Hudson
Owned by Jerry Stube

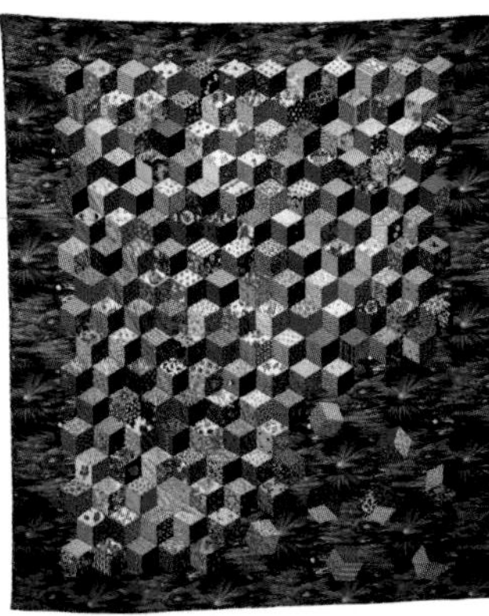

Builder's Block (1947 pattern)
Made in 1999 by Peggy
and Francis Hutinett

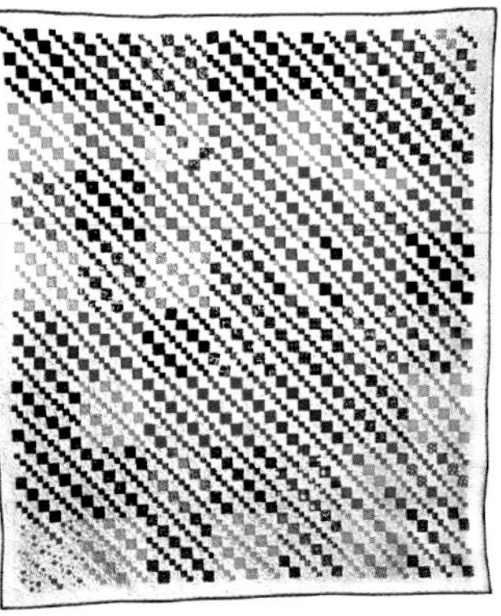

Carrie Nation (1940 pattern)
Made by Lula Tucker
Owned by Lori Huffles

Mystery Snowball **Pieced and owned by Susan Jarsulic** **Quilted by Jean Zyck**

1946-1955

Post-war stars

Interest in quilting, which had thrived during previous years, slowly waned during and after World War II.

Families were looking for more "modern" furnishings for their rooms; handmade quilts, once beloved, now were thought of more as old-fashioned, grandmotherly coverings.

This attitude was true even in the Midwest, traditional heart of the quilting boom. The Kansas Quilt Project recorded fewer quilts dated during the 1950s than in any other decade after 1920.

Only 15 patterns ran in *The Kansas City Star* in 1952, down from a high of 53 in 1930.

But quilting refused to disappear.

In her 1948 book *American Quilts*, author Elizabeth Wells Robertson reported that "in farmhouses in the country, in cabins on the windswept plains, in fine houses surrounded by gardens, in apartments in cities, they are still carrying on this art of the American people. They venture into the difficulties and happy surprises of making their own designs. Like their grandmothers and great-grandmothers, they make pictorial use of their own familiar surroundings and their pets. However, they no longer work only with scraps 'left over,' but with all the wealth of materials and color that America today has at their command."

Kansas women, some in period costume, worked on a Bear's Paw pattern. The pattern was first published in The Star in the late 1930s.

MYSTERY SNOWBALL

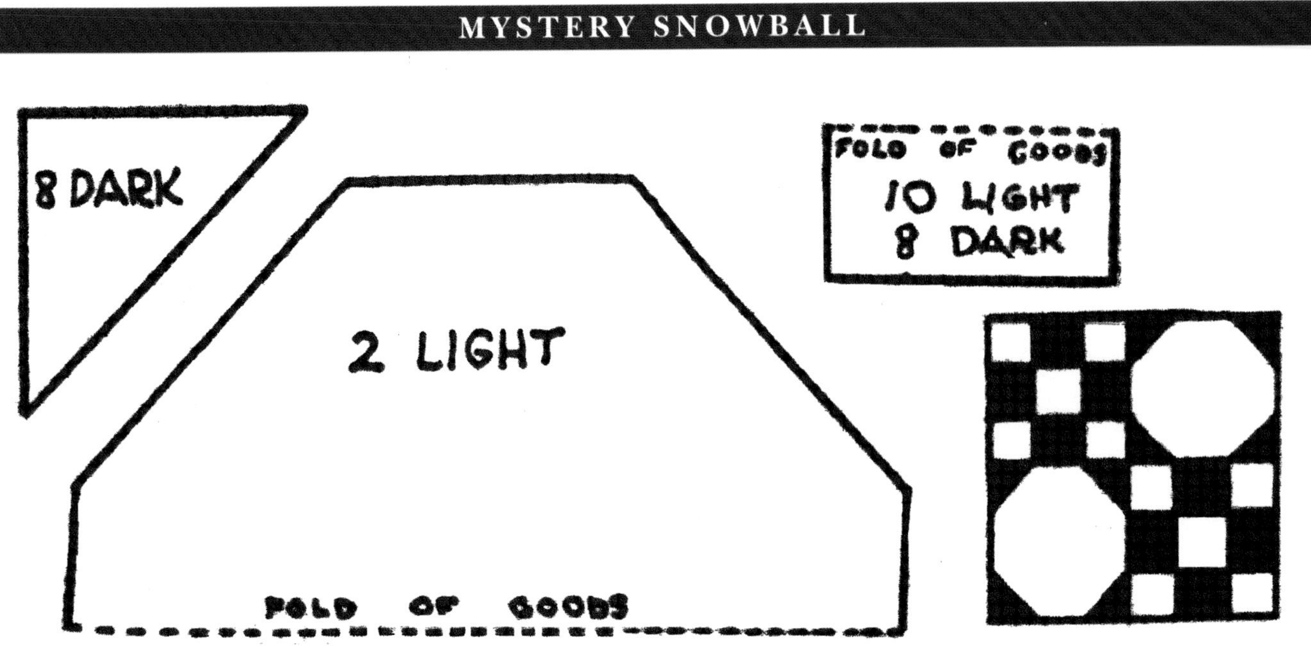

Published June 11, 1947

This Snowball quilt design shows a winter emblem that has added deep shades to its white in its rolling journey.

Mystery Snowball **Jeanne Poore**

■ **Block size:** 12"

■ **Fabrics needed:** Two fabrics, a **light** and a **dark**

Cutting and piecing instructions

■ From **light** fabric, cut:

* Two 6½-inch squares.

* One 2½-inch strip, 25 inches long.

■ From **dark** fabric, cut:

* Eight 2½-inch squares.

* One 2½-inch strip, 20 inches long.

Snowball assembly:

■ **Draw** a diagonal line on the wrong side of eight dark squares, shown here as a dashed line. Place four of them at the corners of a 6½-inch light square, right sides together.

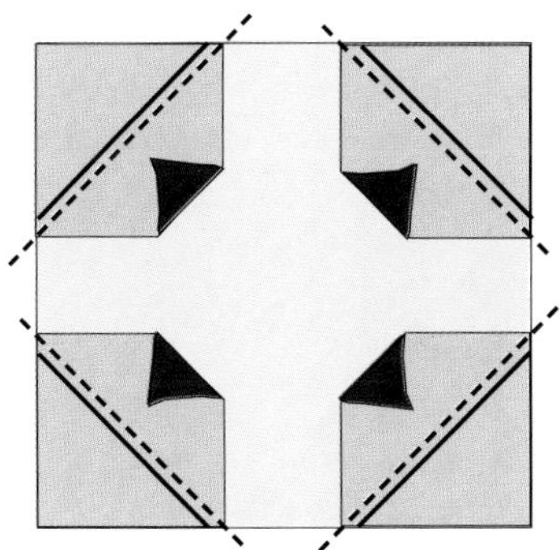

■ **Stitch** along the diagonal line, trim ¼ inch from the line as shown by the solid line and press toward the corners. Repeat this. You now have two snowball assemblies.

9-Patch assembly:

■ **Subcut** the 2½-inch x 25-inch light strip into two 10-inch strips and one 5-inch strip.

■ **Subcut** the 2½-inch x 20-inch dark strip into one 10-inch strip and two 5-inch strips.

■ **Stitch** the 10-inch dark strip between the two 10-inch light strips.

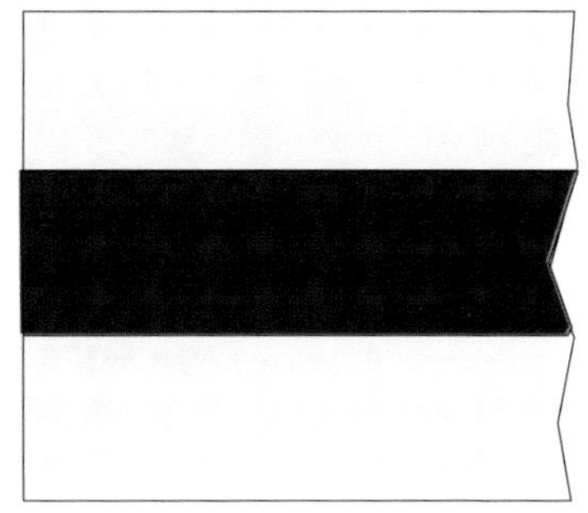

■ **Stitch** the five-inch light strip between the two five-inch dark strips.

■ **Subcut** the strips into 2½-inch sections.

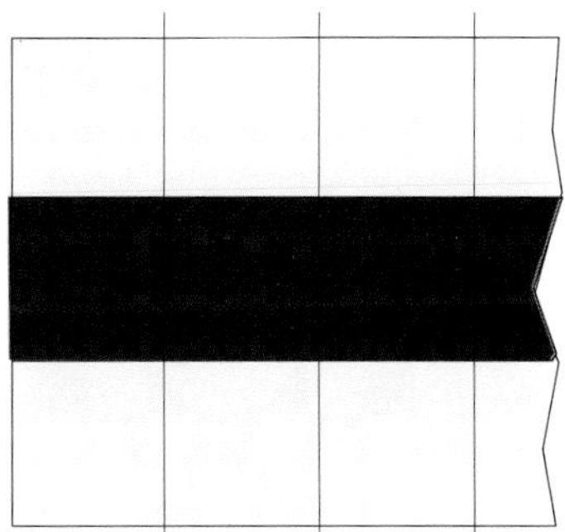

■ **Assemble** the 9-patches like this.

Templates

See appendix for Sq 2½, T 2½, Misc. 10

■ **Stitch** the snowball and 9-patch sections together.

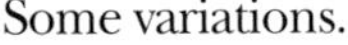

Some variations.

DOUBLE T IS AN INTERESTING QUILT PATTERN

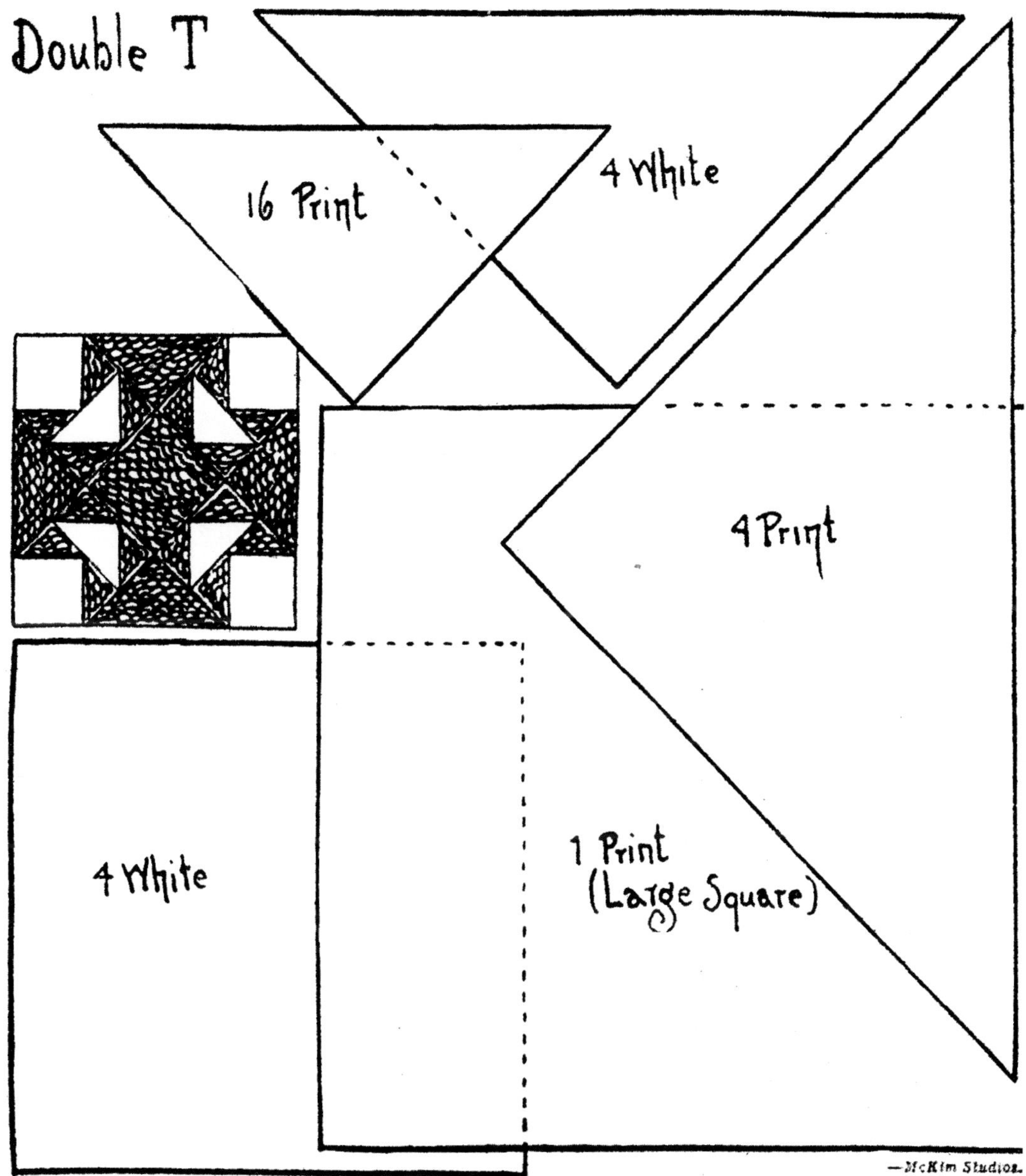

Published Dec. 10, 1947

The Double T quilt pattern is another of those designs which is adapted for use on a patchwork pillow as well as for a counterpane. The completed block is twelve inches square.

These 12-inch blocks may be set together for a quilt with alternate 12-inch plain squares between. Or it is very attractive with strips three inches wide of white or harmonizing color between blocks, either continuing in unbroken lattice work or with 3-inch squares of a contrasting color at each corner.

The patterns shown are of the size needed for the quilt but do not allow for seams. To make cardboard patterns, trace these squares and triangles on cardboard and then cut out the patterns. Place cardboard patterns on the material and trace around these with a pencil line. When you cut them out however, cut beyond the pencil line, allowing for a seam, and then sew back to the line when piecing. The smallest triangle pattern, from which sixteen print pieces are to be cut, should measure 3" inches on the long side, 2 1/2" inches on each of the two short sides.

1947 Double "T"

Double "T" **Quilt maker unknown** **Owned by Cindy Rennels Clinton, Okla.**

1947 Double "T": The Redraft

■ **Block size:** 12"
■ **Fabrics needed:** Two fabrics, a **light** and a **dark.**

Cutting and piecing instructions

■ From **light** fabric, cut:
* Two 4⅞-inch squares.
* Two 5¼-inch squares.

■ From **dark** fabric, cut:
* One 4½-inch square.
* Two 4⅞-inch squares.
* Eight 2⅞-inch squares.

■ **Draw** a solid diagonal line from corner to corner on the wrong side of a 4⅞-inch light square. Place a light square atop a 4⅞-inch dark square, right sides facing.

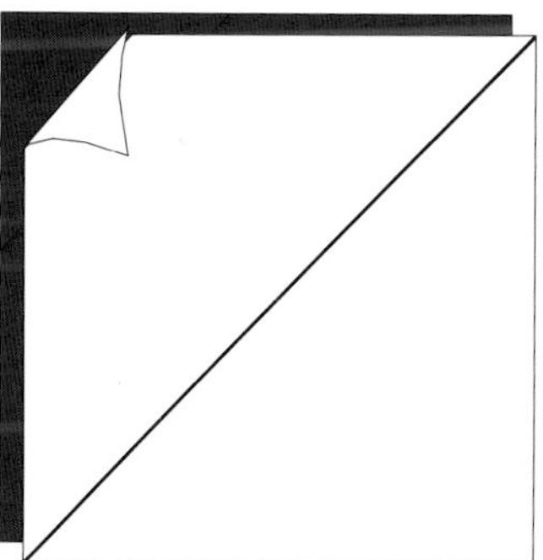

■ **Stitch** ¼ inch on either side of the line and cut along the line.

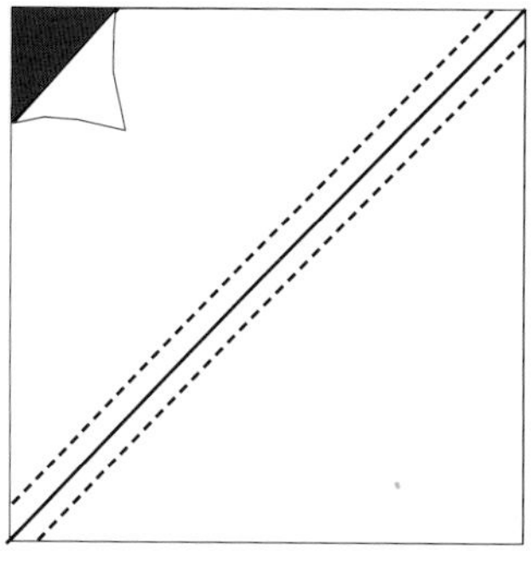

■ **Cut** on the solid line, unfold, and press to dark. Repeat this process with the other 4⅞-inch light and dark square to create four units that look like this:

Flying goose units

■ **Draw** a diagonal line across the backs of two 2⅞-inch dark squares.

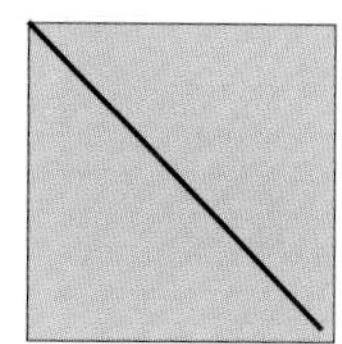

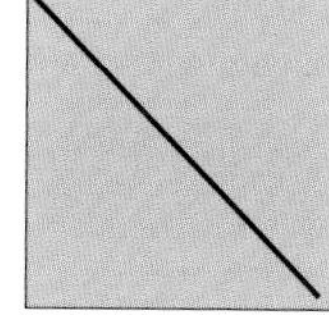

■ **Place** them atop a 5¼-inch light square, right sides facing.

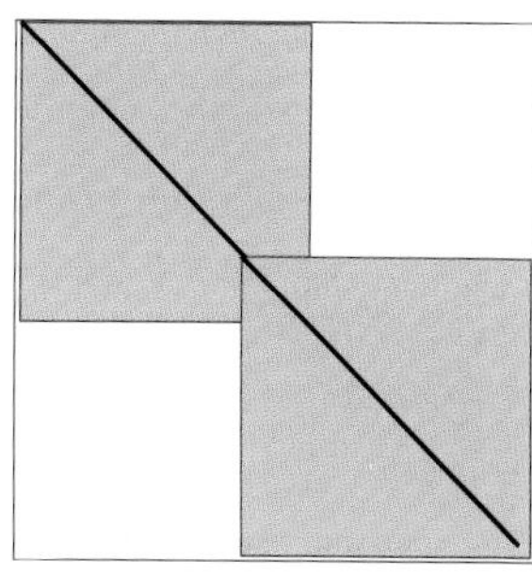

■ **Stitch** ¼ inch on both sides of the line.

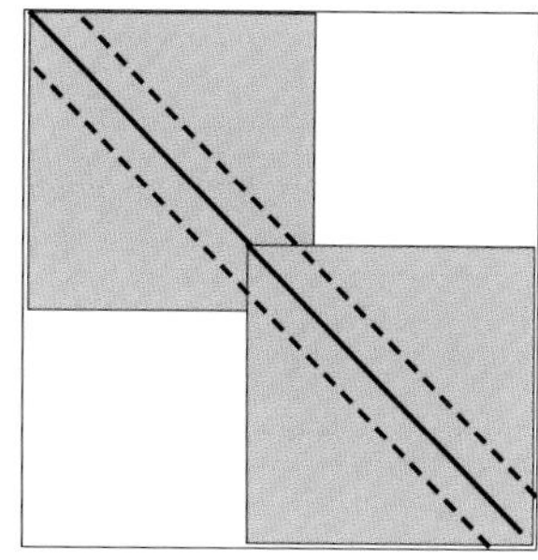

Cut on the line. Place the remaining unit aside.

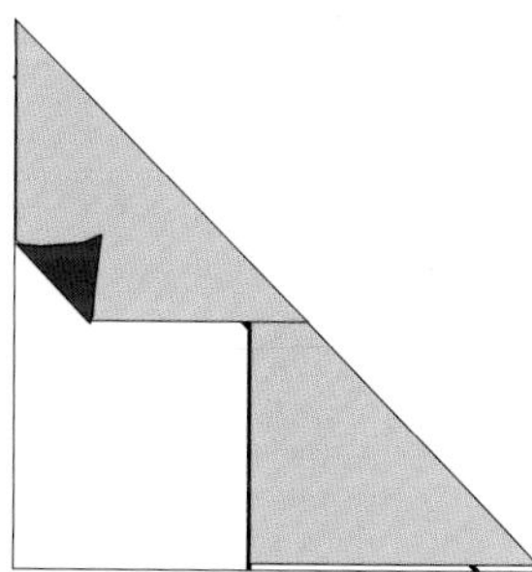

Press to darker unit.

■ **Place** a dark square in the lower left corner, mark a diagonal as shown and stitch ¼ inch on either side.

■ **Cut** along the solid line through all layers of fabric.

Press to darker fabric.

Templates

See appendix for Sq 4½, T 2⅞, T 3¾, T 4⅞

■ **Repeat** with the remaining unit, then with the other light square.

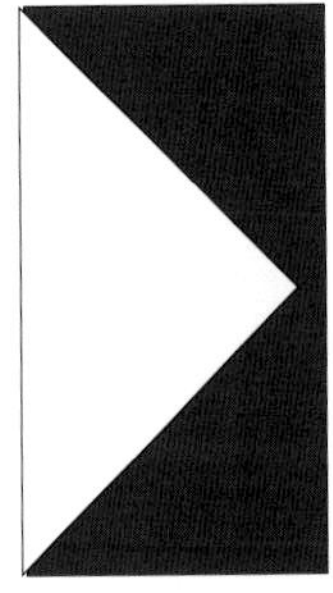

You should get eight units like these.

■ **Assemble** units in rows, then assemble rows as shown below.

1948 Grandmother's Quilt

The center of this "Grandmother's Quilt" consists of 36, 1-inch squares; all points are different fabrics. Quilt instructor Jeanne Poore reproduced this 1948 pattern in 1994, and the Legler Barn Quilters of Lenexa, Kan., hand-quilted it in 1996.

GRANDMOTHER'S QUILT

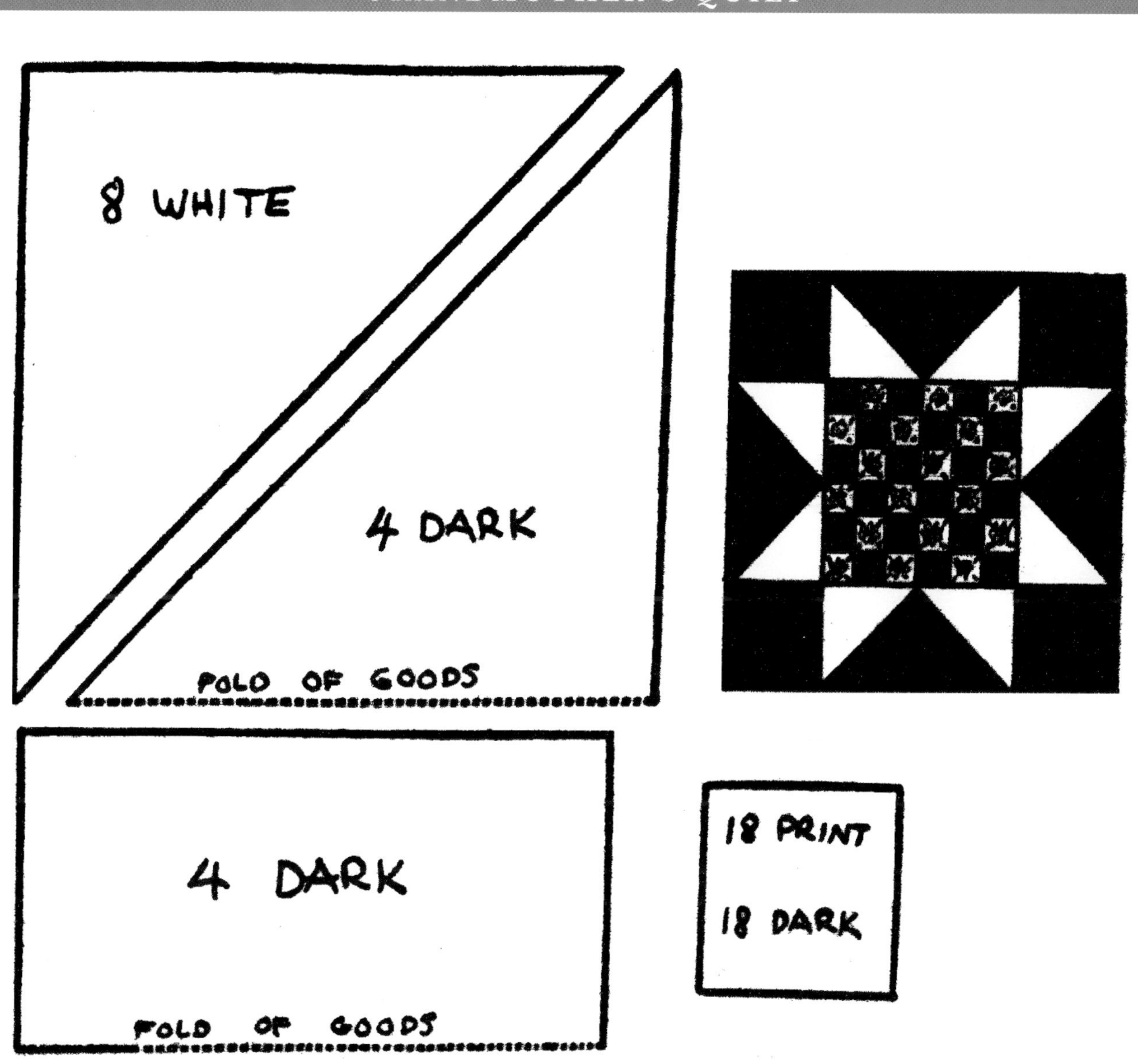

Published Nov. 3, 1948

When Mrs. Claudie Gray, route 1, Qulin, Mo., married in 1903, one of her wedding gifts was a quilt in this pattern, pieced by her husband's mother during the latter part of the nineteenth century, when the design was a general favorite.

■ **Block size:** 12"

■ **Fabrics needed:** Three fabrics, a **light,** a **medium** and a **dark.**

Cutting and piecing instructions

■ From **medium** fabric, cut:

* Four 3½ -inch squares.

■ From **light** fabric, cut:

* Four 3½ x 6-inch rectangles.

* Eight 3½ -inch squares.

* One 1½ -inch strip, 27 inches long.

■ From **dark** fabric, cut:

* One 1½ -inch strip, 27 inches long.

Center assembly

■ **Subcut** strips into 9-inch lengths. Stitch together lengthwise, six strips. Alternate the colors. Measure 1½-inch lengths as shown.

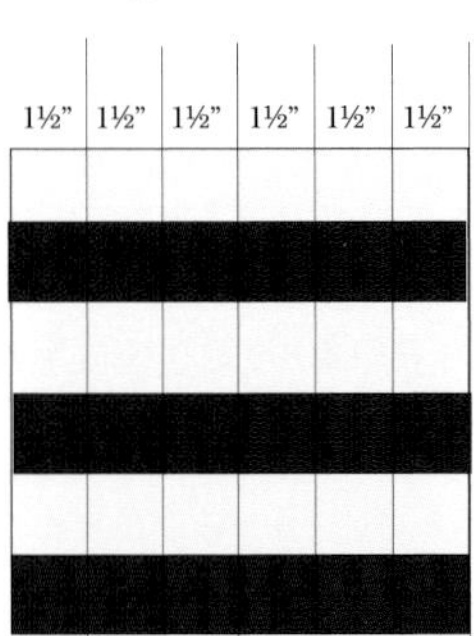

■ **Cut** strips along width, creating six units. Alternate the units as shown and stitch together.

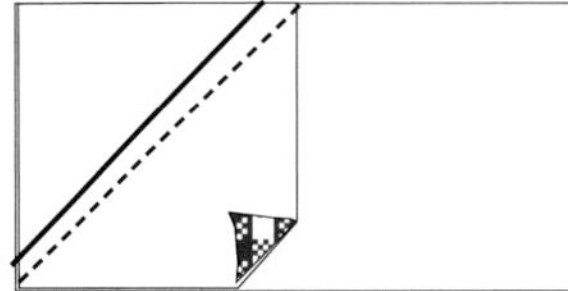

Star-point assembly

■ **Draw** a diagonal line on the wrong side of a 3½-inch medium square, shown here by dotted line. Place the square atop a light rectangle, at one end, right sides facing. Stitch along the line. Trim along solid line as shown, unfold and press toward print. Repeat this process at the other end of the rectangle. Make four units like this.

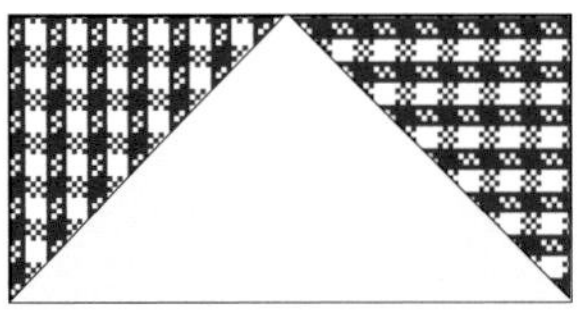

.■ **Attach** 3½-inch light squares to the ends of two of these units.

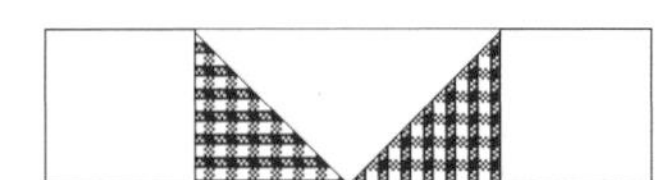

■ **Assemble** block in rows like this.

Adding more colors to the strips can create a more vibrant, even random center.

Templates

See appendix for Sq 1½, Sq 3½, T 5

1948 Grandmother's Quilt: The Redraft

1948 Grandmother's Quilt

Grandmother's Quilt (1948) **Made and owned by Jeanne Poore**

GRANDMOTHER'S QUILT
AKA - POSTAGE STAMP STAR
COMPLETED 1996 88" X 116"
35 BLOCKS, EACH STAR DIFFERENT
CENTERS OF 36 ONE INCH SQUARES
REPRODUCTION FABRICS USED
MACHINE PIECED, BOUND
BY OWNER/MAKER
M. JEANNE POORE
HAND QUILTED BY
LEGLER BARN
QUILTERS

Grandmother's Quilt Made by Jeanne Poore Signature on back of quilt

Monkey Wrench (1929 pattern; other versions printed in 1956 and 1960) **Owned by D. Thomas**

1956-1961

The patterns fade

Quilting activities dwindled during the late 1950s and the Stars slowly departed from the pages of their hometown newspaper. In 1957, 11 patterns ran; by 1961, the final year, only eight saw print.

Some of the captions, which had once been so bright and conversational, were reduced to a few, simple lines of instruction. Several ran with no captions at all.

There's a nostalgic bittersweetness to these final designs. Many older patterns were reprinted. Quilters seemed to be longing for the old days, when their handiwork was prized and their quilt designs cherished.

In 1956 Mrs. T.A. Best of Seminole, Okla., submitted "Monkey Wrench," a design she had clipped from *The Weekly Star* some 20 years earlier. The caption shows that although the art of quilting at times may wane, it never fully dies out:

She was motivated to mail in the pattern, Mrs. Best said, by her "renewed interest in quilt making."

Name on Each Friendship (1956) **Jeanne Poore**

A NAME ON EACH FRIENDSHIP BLOCK

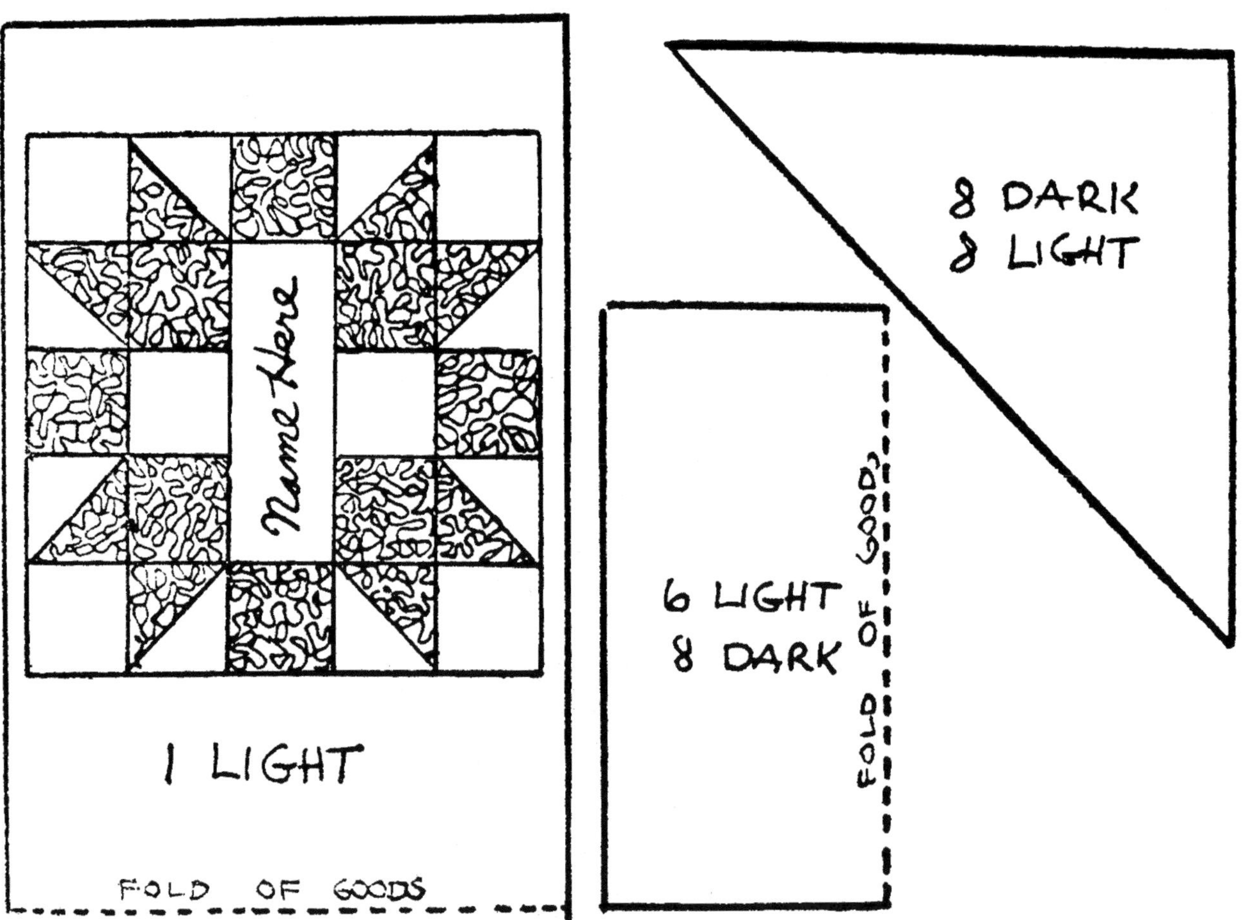

Published Oct. 10, 1956

Her conception of a friendship quilt is expressed by Mrs. Rosella Shaw, route 1, Madill, Okla., in this block edged by squares and triangles.

1956 Name on Each Friendship: The Redraft

This "Friendship Block" was machine-quilted in the 1950s. It belongs to Jeanne Poore. "These blocks were made for my mother, Mildred Enfield, in Washington County, Kan.," Poore says. "The names include my grandmother, aunt, cousin, great aunt, neighbors and the midwife who was with my mother when I was born."

■ **Block size:** 12"

■ **Fabrics needed:** Two fabrics, a **medium** and a **dark.**

Cutting and piecing instructions

■ From the **dark** fabric, cut:
* Twelve 2⅞-inch squares
* Four 3¼-inch squares

■ From the **medium** fabric, cut:
* Two 2⅞-inch squares.
* Four 3¼-inch squares
* One 2⅞ x 7¼-inch strip

■ **Draw** a solid diagonal line from corner to corner on the wrong side of a 3¼-inch dark square. Place together with a 3¼-inch medium square, right sides facing.

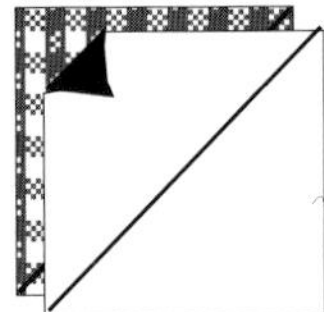

■ **Stitch** ¼-inch on both sides of the diagonal line.

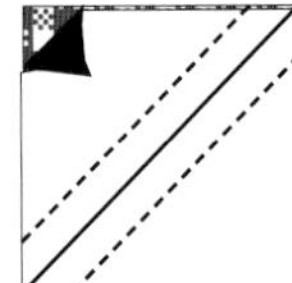

■ **Cut** on the solid line, unfold, and press to dark. Repeat this process with all four 3¼-inch medium and dark squares to create eight units that look like this:

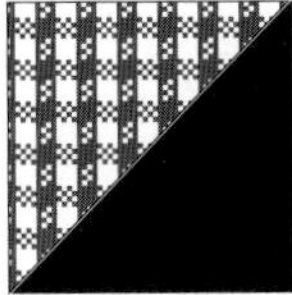

■ **Assemble** two rows that look like this:

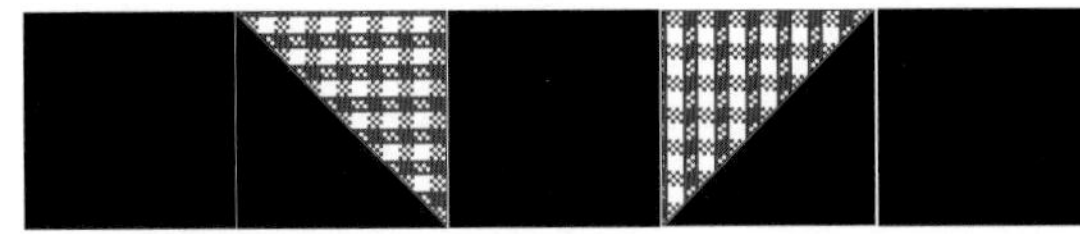

■ **Assemble** two rows that look like this:

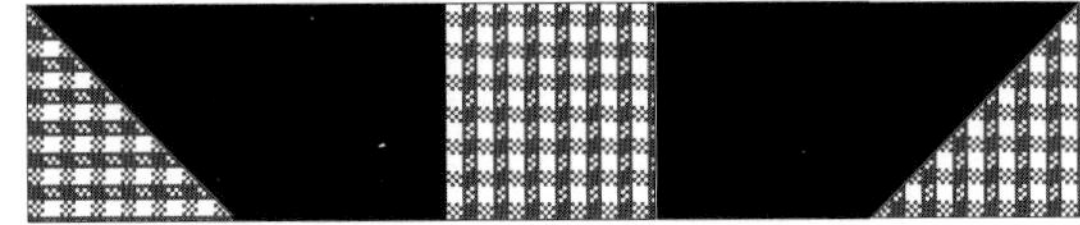

■ **Place** the 2⅞ x 7¼-inch strip (with a friend's name embroidered if desired) between two dark squares to create this unit:

■ **Assemble** the block as shown:

Templates

See appendix for Sq 2⅞, T 3¼, P 2⅞ x 7¼

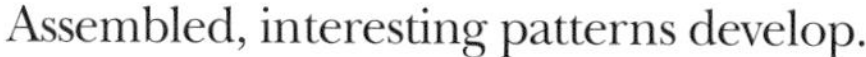

Assembled, interesting patterns develop.

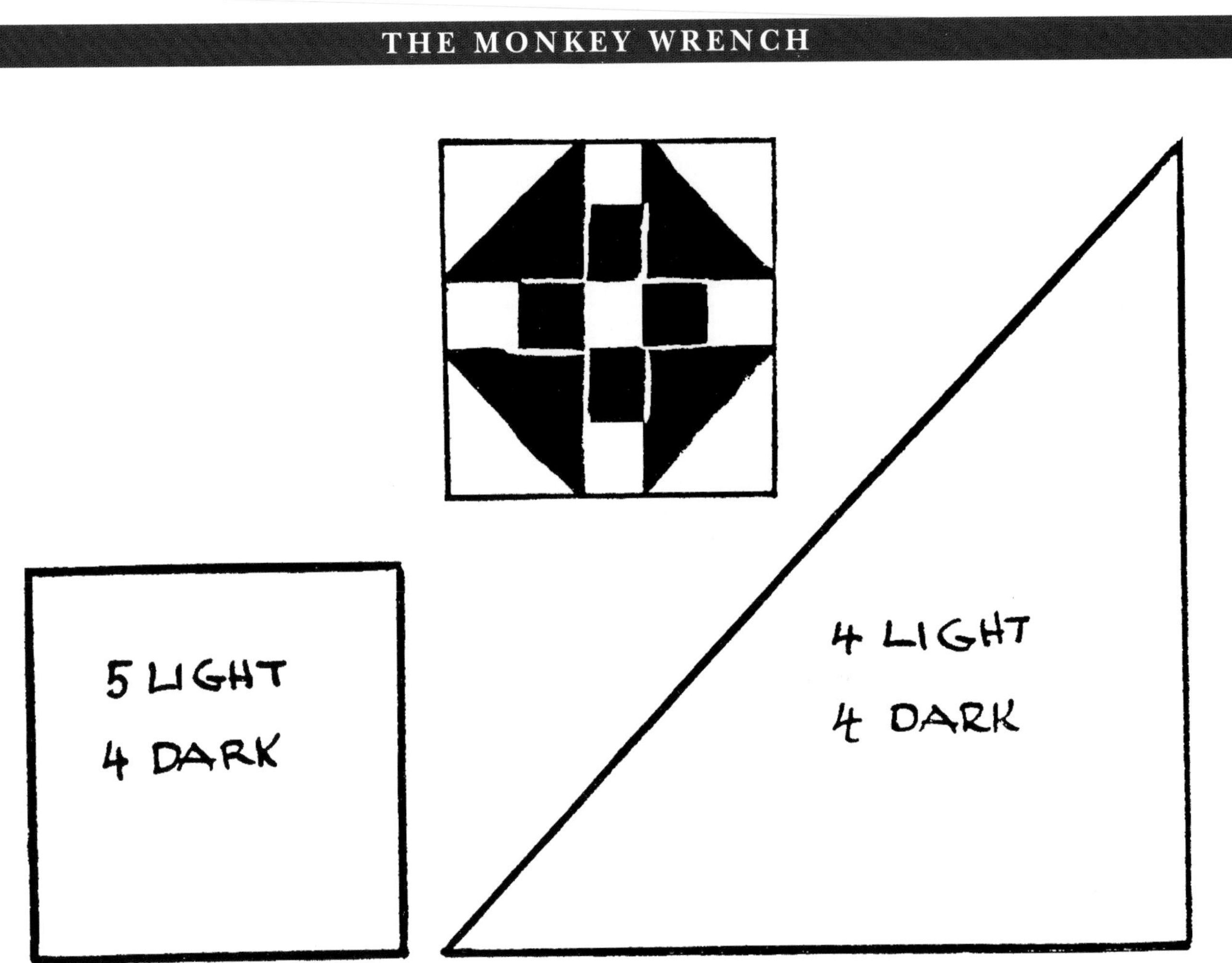

Published Jan. 20, 1960

Two one-tone colors are most pleasingly effective for this design, which the contributor, Mrs. A. H. Ward, route 2, Steele, Mo., has named the Monkey Wrench. One can quickly imagine it serving as a friendship or signature quilt.

Monkey Wrench (1956 pattern) **Owned by Cindy Rennels, Clinton, Okla.**

■ **Block size:** 12"

■ **Fabrics needed:** Two fabrics, a **medium** and a **dark.**

Cutting and piecing instructions

■ From the **medium** fabric, cut:

* Two 5⅝-inch squares.
* Five 3-inch squares.

■ From the **dark** fabric, cut:

* Two 5⅝-inch squares.
* Four 3-inch squares.

■ **Draw** a solid diagonal line from corner to corner on the wrong side of a 5⅝-inch medium square. Place together with a 5⅝-inch dark square, right sides facing.

■ **Stitch** ¼-inch on both sides of the diagonal line.

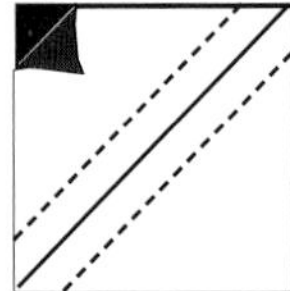

■ **Cut** on the solid line, unfold, and press to dark. Repeat this process with the other 5⅝-inch medium and dark squares to create four units that look like this:

■ **Sew** together five of the 3-inch units, alternating medium and dark

■ **Sew** together two of the 3-inch units, alternating medium and dark. Repeat this process to produce two new units.

■ **Sew** two of the triangle units with the 3-inch square units in between.

Make two of these units.

■ **Assemble** in rows, as shown:

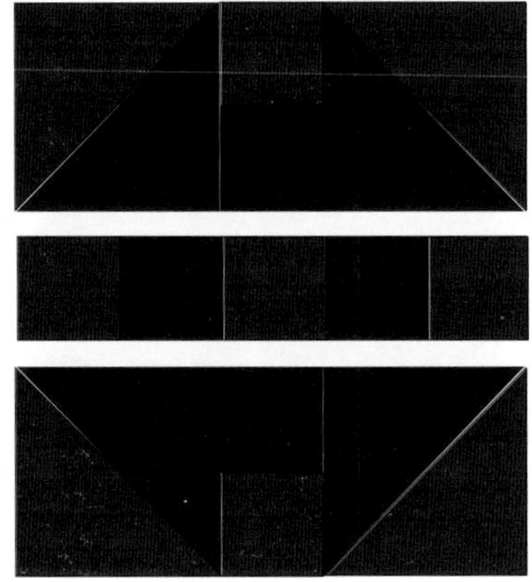

Templates

See appendix for Sq 3, T 5⅝

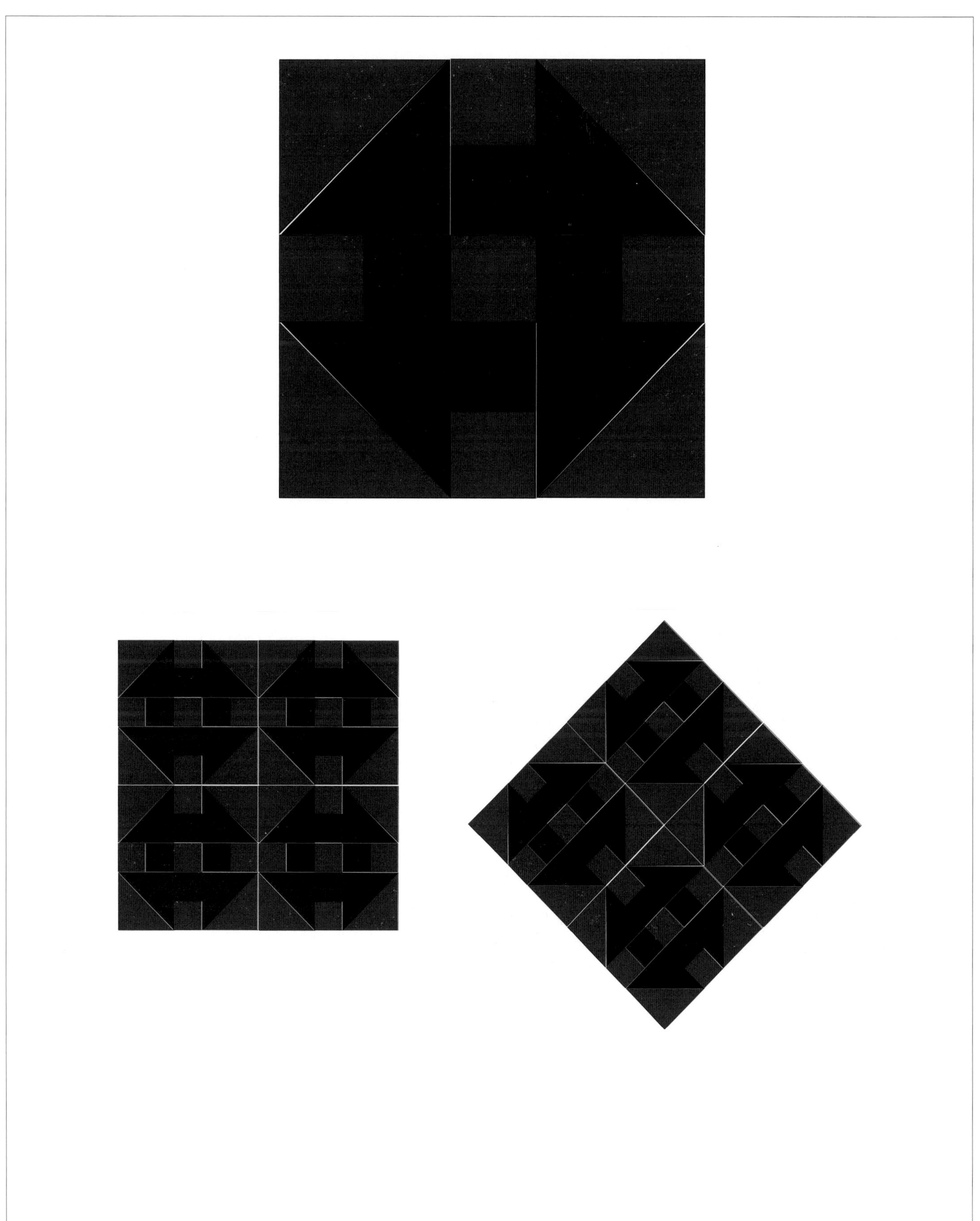

Rope and Anchor block **Jeanne Poore**

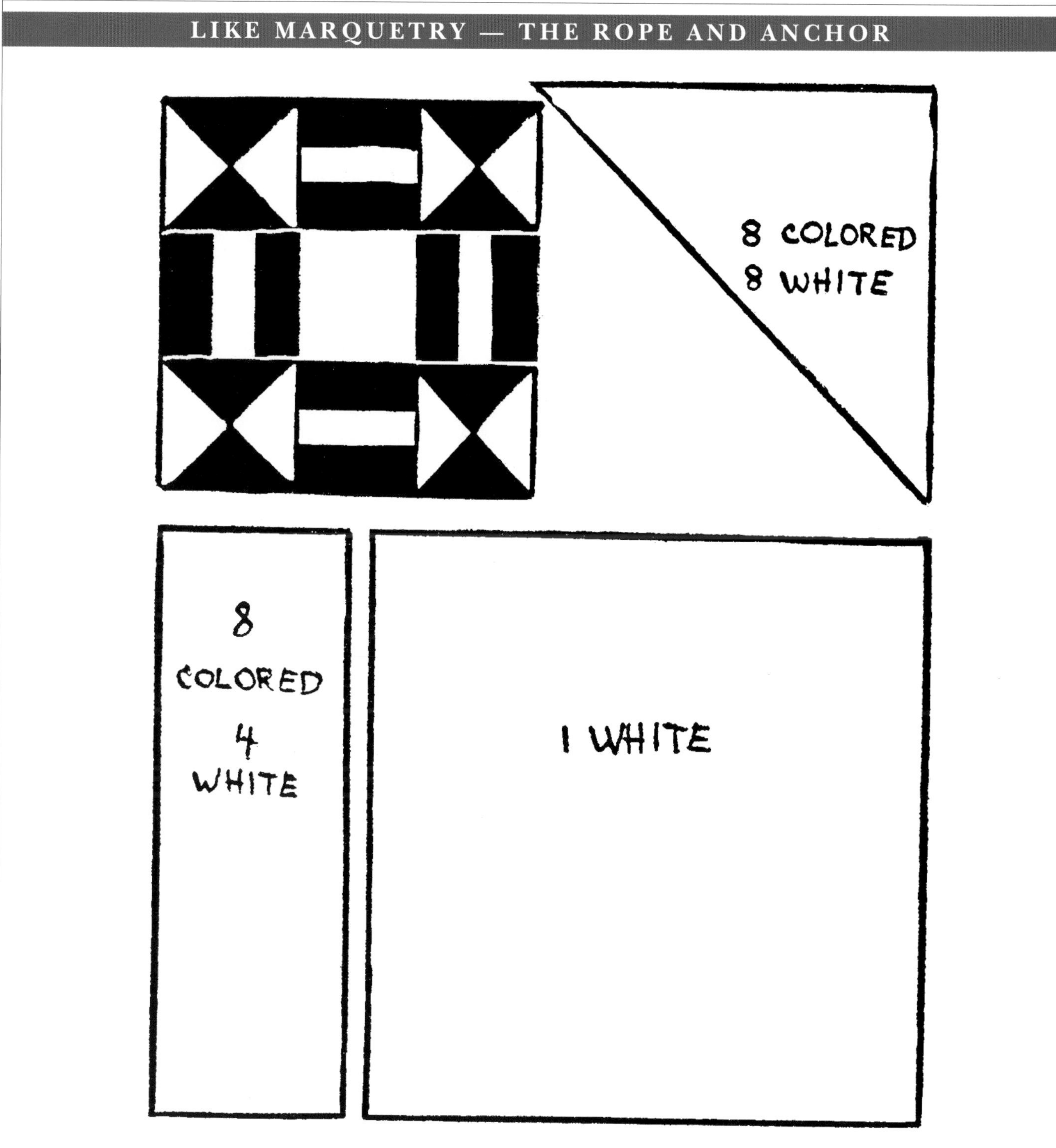

Published June 11, 1960

This maritime theme, the Rope and Anchor, is most effective when developed in two colors. Like any marquetry skill is required in cutting the pieces and in putting them together to preserve the straight lines. The design is an offering of Amelia Lampton, Aguilar, Colo.

■ **Block size:** 12"

■ **Fabrics needed:** Two fabrics, a **light** and a **dark.**

Cutting and piecing instructions

■ From the **light** fabric, cut:

* One 3½" square
* Two 4¼" squares
* One 1½ x 15-inch strip

■ From the **dark** fabric, cut:

* Two 1½ x 15-inch strips
* Two 4¼" squares

■ **Draw** a solid diagonal line from corner to corner on the wrong side of a 4¼-inch light square. Place together with a 4¼-inch dark square, right sides facing.

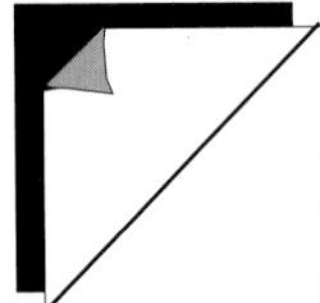

■ **Stitch** ¼-inch on both sides of the diagonal line.

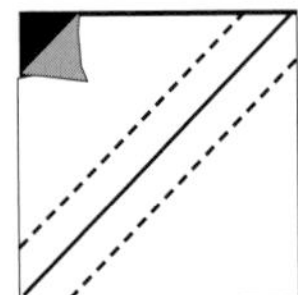

■ **Cut** on the solid line, unfold, and press to dark. Repeat this process with all 4¼-inch light and dark squares to create four units that look like this:

■ **Place** the half square triangle units right sides together. Draw another line on the back

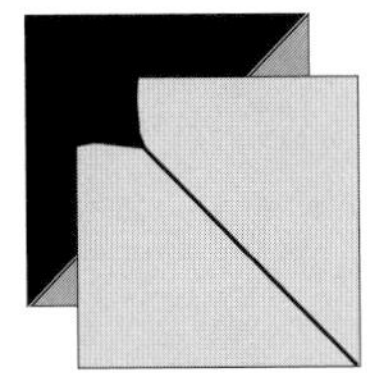

■ **Stitch** ¼-inch on both sides of the drawn line. Cut on line, press to one side.

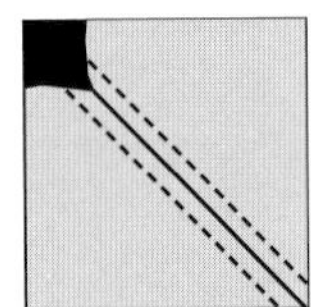

■ You now have four quarter square triangle units.

■ **Stitch** together the two 1½ x 15-inch strips of dark fabric and the 1½ x 15-inch strip of light fabric along the lengths, as shown:

■ **Subcut** the 15-inch strips into four units, each 3½-inches wide.

■ **Stitch together** two of the triangle units with a strip unit between. Make two of these units.

■ **Stitch together** two of the strip units with the center square in between.

■ **Assemble** the block as shown.

Templates

See appendix for Sq 3½, T 3⅛, P 1½ x 3½

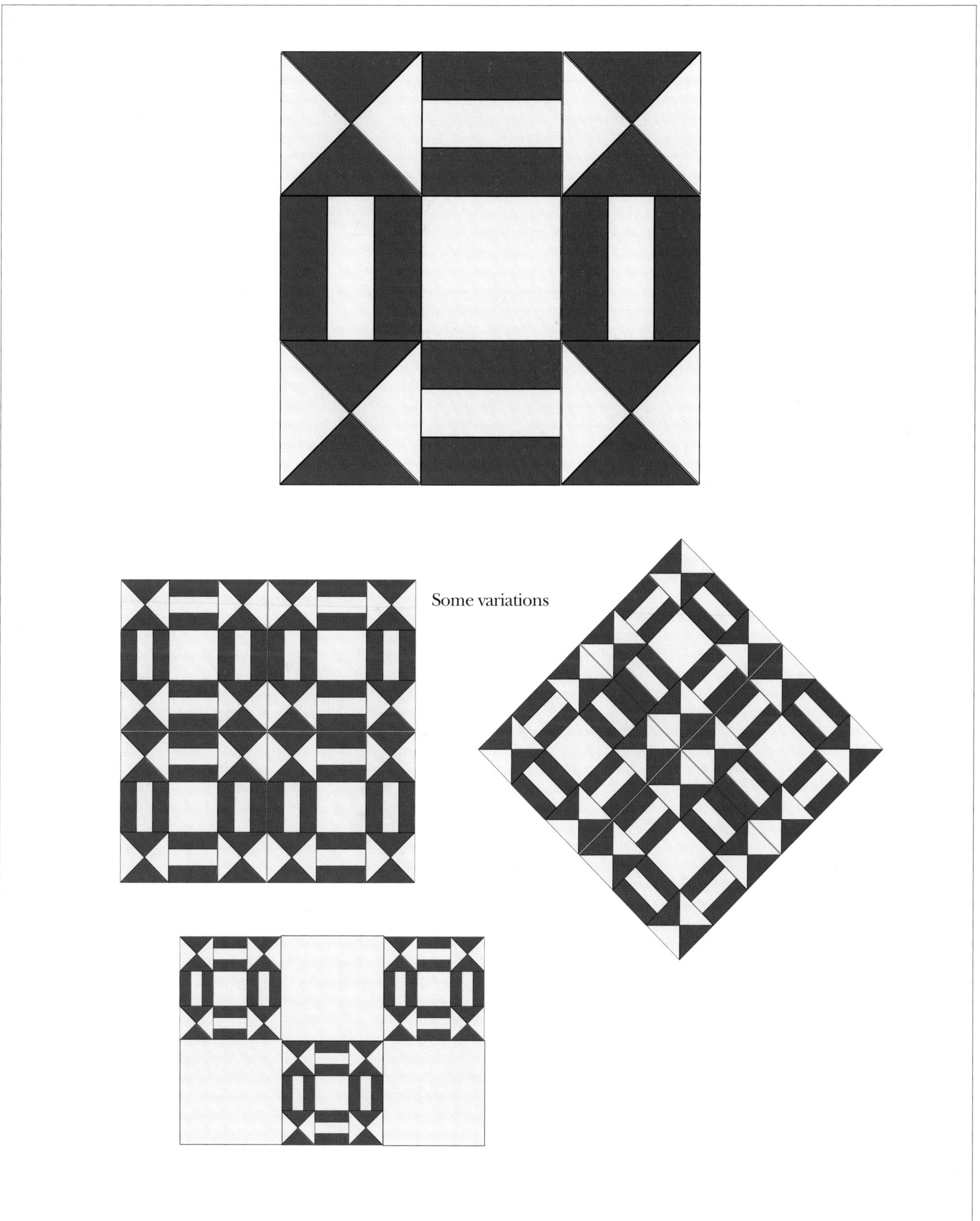
Some variations

Big crowds attended the National Quilting Association, Inc., show in Omaha, Neb.

Electric Quilt 4 demonstration at the National Quilting Association, Inc., show in Omaha, Neb.

The Stars live on

The Stars are many things: Historical, utilitarian, fascinating.

Most of all they are resilient.

In 1928, when the first patterns appeared in *The Kansas City Star*, quilting was a domestic task often taught to daughters by mothers and grandmothers. By 1961, when the last pattern ran, many daughters and granddaughters weren't very interested in quilts anymore.

But quilters kept on stitching the Stars.

America's bicentennial in 1976 brought about a quilting renaissance. Since then, quilting has grown into a sophisticated art form. Now there are hundreds of quilt books, dozens of quilt magazines, all kinds of quilt design software for computers, endless Internet quilt sites.

And still, the Stars remain wildly popular.

The patterns have evolved past simple bed covers. Blocks are embedded in the sidewalks of one Kansas town. An Oklahoma woman has stitched dozens into intricate, framed artworks. And the Oklahoma Quilters Guild has hand-sewn more than 1,000 blocks, which are exhibited at quilt shows throughout the country.

The Stars haven't lost their shine.

Quilting bees, those old-fashioned gatherings, still take place every day around the world. Women meet to quilt, swap blocks, exchange gossip and sewing tips, discuss child care and husband care.

All on the Internet.

Debbie Hanlan of Stewartsville, Mo., is a hostess for one such "chat room" on the Crazy Quilters Web site (**www.crazyquilters.com**).

"It's a fun place to go," says Hanlan, who meets with quilters from all over the world through her home computer. "A place to chitchat."

Participants keep quilting projects right next to their computer. That way they can follow Internet conversations and classes and stitch at the same time.

Hanlan helped organize an "FTF" meeting — that's "face to face" in computer jargon — for dozens of the women in 1999 in Kansas City. Participants flew in from as far away as Australia, California, Florida and Pennsylvania.

One highlight of the weekend's activities was a block lotto. Quilters who attended contributed a block (or blocks) of Cross and Crown, a 1930 *Star* pattern drawn by Ruby Short McKim, and were eligible to go home with a bundle of the blocks.

The quilters all used reproduction 1930s fabric.

Hanlan has quilted other *Star* patterns, too. "I did a Churn Dash in flannel that's oh-so comfy," she says.

That *Star* quilt also was created through a block swap on the Internet site. "I have blocks in there from Australia, Canada and all over the U.S.," Hanlan added.

Most downtown revitalization projects mean cleaning up old buildings, bringing in new businesses.

But Great Bend, a town of 16,000 in central Kansas, wanted something unique for its courthouse square redevelopment in the early 1990s.

"A design firm we hired came to us with a few proposals, and one was to put quilt blocks in the sidewalks," said Chris Collier, executive director of the Great Bend Convention and Visitors Bureau. "That kind of caught everyone because being a part of Kansas and having that pioneer history, quilts are a big part of that."

Local quilters researched patterns that would be most appropriate, to best reflect the Kansas heritage. Several they chose appeared as Stars: Windmill Quilt (1939), Kansas Trouble (1934) and Kansas Dugout (1942).

Colored concrete was poured into molds to form the seven inlaid block patterns, which were placed around the city's picturesque Lafayette Park.

Now the Quilt Walk is so popular that the Convention and Visitors Bureau sells redrafted patterns of the blocks to many visitors.

"We're getting ready to gear up again and add some more blocks to surrounding sidewalks," Collier says. "Then we'll have between 20 and 30."

Kansas City native Lucretia Hallam has had an adventurous life. She was a fashion model in the early 1950s, then a stewardess for Trans World Airlines. She married an Air Force man and moved to England. She became a psychiatric social worker and toured China in the 1980s with a team of psychiatrists.

But she always missed her hometown and the memories it held for her.

Her mother and grandmother were both avid quilters.

"I remember back when I was so small I could run under the quilt frame," Hallam says. She sat quietly and listened to the women chatter as they stitched quilt after quilt, many from *Star* patterns.

The Great Bend, Kan., Quilt Walk.

So when Hallam retired in 1995 in Lawton, Okla., she knew what she wanted to do. She decided to create the Stars in miniature and sell them back in her hometown. "I gave myself permission to be a folk-artist full time," she said.

She's been doing that for several years. She completes about 12 patterns a year and sells them through the Toy and Miniature Museum in Kansas City.

"It takes awhile to figure out a color scheme and fabrics," she said. "Prints have to be so tiny because many pieces are just a quarter-inch big." She uses special silk thread.

Patterns she's completed so far include Fence Row (with more than 400 pieces of 35 miniature-print fabrics), Double "V," Basket and SheepFold Quilt.

The finished works are about 8 by 10 inches and come matted and framed. Hallam has even "aged" some so they look antique.

The tags on her Stars feature a photograph of her grandmother and great-grandmother, Kansas pioneers.

Customer at vendor's booth "Cindy's Quilts" inspecting antique quilts and quilt tops for sale at National Quilting Association, Inc., show at Omaha, Neb.

Betty Jo Haines still lives in her family's Oklahoma farmhouse, "just east of Hydro right on Old 66."

Her grandmother earned a living by piecing quilts.

"For instance, in the 1930s she made a Wedding Ring Quilt and was paid $25," Haines says. "That was a lot of money back then."

In 1985, Haines saw a copy of Wilene Smith's index to the *Star* patterns and had an idea: She wanted to preserve and pay tribute to the many *Star* patterns that her mother and grandmother quilted.

Haines approached a group that she had founded, the Central Oklahoma Quilters Guild, with an idea. She wanted members to help quilt each and every original *Star* block.

"They seemed excited," Haines said.

As quilters around the country heard about the project, Haines began receiving hundreds of the original patterns in the mail. In January 1986 kits were assembled for the 202 (out of 285) members who wished to quilt the patterns. Each received a copy of the original pattern, a re-draft, muslin for backing and batting. One member, Judy Reeder, made 60 blocks.

Members supplied the fabric, following the original recommendations on the patterns as to the size of block and colors.

For months the women stitched.

The last blocks were completed in December 1989. They were mounted on 42 black felt panels and continue to be displayed at quilt shows around the country.

When back home in Oklahoma, the panels are stored in acid-free boxes in a special temperature- and humidity-controlled warehouse.

Thus they are preserved for future generations of fans of the Kansas City Stars.

Acknowledgments

This book would not have been possible without the work of Jeanne Poore of Overland Park, Kan., who graciously provided her personally redrafted Kansas City Stars as well as her knowledge of the history and art of quilting. Also indispensable was Edie McGinnis of Kansas City, Mo., who lent her time, ideas and enthusiasm. We are also grateful for the encouragement and assistance of members of the quilting community nationwide, especially (in alphabetical order): Jenny Alcasid, Nancy Cameron Armstrong, Lois Embree Arnold, Barbara Brackman, Betty Calcara, Anne Copeland, Kris Driessen, Beverly Dunivent, Lisa Erlandson, Jill Sutton Filo, Judy Fleischmann, Roy and Lougene Geary, Harold and Dorothymae Groves, Christine Husak, Bonnie Gardner Ingram, Roderick Kiracofe, Raeann Lenzini, Jayna Marrinan, Lorrie Oltman, Vicki Paullus, Gayle Sternheim, Jeannie Spears, Jerry Stube, Emma Talbot, Cynthia Tucker, Nancy P. Wakefield. Thank you to Janelle Hopkins and Derek Donovan of *The Kansas City Star* library.

Bibliography

Wilene Smith, *Quilt Patterns: An Index to The Kansas City Star Patterns, 1928-1961.* Mennonite Press, 1985. For more information write: Wilene Smith, 815 W. 61st North, Wichita, KS, 67204; or e-mail WileneSmth@aol.com.

Central Oklahoma Quilters Guild Inc., *The Ultimate Illustrated Index to the Kansas City Star Quilt Pattern Collection.* 1990. For more information write: Central Oklahoma Quilters Guild, P.O. Box 23916, Oklahoma City, OK, 73123.

Harold and Dorothymae Groves, editors and compilers, *The Kansas City Star Classic Quilt Patterns: Motifs & Designs* . 11 volumes, Groves Publishing Co., 1988. For more information write: Groves Publishing Co., P.O. Box 33068, Kansas City, MO, 64114

Barbara Brackman, Jennie A. Chinn, Gayle R. Davis, Terry Thompson, Sara Reimer Farley and Nancy Hornback, *Kansas Quilts and Quilters.* University Press of Kansas, 1993.

Elizabeth Wells Robertson, *American Quilts.* The Studio Publications Inc., 1948.

Fiona Courtenay-Thompson and Kate Phelps, editors, *The 20th Century Year by Year: The People and Events That Shaped the Last Hundred Years.* Barnes & Noble Books, 1998.

Joyce S. Steward, compiler,*Quilting: Quotations Celebrating an American Legacy.* Running Press Miniature Edition, 1994.

Photography credits

COVER PHOTOGRAPH: Tammy Ljungblad, *The Kansas City Star*

Pages i, v, 3-6, 12, 15, 18, 24, 27, 32, 36, 38, 40, 45, 49, 53, 57, 60, 64, 68, 72, 76, 79, 83, 86, 90, 93, 94, 97, 105, 107, 111, 114, 116, 124, 128, 130, 131, 133, 140, 146, 166, 172: Tammy Ljungblad, *The Kansas City Star*

Pages ii, iii and 3: *The Kansas City Star* archives

Page 2: Courtesy Kansas Quilt Project

Page 7: Ruby Short McKim photograph courtesy of Chris Jones, Independence, Mo.

Page 7: Edna Marie Dunn photograph from T*he Kansas City Star* archives

Pages 8, 13: Library of Congress, Prints and Photographs Division, FSA-OWI Collection

Page 21: Photograph by Edie McGinnis, *The Kansas City Star*

Page 95: Photographic archives, Ekstrom Library, University of Louisville, Louisville, Ky.

Pages 105: Jim Barcus, *The Kansas City Star*

Page 115: AP/Wide World

Pages 120, 137, 150, 151, 153,: Susan Pfannmuller, special to *The Kansas City Star*

Page 152: Courtesy of the Convention and Visitors Bureau of Great Bend, Kan.

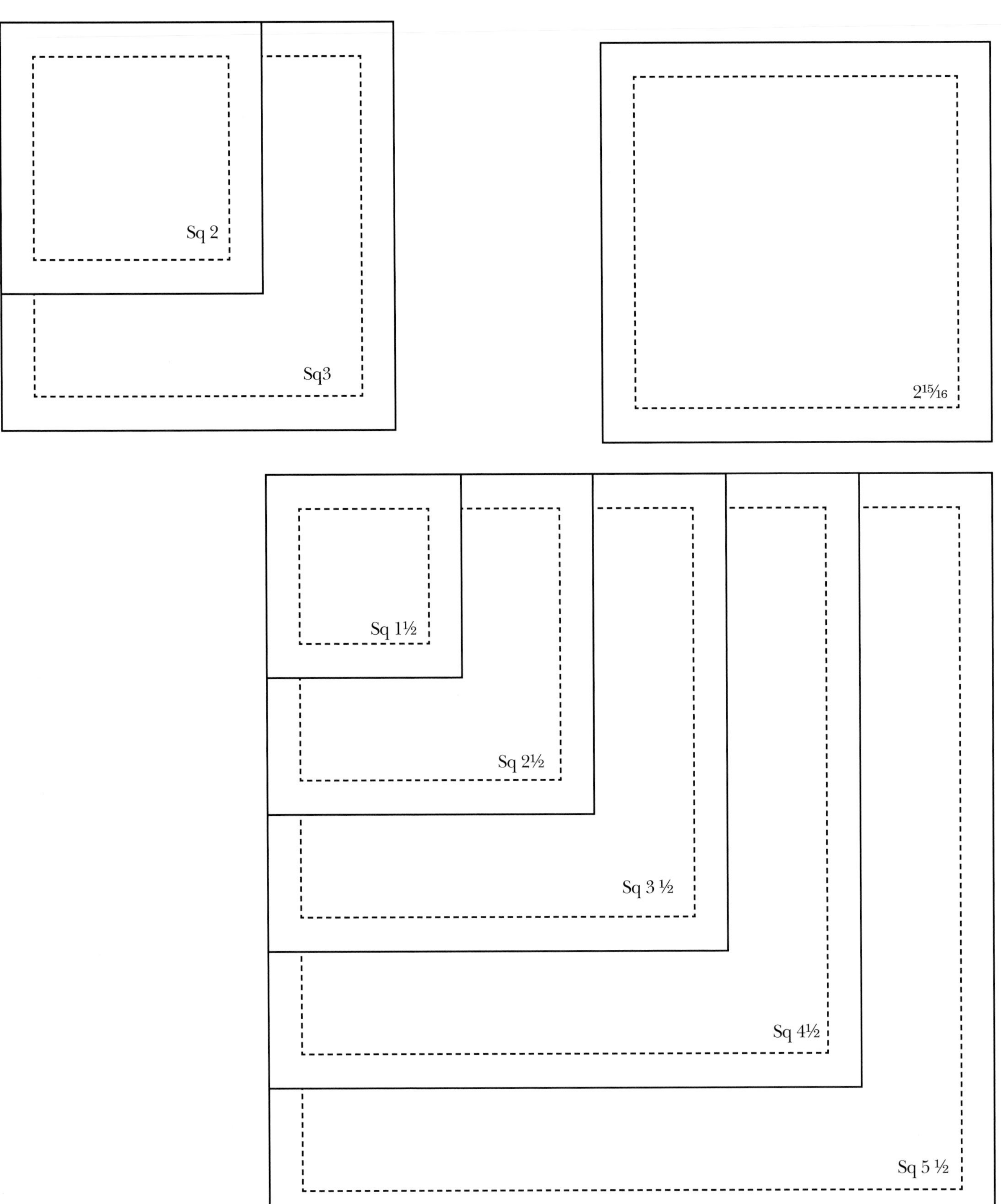
Sq 2
Sq3
$2^{15}/_{16}$
Sq 1½
Sq 2½
Sq 3 ½
Sq 4½
Sq 5 ½

Sq 2¼
Sq 3¼

Sq 1⅜
Sq 1⅞
Sq 2 ⅞
Sq 3⅜

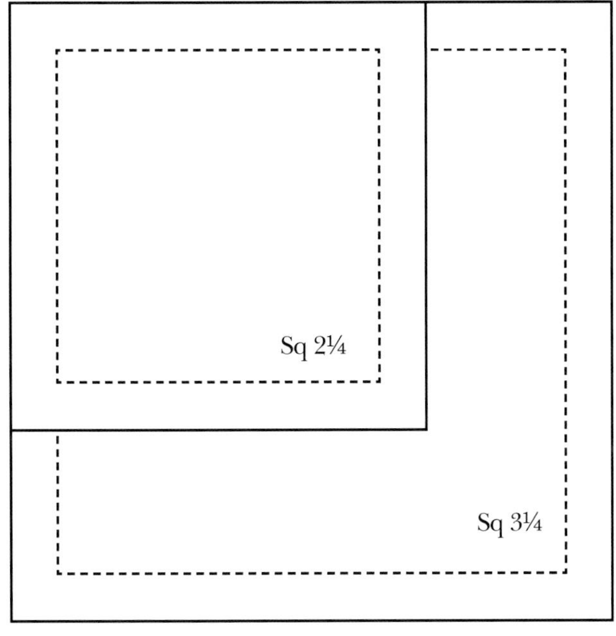

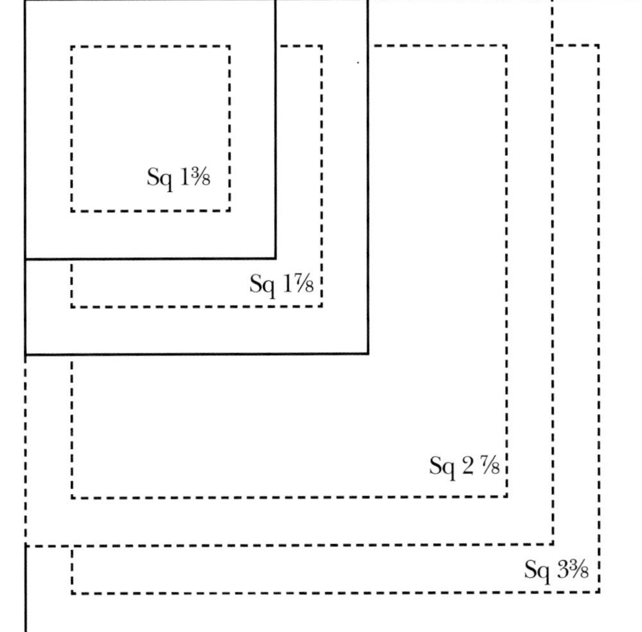

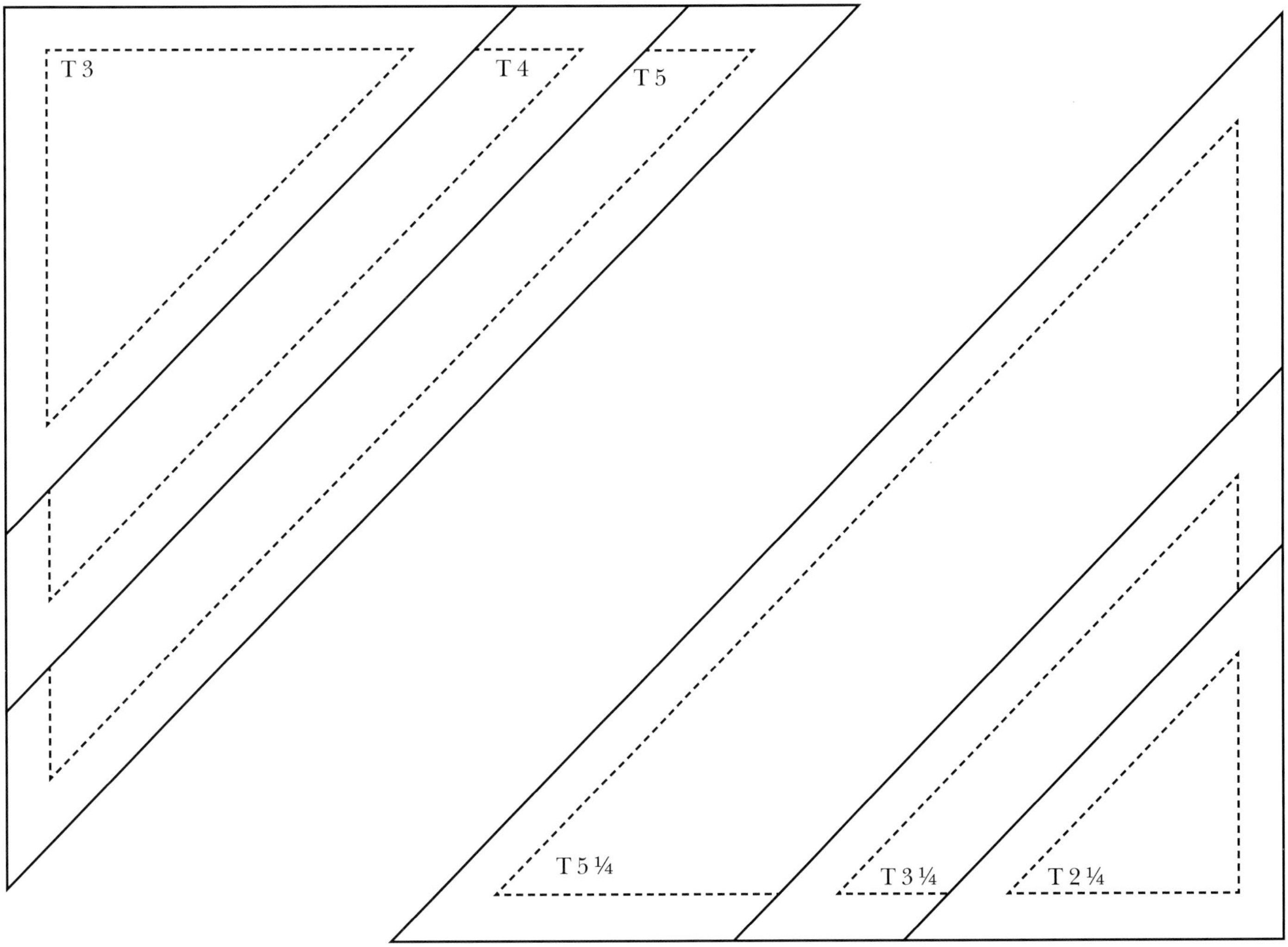

T 3
T 4
T 5
T 5 ¼
T 3 ¼
T 2 ¼

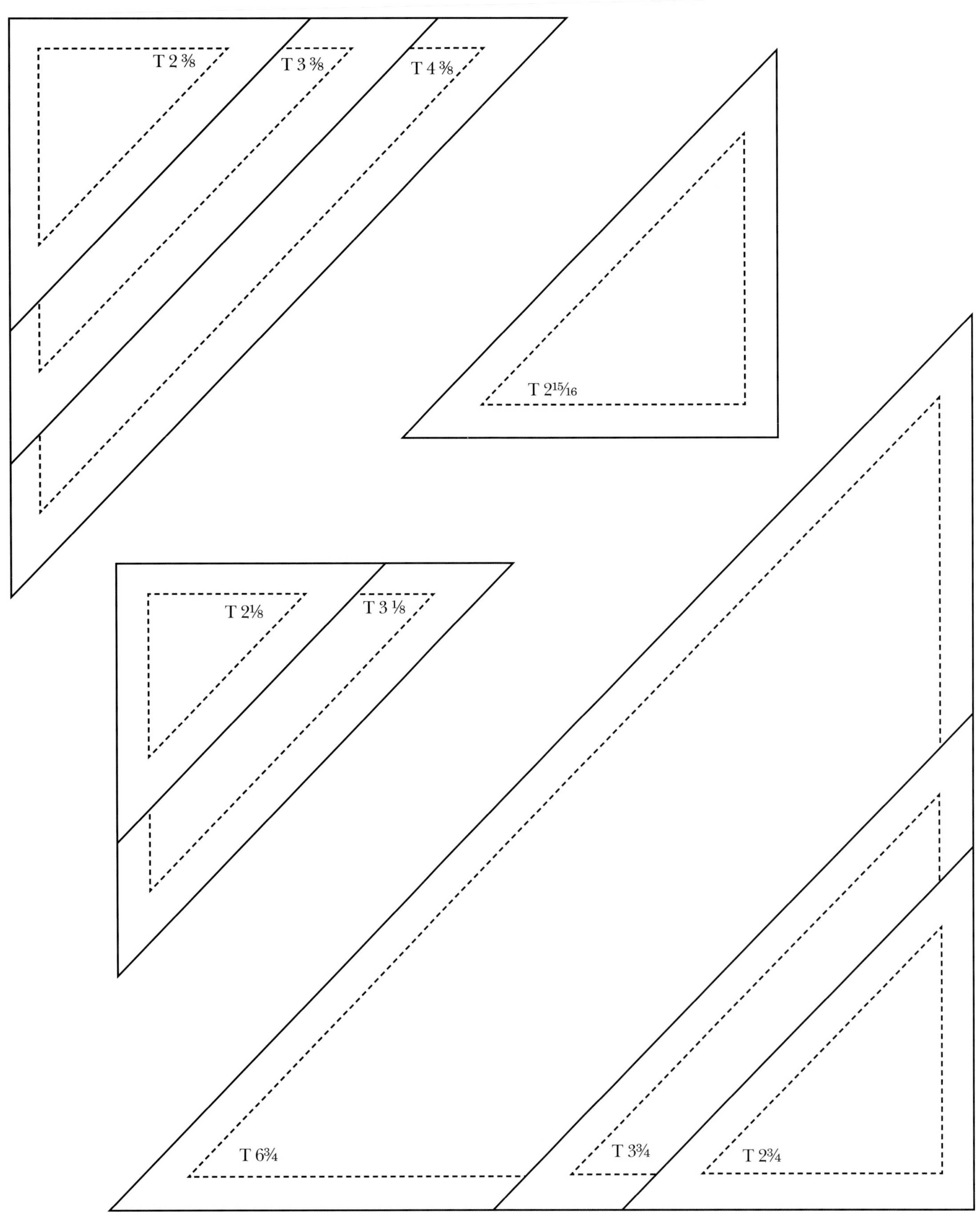
T 2⅜
T 3⅜
T 4⅜
T 2¹⁵⁄₁₆
T 2⅛
T 3⅛
T 6¾
T 3¾
T 2¾

T 5⅝
T 4⅝
T 2⅝
T 2⅞
T 3⅞
T 4⅞
T 5⅞
T 6⅞

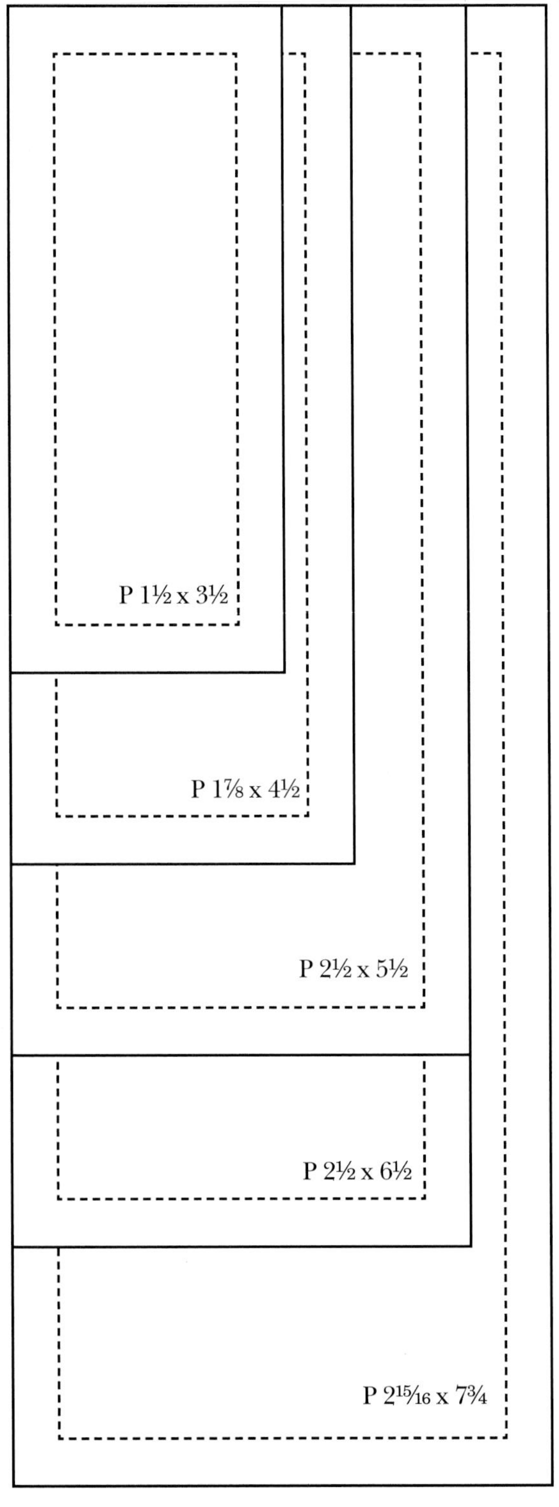
P 1½ x 3½
P 1⅞ x 4½
P 2½ x 5½
P 2½ x 6½
P 2¹⁵⁄₁₆ x 7¾

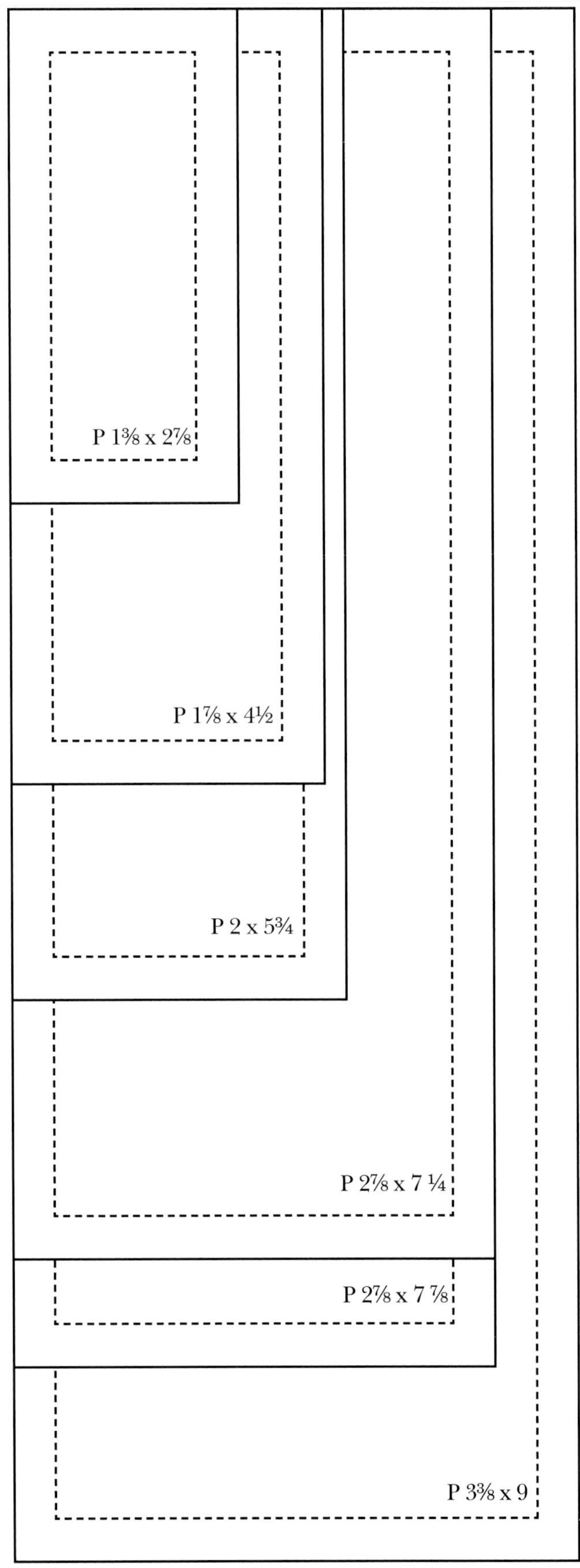
P 1⅜ x 2⅞
P 1⅞ x 4½
P 2 x 5¾
P 2⅞ x 7 ¼
P 2⅞ x 7 ⅞
P 3⅜ x 9

P 4 x .75

Misc 1

Misc 2

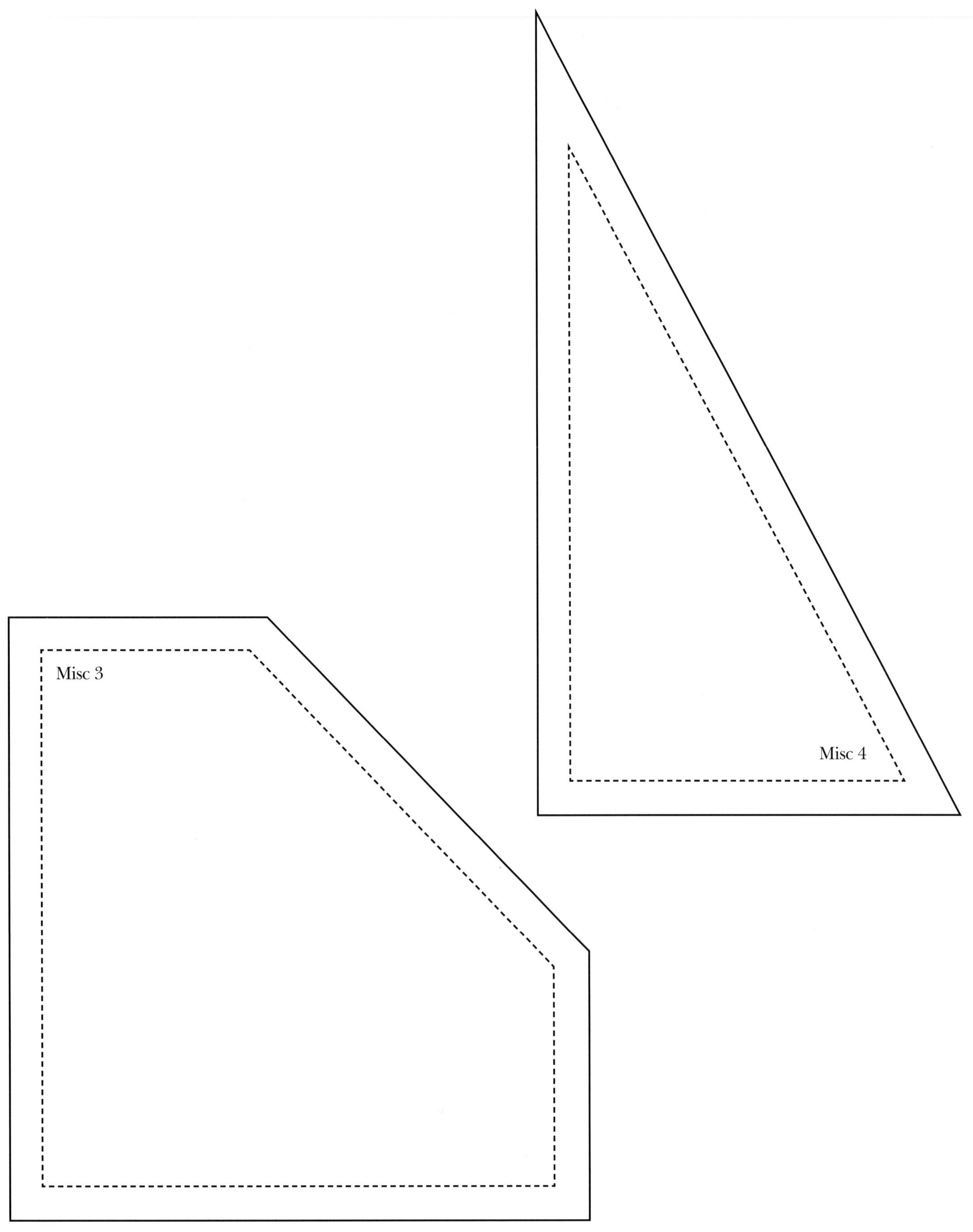
Misc 3
Misc 4

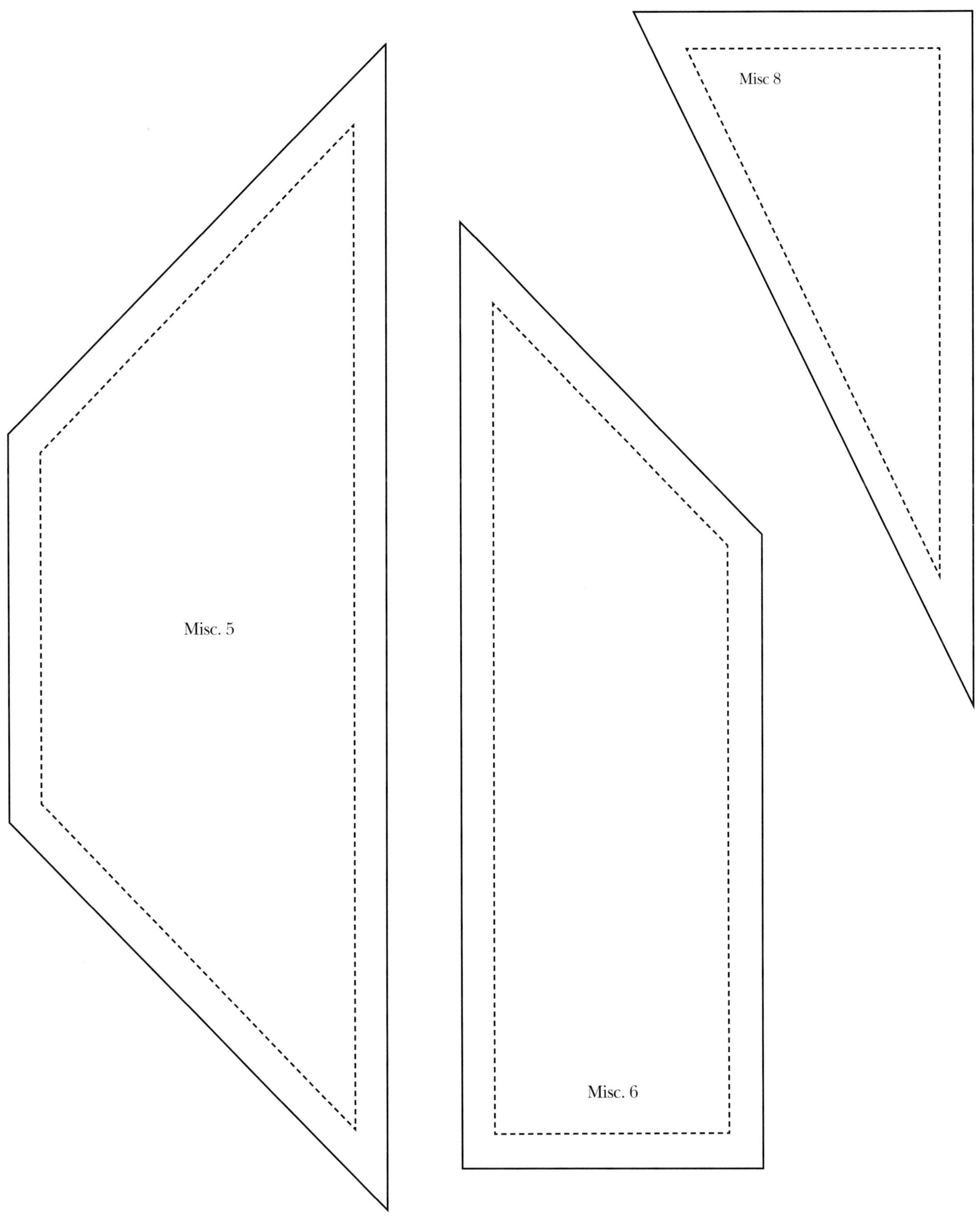
Misc 8
Misc. 5
Misc. 6

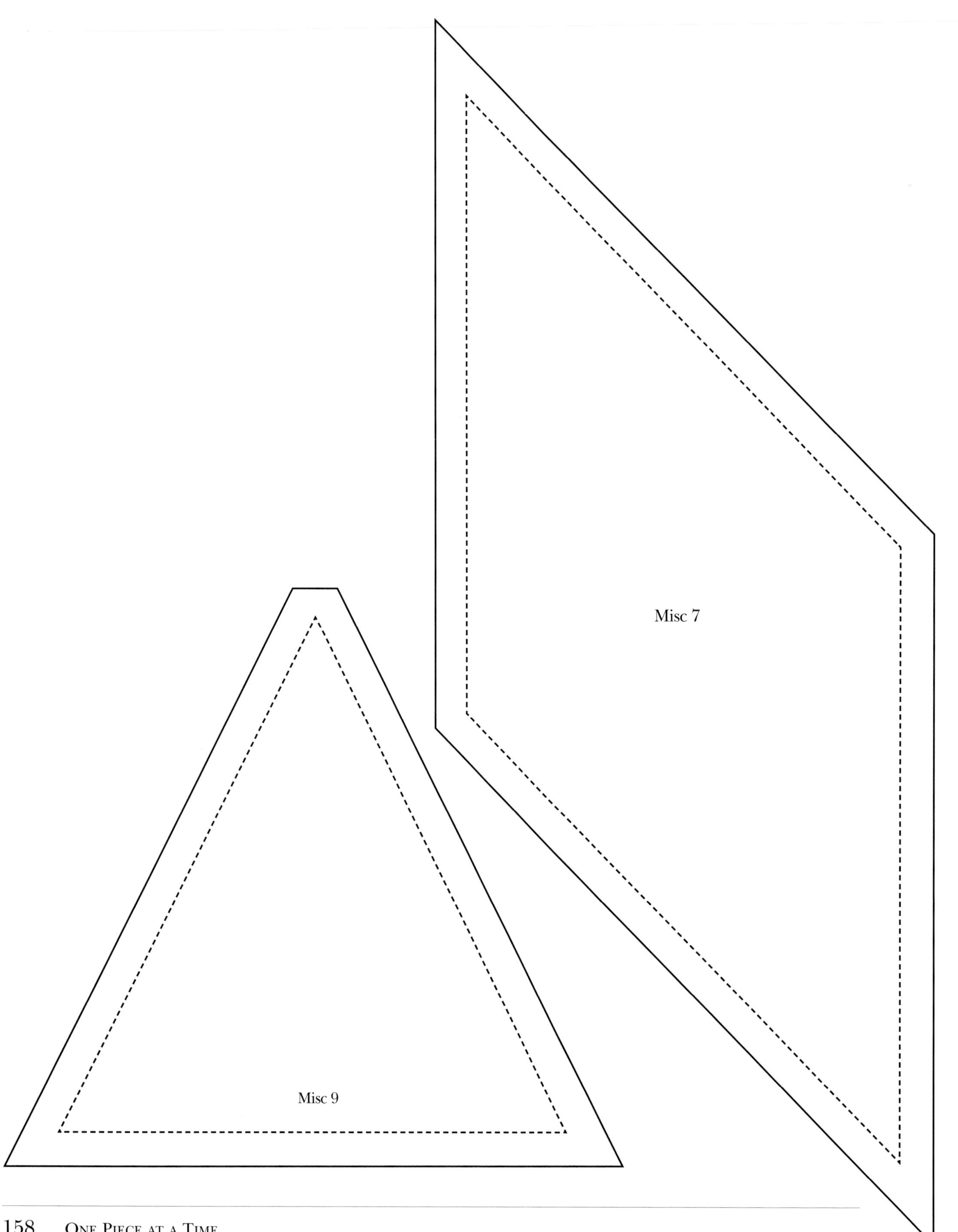
Misc 7
Misc 9

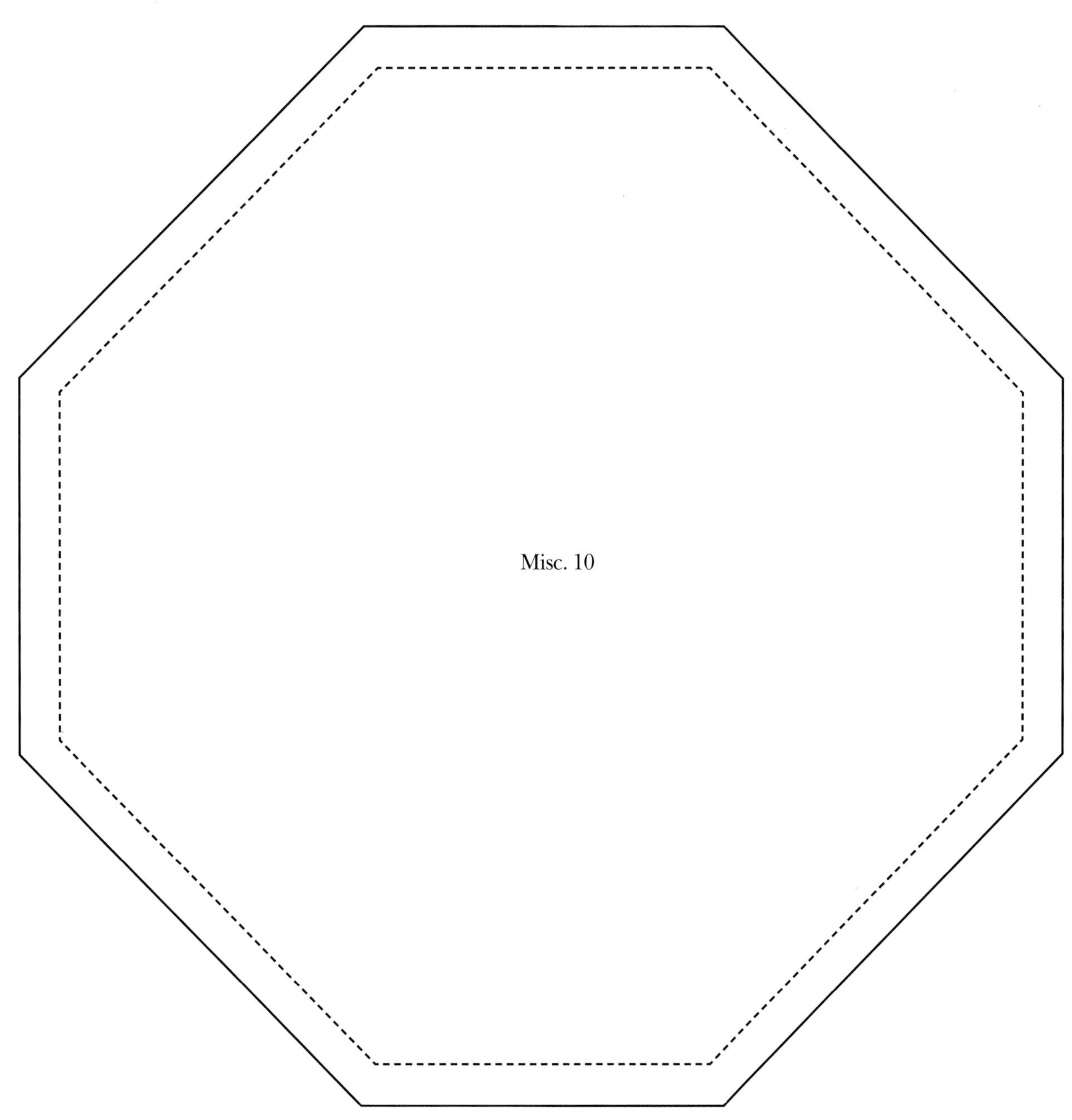
Misc. 10

Circle Upon Circle (1933 pattern)
Made about 1940 by Sue Wakefield and Mattie Carrell
Owned by Nancy P. Wakefield

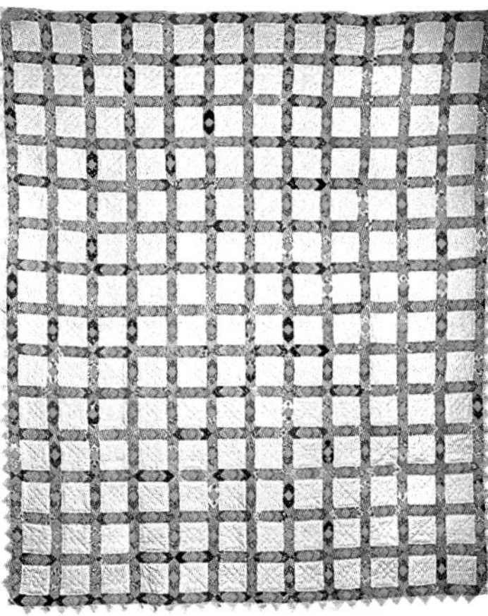

Cupid's Arrow Point (1929 pattern)
Owned by Cathy Wutke

English Flower Garden (1930 pattern)
Made by Avis Landess Kneale
Owned by Marilyn Kneale Henderson

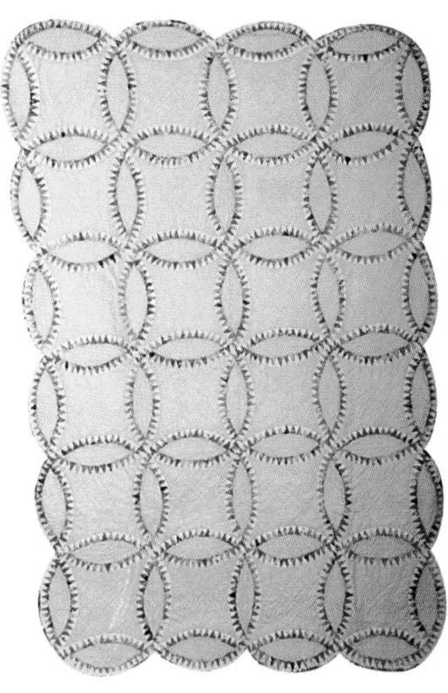

Pickle Dish (1931 pattern)
Made in 1938-1940 by Avis Landess Kneale
Owned by Marilyn Kneale Henderson

The Star (1936 pattern)
Made in the 1940's by Ellen Groves
Owned by Harold Groves

Wheel of Mystery (1931 pattern)
Made circa 1935 by Alice M. Pager
Owned by Nancy P. Wakefield

Fence Row (1931 pattern)
Made and owned by Roy Dale Geary

Memory Bouquet (1930 pattern)
Made by Charlene Dodson
Owned by Dorothymae Groves

Lone Star of Paradise (1933pattern)
Made by Angie Eads
Owned by Lougene Eads Geary

Ocean Wave (1928 pattern)
Made in 1931 by Mrs. Wheller
Owned by Agnes Shellhammer

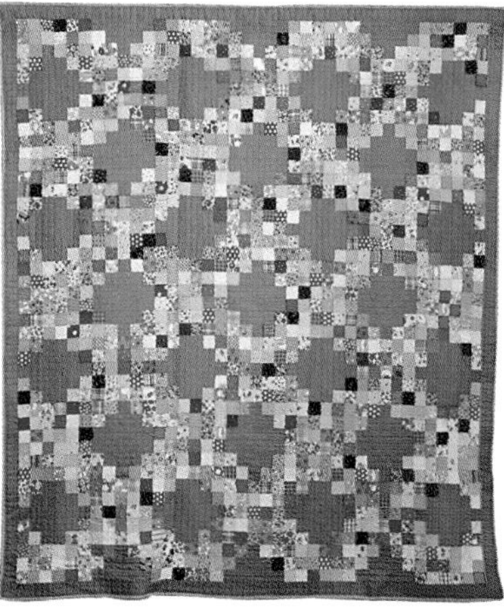

Irish Chain (triple) (1929 pattern)
Made by Mattie Nichols
Owned by Janet Majure

Casement Windows (1931 pattern)
Made by Grace Rollins
Owned by Donna M. Robertson

THE QUILTS, YEAR BY YEAR

Here is a chronological list — including repeats — of the quilt patterns and designs published by *The Kansas City Star* from 1928 through 1961.

If you'd like to see the patterns on the pages of the newspaper, microfilm copies of *The Star* are available at the Kansas City Public Library's Main Branch, 311 E. 12th St., Kansas City, Mo.

For an alphabetical list of the designs, see Wilene Smith's *Quilt Patterns: An Index to The Kansas City Star Patterns* (details in Bibliography).

For a thumbnail sketch of each pattern, see Volume 5 of *The Ultimate Illustrated Index to The Kansas City Star Quilt Pattern Collection* by the Central Oklahoma Quilters Guild (details in Bibliography).

Months not listed here had no published quilt patterns.

1928

■ **September**
Pine Tree
Album Quilt

■ **October**
French Star
Log Cabin
Rob Peter and Pay Paul
Cherry Basket
Wedding Ring

■ **November**
Jacob's Ladder
Greek Cross
Sky Rocket
Double T

■ **December**
Ocean Wave
Wild Goose Chase
Old Maid's Puzzle
Rambler

1929

■ **January**
Weathervane
Monkey Wrench
Spider Web
Irish Chain

■ **February**
Rising Sun
Princess Feather
Double Nine Patch
Eight-Pointed Star

■ **March**
Goose in the Pond
Dove in the Window
Beautiful Star
Broken Circle
Beggar Block

■ **April**
Cupid's Arrow Point
Noon Day Lily
Lafayette Orange Peel
Necktie

■ **May**
Duck and Ducklings
House on the Hill
Crossed Canoes
Turkey Tracks

■ **June**
Ribbon Border Block
Posey
Bird's Nest
Crosses and Losses
Double Star

■ **July**
Jack in the Box
Aircraft
Springtime Blossoms
Sunbeam

■ **August**
Saw-Tooth
Cross and Crown
Hands All 'Round
Honey Bee
Flower Pot

■ **September**
Susannah
Goose Tracks
Fish Block
Wedding Ring

■ **October**
Swastika
Seth Thomas Rose
"V" Block
Little Beech Tree

■ **November**
Palm Leaf
Tulip Applique
Mill Wheel
Order No. 11
Old King Cole's Crown

■ **December**
Strawberry Block
Old King Cole
Little Wooden Soldier
Road to Oklahoma
(The "Santa's Parade Quilt" series ran in December 1929).

1930

■ **January**
Churn Dash
Corn and Beans
Rose Cross
Milky Way

■ **February**
True Lovers Buggy Wheel
Indiana Puzzle
Blazing Star
Aster

■ **March**
Sunflower
Grape Basket
Steps to the Altar
Kaleidoscope
Dutchman's Puzzle

■ **April**
English Flower Garden
Single Wedding Ring
Pin Wheels
Cross and Crown

■ **May**
Missouri Puzzle
Merry Go-Round
Lone Star
Missouri Star
Sail Boat

■ **June**
Virginia Star
Rail Fence

■ **July**
Mexican Star
Basket of Oranges
Rose Album
Clay's Choice

■ **August**
Maple Leaf
Sunbonnet Sue
Compass
Kaleidoscope
Rainbow Tile

■ **September**
Goblet
Calico Puzzle
Broken Dishes
Swallows in the Window

■ **October**
Secret Drawer
Spider Web
Marble Floor
Pinwheel
(The "Memory Bouquet Quilt" series ran in October 1930.)

■ **November**
Grandmother's Favorite
Indian Emblem
Friendship
Puss in the Corner
Sage-Bud
(The "Memory Bouquet Quilt" series ran in November 1930).

■ **December**
Turnabout "T"
Snow Crystals
Sweet Gum Leaf
Rose Dream

1931

■ **January**
Silver and Gold
Tennessee Star
Flower Pot
Greek Cross
Sheep Fold

■ **February**
Amethyst
Wheel of Mystery
Pontiac Star
Baby Bunting

■ **March**
Seven Stars
Rebecca's Fan
French Bouquet
Casement Window

■ **April**
Basket of Lilies
King's Crown
June Butterfly
Fence Row

■ **May**
Indian Trail
English Ivy
Jackson Star
Dutch Tulip
Love Ring

■ **June**
Ararat
Iris Leaf
Ozark Diamond
Kite Quilt

■ **July**
Cactus Flower
Arrowhead Star
Giddap
Sugar Loaf

■ **August**
Cross Roads
Bachelor's Puzzle
Morning Star
Pineapple Quilt
Dresden Plate

■ **September**
Stepping Stones
Tennessee Star
Chips and Whetstones
Boutonniere

■ **October**
Prickly Pear
Castle Wall
Butterfly
Pickle Dish
Dutch Tile

■ **November**
Cottage Tulips
Formosa Tea Leaf
Bridge
Evening Star

■ **December**
Poinsettia
Goldfish
Christmas Star
Crazy Daisy

1932

■ **January**
Friendship Knot
Circular Saw
Heart's Desire
Job's Tears
Necktie
(The "Horn of Plenty Quilt" series also ran in January 1932).

■ **February**
Autograph Quilt
Hour-Glass
Spring Beauty
Grandmother's Basket
(The "Horn of Plenty Quilt" series also ran in February 1932).

■ **March**
Grandmother's Favorite
Quilting Design
Shamrock
Magnolia Bud

■ **April**
Nose-Gay
Diamond Field
Red Cross
Solomon's Puzzle
"4-H" Club

■ **May**
Russian Sunflower
Storm at Sea
Crow's Nest
Garden Maze

■ **June**
Cowboy's Star
Ducklings
Lend and Borrow
Wheel of Fortune

■ **July**

Index of Patterns

Index of Patterns

Index of Patterns

Index of Patterns